The Stewardship Companion

THE STEWARDSHIP COMPANION

Lectionary Resources for Preaching

David N. Mosser

Foreword by William H. Willimon

Westminster John Knox Press
LOUISVILLE • LONDON

© 2007 David N. Mosser
Foreword © 2007 Westminster John Knox Press

Scripture quotations, unless otherwise indicated, are from the New Revised Standard Version of the Bible, copyright © 1989 by the Division of Christian Education of the National Council of the Churches of Christ in the U.S.A., and used by permission.

Book design by Sharon Adams
Cover design by Night & Day Design

First edition
Published by Westminster John Knox Press
Louisville, Kentucky

This book is printed on acid-free paper that meets the American National Standards Institute Z39.48 standard. ♾

PRINTED IN THE UNITED STATES OF AMERICA

07 08 09 10 11 12 13 14 15 16 — 10 9 8 7 6 5 4 3 2 1

Library of Congress Cataloging-in-Publication Data

Mosser, David.
   The stewardship companion : lectionary resources for preaching / David N. Mosser ; foreword by William H. Willimon. — 1st ed.
      p. cm.
   Includes index.
   ISBN 978-0-664-22993-1 (alk. paper)
   1. Stewardship, Christian—Sermons. I. Title.

BV772.M67 2007
251'.6—dc22

2007007075

People along life's path teach us of what stewardship consists by simply living as generous human beings—and as believers.

To the sacred memory of Gary Carroll, Timothy A. Russell, James L. Kinneavy, Bobby Dean Baggett, and Albert Cook Outler

To the honor of Tom Butts, O. L. Davis Jr., and James W. (Jay) Darnell

Contents

Foreword

William H. Willimon

"The earth is the LORD's and all that is in it, the world, and those who live in it."

(Ps. 24:1)

This claim of divine ownership is axiomatic for anything we say about Christian stewardship. The earth is the Lord's. God creates and owns all of it. Whatever we have, including life itself, is on loan. This Christian life is one long process of learning that we don't "have" anything of any value and that anytime we use the word "mine" we are on shaky ground. Life, time, possessions, family, nature, pension funds, friends—all are held in trust by us, all are on loan from God to us. God graciously gives, but God does not let go of what God owns. Our God is a "jealous God," as the Scriptures sometimes put it. This God is gracious, but at the same time possessive. Learning to acknowledge God's claim upon us is the beginning of wisdom.

Furthermore, Jesus tells us that we are held accountable for everything we have received—every cent, every minute, every thing. God loves us enough not only to give us good things but also to hold us accountable for the gifts. As the Germans say it, every gift (*Gabe*) is an assignment (*Aufgabe*). God's grace is both free and costly. There is, with this gracious God, always that time, sometime, when we are asked simply, "What have you done with what you have been given?"

David Mosser knows all this. He brings a pastor's heart and a preacher's skill to the task of biblical interpretation. He pours a lifetime of stewardship education into this book. His interpretation of the Revised Common Lectionary's pericopes demonstrates the fruitfulness of reading Scripture from a distinctive perspective. In all too many cases, many of us pastors have been trained to read Scripture in the mode of the academy—keep detached from the biblical text, attempt objectivity, keep as great a distance as possible from the text, read hoping for intellectual understanding rather than expecting divine obligation. When Mosser looks at a given text from the standpoint of stewardship, he sees both gift and assignments everywhere. Mosser playfully, obediently listens to each text confident that he will hear a contemporary discipleship claim from it. He reads not only to understand but also to receive a God-given task that may cost something.

I was invigorated by Mosser's insights, time and again surprised by unexpected stewardship implications of the biblical texts. I also got a sense that God's stewardship expectations of us are not onerous burdens but rather gracious gifts. God graciously treats us as if we were the responsible disciples we have been called to be. In Jesus Christ we become coworkers with a creative God. Whatever God is doing in the world, God chooses not to do it alone. Something good is left for us to do. Our little lives are swept up into the grand drama of God's redemption of the world. In reading Mosser's commentary I was freshly reminded that the ability to know God's will and to join in God's work is surely one of the greatest of God's good gifts.

A friend of mine says that the whole gospel can be encapsulated in the phrase "God is going to get back what belongs to God." A major means of getting what God wants in the world is through our stewardship of what God has given. Stewardship is a primary way that good news is enacted and embodied. As a good steward, David Mosser repeatedly brings something new out of something old, he locates the gospel in your congregation and mine, he hears what we have failed to hear before, and he gives us all something good to say on Sunday, something good that is not of our own devising.

Well done, good and faithful steward.

William H. Willimon
Bishop, North Alabama Conference of the United Methodist Church
Visiting Research Professor, Duke Divinity School

Introduction

The chief focus of this stewardship commentary, based on the Revised Common Lectionary, is for any preaching occasion called for by the church's liturgical calendar. More creatively, this commentary may also engage those teaching stewardship to particular groups, such as administrative boards, church councils, sessions, stewardship committees, Sunday school classes, or even a church staff. An in-depth, churchwide study on what the Bible relates concerning a Christian's use of possessions might be another profitable application. Pastors or other church leaders might also use this commentary to craft letters, parish bulletins, or other communication forms that highlight our use of God's gifts—time, treasure, and talent. Churches could base their annual budget campaign on this resource—clearly the book's most pragmatic use.

Across denominational and nondenominational lines, most pastors understand stewardship both theologically and biblically. Troubles arise, however, when preachers or leaders try to articulate faith in God and its accompanying discipleship via stewardship. Too often preachers and church leaders carry a concealed anxiety that laypeople will raise those old well-worn defensive chestnuts: "All the church talks about is money" or "The church needs to focus on spiritual matters, not on money matters."

Nonetheless, a quick perusal of the Bible should lay these threadbare allegations to rest. In fact, my best stewardship teachers have been discerning laypeople who understood the weighty connection between what we profess and how we live that profession. People who have mastered Christian stewardship principles know far too much than to confuse a congregation's annual budget drive with a genuine biblical understanding of stewardship. Our stewardship reaches into every corner of our life of faith, which of course includes but is not limited to our purses. I hope that this stewardship commentary can further conversation about the nature of stewardship and the claim that God has laid on us as stewards. Many of God's gifts and claims will be discussed within the pages of this commentary.

Twenty-five years ago I inherited a remarkable little book by Roy L. Smith titled *Stewardship Studies*. The inheritance came from the library of a minister in the Christian Church (Disciples of Christ), Floyd Diehm, by way of his son Ken, a United Methodist minister. Smith's book contained about 235 short sermonic essays on biblical stewardship from Genesis to Revelation. It was a gift that changed my ministry. Over the years as I contemplated how to preach stewardship to congregations in Corsicana, Burleson, De Leon, Georgetown, Graham, and Arlington (all in Texas), I realized the book's value but also its relative obscurity. I thought that Roy Smith's book might be a great asset to other preachers. Yet the book needed substantial updating.

Mindful of these matters, I approached the always approachable and even more patient editor at Westminster John Knox Press, Jon Berquist. I asked Jon about writing a twenty-first-century version of Smith's earlier work. Jon gamely agreed to take it to the editorial committee. He soon returned the committee's positive affirmation but with one major stipulation in the guise of a question: "Do you think you could write about stewardship, but use the Revised Common Lectionary as a guide?"

Of course I said yes—what was my alternative? But as I mulled over my agreement to the task, I realized that I had been given a tall order. Yet as I discovered reading and writing through the three-year lectionary cycle, the task was not as difficult as I first imagined. Stewardship is a mainstay of the Christian life. Therefore, Scripture is shot through and through with diverse perspectives on what Christian stewards do with what God has loaned us by way of gifts and graces. In fact, on many preaching days multiple stewardship themes emerge from the lectionary's four readings for preaching occasions. I have merely scratched the Bible's surface on the manifold stewardship themes found therein.

While this book is written under the rubric of the Revised Common Lectionary, it need not be used exclusively by lectionary preachers. Each entry stands alone with its text. For this reason, both lectionary preachers and non-lectionary preachers can reference this commentary. Preachers can address today's vital stewardship topics with material that comes straight from the Bible. Each of the three lectionary cycles in this commentary has about sixty-two or so entries. This variance between the years occurs because several preaching days in the liturgical calendar, Ash Wednesday for example, have an identical set of readings for each year in the three-year cycle. Even so, this commentary addresses no fewer than 180 distinctive biblical texts that provide a broad range of preaching possibilities. I have taken care to cover not only the Gospels but also the Hebrew Bible texts, the Epistles, and the Psalter. I have tried to attend to the full reach of the Bible.

Within the matching liturgical day in all three cycles, I selected texts from different genres of the options for the day. That is, over the three-year cycle on a given day—for example, Easter Day—the commentary text explores the Epistle (Year A), Acts (Year B), and the Psalter (Year C). For another example, the commentary on the First Sunday after Christmas Day covers the Gospel (Year A), the Epistle (Year B), and the Psalter (Year C). Although the text selections may appear random, I chose them in order to support preachers who want to use the entire Bible when addressing one of the Scripture's most elemental themes.

Year C has a higher incidence of commentary devoted to Gospel lections because of Luke's paramount concern with people and their relationship to possessions. This also accounts for the many texts from Luke's book of Acts as well.

I would like to thank a dedicated group of laypeople at First United Methodist Church in Arlington, Texas, for sacrificing more than a few long Saturdays to explore Christian stewardship in the context of both Scripture and modernity. Specifically, my appreciation goes to the late Clancy Morris, as well as to Carrie Palmer, Cynthia Ellis, Dick and Joyce Kahler, John Bradshaw, Joy McKee, Lannie Forbes, Lynda Sherrieb, Pam Cunningham, Sara Marshall, Suzy Lundquist, and Beth Kelly. This collection of bright Christians helped move stewardship from an academic and ecclesial field into real life, where God is incarnate.

I also want to offer my heartfelt thanks to Susan Patterson-Sumwalt, David Jones, and Bill Obidil for several helpful suggestions along the way. Bill brought to my attention a superb book by Douglas John Hall, *The Steward: A Biblical Symbol Come of Age* (revised edition, 1994). Hall suggests that "steward" is a metaphor that approaches in depth and adequacy our whole relationship with God, "a summing-up of the meaning of the Christian life." Further, Hall suggests that many outside the church have a more positive and holistic understanding of stewardship than many inside the church, where the church tends to retain a technical and institutional framework for fund-raising.

Bill told me, "Your commentary, which speaks of the stewardship of all the gifts of God to us, provides a preacher with resources to speak to the under-churched in authentic biblical terms that resonate with the postmodern spirit." Bill is an example of parish pastors who are faithful in their stewardship understanding and who grasp the need to communicate the good news and our part in it.

Through all the drafts of the commentary, Sandra Boedeker searched for typos and unparallel construction, but most of all she asked highly penetrating theological questions about my biblical interpretations of Holy Scripture. All of these people, in their own distinctive ways, made this a better book.

David N. Mosser
February 2, 2007
The Presentation of Our Lord Jesus Christ in the Temple

YEAR A

Advent and Christmas

First Sunday of Advent

Isaiah 2:1–5   The High Cost of War

"The nations . . . shall beat their swords into plowshares."
(Isa. 2:4)

Today's text from Isaiah launches Advent and links Israel's obvious prophetic tradition to the torah tradition. Although Christians often interpret the word *torah* as "law," its earliest context defined the term just as accurately as "teaching." Consequently, Isaiah stresses God's teaching from the mountain. This teaching is so vital to both Israel's and God's identity that "many peoples shall come." Thus, God's people steward God's teaching, preserving it for "the nations."

The text's original focus consists of God's promise "in the days to come." When that day is, Isaiah does not say, and perhaps we await the fulfillment of this promise even today. Regardless, the prophet's confidence rests in the promise maker. What is unusual about Isaiah's prophecy is that the promise precedes the denunciations of Judah (see, for example, Isa. 3). Internal and external threats

3

menace Judah and Jerusalem, from Isaiah's perspective. The internal menace consists of a people, the residents of Judah and Jerusalem, who have deserted the Lord's ways. The external threat to Judah, now posed by the adjacent national superpowers, continually bedevils both Judah and Israel, as it has for some time. But before Isaiah turns to the prophetic denunciation of the people, he first offers the divine promise—the assurance today's text offers.

The promise resides in the Lord's power or the teaching from Zion. The teaching is so persuasive, at least in Isaiah's vision, that the nations (or Gentiles) will flow up to the mountain to receive such divine instruction. Not only will God arbitrate between nations so that people no longer deem war as necessary, but God will teach all people to turn their implements of war into implements of agriculture. Equipment previously used to make war now will serve to feed hungry people, plainly Isaiah's vision of "a peaceable kingdom."

More than one social commentator has observed that the twentieth century was the most violent in humankind's history. No up-to-date evidence suggests that our present century will be any less inhumane. Nations wage war at the expense of those least able to bear its burden—the children, the poor, and the elderly. This particular segment of a nation's community bears the disproportionate weight of war. Those nations and leaders who wage war are poor stewards of God's bountiful resources. Isaiah's vision reminds Judah and Jerusalem that although things are as they are, "in the days to come" God will present a better passageway to abundant and vital life.

Advent, at least in one significant way, celebrates and teaches believers "why" God sends the world a messiah. Unless we learn from God the divine purpose of creation, which is to till and keep God's garden, then a perpetual battle for national pride, land, and natural resources will persist. Yet Isaiah's prophetic vision of swords into plowshares and spears into pruning hooks triggers our memories, faint as they may be, regarding God's intention at creation. God created people to live in a community based on mutual respect and peace—a community that is bent on feeding its members from the least to the greatest. Faithful stewards continue to preserve this teaching of the Lord. The First Sunday of Advent holds up the promise that when the Messiah comes, God will bring the divine intention for God's people to fruition.

Second Sunday of Advent

Psalm 72:1–7, 18–19   Leadership in God's Realm

"In his days may righteousness flourish and peace abound."
(Ps. 72:7)

Stewardship is, by definition, the management of an owner's household. Christian stewards are people who manage any number of households. A "household" contains the talents we possess that God has loaned us while we are among the gathered people we call "the church militant." Some of the stewardship households we manage consist of our caring, education, giving, praying, spiritual discernment, and the like. A pragmatic understanding of stewardship teaches that all Christians have households to manage.

The church gives over the second Sunday in the liturgical season of Advent to describing the odd behavior, not to mention the odd diet and apparel, of John the Baptizer. John was a prophet and cousin of Jesus about whom Matthew writes, "Now John wore clothing of camel's hair with a leather belt around his waist, and his food was locusts and wild honey" (Matt. 3:4).

Psalm 72, however, is the text we will explore here. Israel's hope had faded for David and David's kingdom. Of course, many historic circumstances accounted for Israel's demise. Israel was a people in trouble. Yet the nation began to look to the future. God and the people of Israel tie that future to the coming of a new king. Perhaps for this reason the superscription over Psalm 72 bears Solomon's name. Could someone like Solomon provide hope for Israel?

A friend who worked for IBM once disclosed to me that a reason for the company's phenomenal success was that it controlled every aspect of the business, from the boardroom to the distribution centers. He went on to say that IBM had exhaustive job descriptions for every employee. This was true from the corporation's top to its bottom.

A job description lists the broad functions and tasks of a position. Usually job descriptions include to whom the position reports, details such as the qualifications required of the employee, and the position's salary range. The job description also explores the areas of knowledge and skills needed for the job. Job descriptions help working stewards focus on their tasks.

Psalm 72 is essentially "a king's job description," originally for a sovereign with sensitivities to God's will. However, our Christian tradition has appropriated this kingly job description and fashioned it into a prayer for the expected Messiah. This Messiah we both announce as Jesus and wait for with anticipation.

The church has always been adept at adapting. What if Christians took the job description for a king and adapted it as a mandate for a stewardship of leadership? Leadership is clearly a "household" that many Christians manage. Often this leadership is within the confines of a congregation, but the church also produces leaders in its community. What would our communities look like if our political leaders would "defend the cause of the poor" and "give deliverance to the needy"? What would our schools look like if our educational leaders imparted to students the need to let "righteousness flourish and peace abound"? What if, in our criminal justice system, we created a judiciary that arbitrated cases "with righteousness"?

Faithful stewards have the mandate to take the job description of a king and put it to use for the King. Perhaps this is our Advent call to be disciples and stewards.

Third Sunday of Advent

James 5:7–10   Patience Is a Virtue

"The farmer waits for the precious crop . . . , being patient with it."
(Jas. 5:7)

Today's lectionary text counsels its recipients to "be patient . . . until the coming of the Lord." In an odd way, as most current churches celebrate Christ's impending birth at Advent, James provides a word for those who wait for the Parousia, the coming of the Lord. Because James wrote his epistle several decades after Jesus' death, he may mean "the second coming," which is often the meaning of *Parousia* in Christian theology. Yet this idea is uncommon in the New Testament (see John 14:3; Heb. 9:28). Thus, as the modern church anticipates Christ's birth, James adds an element of ethical guidance for those who wait for Jesus as judge and savior.

For conscientious and diligent people who wait, there could be no more painful expressions than "killing time" or "wasting time." Yet how do people who wait for something as anticipated as Jesus wait with useful expectation without wasting or killing time? In other words, how does the believer wait as a good steward of time?

James offers some principled advice concerning how the church lives while waiting "for the coming of the Lord." As James frequently does, the letter speaks to grumbling speech and an unbridled tongue (1:26; 3:5–10; 4:11). By avoiding grumbling against one another, believers evade divine judgment. In addition, James furnishes the prophets as exemplars of those who suffered with patience.

James's effective icon for faithful waiting inheres in "the farmer" image. Societies have long recognized farming as an endeavor that epitomizes patience. Farmers prepare the soil, plant the seed, and then wait for nature to take its course. There is no way to speed up the natural process. Growth happens when it happens. The farmer can only wait—and hope for rain or no locusts and the like. James, in addition, uses the phrase "the early and the late rains." This phrase signifies the hope that the farmer clings to, for without the rains, the whole farming enterprise devolves into dust. Significant rain came commonly twice to Palestine. Deuteronomy too recalls "the early rain and the later rain" (11:14). James surely drew on this awareness. The promise of rain relies on the goodness of God, whose promise the faithful farmer counts upon.

I once asked a peanut farmer what he did while waiting between the time of planting and the time of harvest. I showed my ignorance by this question, no doubt. But he good-naturedly explained all the things he did between planting and harvest. He said that he readied himself for the next planting season by determining which crops to plant and which fields he would let lie fallow, buying the suitable seed to plant, maintaining his farming machinery, and studying the latest techniques of farming. In other words, he put his time to good use and did his homework. This farmer was a good steward of the time he had. I assumed, as the uninitiated, that farmers did not have much to do. In fact, good farmers are always busy anticipating the next planting cycle.

James's admonition to his hearers was that they be good stewards and redeem their time prior to the Lord's return. Like the farmer, they were to use the time at hand for faithful pursuits and leave to God the things that only God provides. Being a community that understands suffering and patience makes us more faithful believers. Perhaps James's guidance is a good one for us moderns too as we become better stewards of the time we have until the Lord returns. Advent is an annual reminder that as God is patient with us, so too may we be patient in waiting for the God revealed in Jesus Christ.

Fourth Sunday of Advent

Psalm 80:1–7, 17–19   Salvation as a Gift

"Restore us, O God; let your face shine, that we may be saved."
(Ps. 80:3)

At this late stage in Advent, few congregants have not directed their attention completely to Christmas. Christmas's focus varies depending upon whether one ponders the meaning of Christmas in a more cultural sense or, as Christian stewards, in a firmly theological sense. However, the concept of gifts and gift giving may help us bridge this perceived dichotomy between the cultural and the theological.

Psalm 80 is a prayer for the gift that only God can give—the gift of salvation. Here the creators of the Revised Common Lectionary have offered a psalm that reminds us, among tinsel and brightly colored lights, that the true circumstance under which humans toil is a condition that is nothing without God. Clearly this psalm carries the plaintive cry of a people who feel distant from God. Readers sense this emotional content when we read Psalm 80's question, "How long will you be angry with your people's prayers?" The prayer's deepest yearning is for reconnection with God. The evidence for a reforged bond between divinity and humanity is the state of salvation. Salvation here not only means redemption but also conveys God's making the people whole and well. Those who pray want well-being, which they perceptively understand comes only from God's hand.

Throughout Psalm 80 the refrain "Restore us, O God; let your face shine, that we may be saved" rings out (vv. 3, 7, 19). God's face shining upon the people is nothing other than an indication of divine favor. This divine favor is what the prayer seeks. In an optimum understanding of Christian theology, salvation is a gift—given without an agenda and without an angle. For a gift to be truly a gift, the giver offers the token without stipulation—free and clear. Psalm 80 explicitly prays for the gift of salvation.

Stewardship is all about gifts and gift giving. In this sense, perhaps, we can speak of God as a steward of God's good gifts. The psalmist believes in God's ability to deliver the gift of salvation, and trusts in the efficacy of prayer. The psalmist prays three times, "Restore us, O God; let your face shine, that we may be saved." The prayer counts upon God's grace to bestow a gift that only God can provide.

Believers need two functional attributes in order to exercise their stewardship. The first is possession of the wherewithal to offer the gift. The second is possession of a heart to give. Psalm 80 understands that God possesses the gift of salvation, and thus the prayer is a plea that God furnish this gift to God's people.

On this last Sunday of Advent, as we stand at the edge of Christmas, we "cultural" Christians tend to be preoccupied with gifts and gift giving for those on our "lists." However, after all the selling and buying that dominates this season, we remain needy human creatures. Our relationship with God—the ultimate steward of divine grace—is the only gift that can offer us what we need. In other words, perhaps one of the gifts that this psalm offers us is the truth that we need God's grace and mercy just as much in Advent as we do at Lent.

We are tempted during Advent (and Christmas) to overlook our human condition. This human circumstance necessitated God's sending Jesus in the first place. Advent is an excellent season to remember Paul's words: "For while we were still weak, at the right time Christ died for the ungodly" (Rom. 5:6). Perhaps God, too, is a steward.

Christmas Eve (A, B, and C)

Titus 2:11–14   Responding to the Gift of Salvation

"[Jesus] gave himself for us that he might redeem us from all iniquity and purify for himself a people of his own who are zealous for good deeds."
(Titus 2:14)

I suspect that most preachers would claim that among the many difficult days to preach the gospel, Easter and Christmas Eve are among the most demanding. One likely reason is that worship attendees on these two liturgical occasions little expect that the preacher can supply any surprises. After all, the preacher's message "He is risen" or "He is born" lacks astonishment. Most of us have heard these words for years.

On Christmas Eve the candlelight and recognizable music carry the worship freight. We all know that people bring more emotional and fewer rational expectations to Christmas Eve worship than usual. Despite this reality, Titus offers preachers a text that furnishes ample theological content for Christmas Eve worship. It is worth noting that the lectionary employs only one lesson from Titus during its three-year cycle—and Christmas Eve is the occasion. One of Titus's premises is that God's promise enables us to live as redeemed stewards. Only the redeemed can truly be stewards.

When Titus writes that "the grace of God has appeared, bringing salvation," he is referring to the appearance of Jesus. Jesus for this writer embodies God's grace. Moreover, the appearance of grace means that God offers salvation to

God's people as a gift. Whether one subscribes to different generation's doctrine of etiquette, both would urge a small gift for the host on the occasion of a visit to that person's home. In a sense, when God visits God's creation and creatures, God sends the gift of Jesus for the occasion. Thus, when Jesus arrives as the incarnate Christ, God offers the gift of salvation. Gifts are signs and symbols of a solid relationship. In the reading from the Psalter for Christmas Eve, Psalm 96:8 instructs the people to "ascribe to the Lord the glory due his name; bring an offering, and come into his courts." Our gifts represent an emblem of our firm relationship found in God's prior gift of Christ.

With Psalm 96's concept of bringing offerings in mind, we learn from Titus that even more is involved for the believer. The text's final verse gives a theological rationale for what those receiving the gift of salvation can return to God. In the first mention of God's appearance in Christ (v. 11), we recognize that God brings salvation as a gift.

Later we read that Jesus "gave himself for us that he might redeem us from all iniquity and purify for himself a people of his own who are zealous for good deeds." This is the text's second allusion to Christ's coming—an assertion fusing theology and ethics. Jesus redeems people from iniquity by "buying them back," just as people emancipated slaves in biblical times. As a result, Jesus saves us from all iniquity. Paul too uses redemption language: "Since all have sinned and fall short of the glory of God; they are now justified by his grace as a gift, through the redemption that is in Christ Jesus" (Rom. 3:23–24). People are redeemed from the slavery to sin and death, and this is an aspect of salvation.

Even so, there is an even more positive aspect related here in Titus. Beyond redemption from iniquity, Titus offers believers a proactive way of living in the world. Titus writes that Jesus creates "a people of his own who are zealous for good deeds." Thus, as God redeems us *from* sin, God also redeems us *for* good deeds. The Christian life is more than a belief system; it is a way of living in God's world. People being "redeemed from" and "redeemed for" work in concert in God's realm. God's promise enables us to live as redeemed stewards.

Christmas Day
[See Year B]

First Sunday after Christmas Day

Matthew 2:13–23   The Stewardship of Dreams

> *"Joseph got up, took the child and his mother . . . and went to Egypt."*
> (Matt. 2:14)

Many Christians picture stewardship as pertaining to material substance. For example, we readily understand stewardship in terms of our financial resources or our use of time. This concrete understanding clearly limits the concept of stewardship, for stewardship encompasses all the households we manage as gifts from God. Included in these households may be a believer's power of persuasion, prayers, or even modeling faith. There is something intangible in the notion of stewardship. Yet this intangibility endows stewardship with a great deal more power than we might otherwise normally grant it.

Have you ever considered a dream as a gift? The dreams in Matthew's Gospel lesson are no doubt unsettling. Even so, the three dreams in this lesson, which all come to Joseph, visibly guide the steps of the Holy Family. In what respect could we suggest that God guides us through the agency of dreams?

In recent decades psychologists and psychiatrists have given dream interpretation a "born again" prominence. Modern scholars take Jung's work in dream interpretation with a fresh seriousness, and scientific research has been conducted into nature's dreaming function.

But the modern scientific study of dreams merely supports what biblical writers long ago knew. Dreams played a major role in the stories about Abraham, Jacob, Daniel, and Jacob's son Joseph, among others. Early Christian literature is likewise full of dream references. For example, Tertullian writes, "Almost the greater part of mankind derive their knowledge of God from dreams."* Augustine even developed a "theory of dreams." Expanding the operational definition of dreams to include such terms as *vision, trance,* and *being in the spirit,* there are more than seventy references to dream phenomena in the NRSV, and they involve children, women, and men.

Christmas reminds us that the incarnation comes to us as a gift. The promptings of God's spirit come to us as gracious parts of God's holiness and wholeness. Often we require the gift of discernment in order to receive this gift. Thus, we become stewards of the dreams that God sends us. Ironically, by following his dreams' directives, Joseph becomes a savior to the Savior.

In the end, Joseph prevailed on behalf of his family at the most practical level because he was willing to trust and heed the voice and direction of God. We will never be too modern for this gift. To steward a God-given dream is a remarkable task. Although it seems an awesome responsibility, our dreams erect a wide tent over the lives of other people. To manage or steward the dreams that God sends our way may certainly appear an intangible task, but to pursue the authentic dreams that God sends also provides concrete consequences.

January 1–New Year
[See Year C]

---

*Tertullian, *De anima,* xliv.

Epiphany

Epiphany of the Lord
(January 6 or first Sunday of January; A, B, and C)

Isaiah 60:1–6   The Light God Passes through Us

"The abundance of the sea shall be brought to you, the wealth of the nations shall come to you."

(Isa. 60:5)

Epiphany can sometimes easily become a lost liturgical season. It is a season lodged between the splendor of Advent/Christmas and the well-known stories of temptation, crucifixion, and resurrection related during the seasons of Lent and Easter. As a result, we recognize Epiphany as a season in Ordinary Time. Yet Epiphany's message to the church remains both potent and important. Epiphany is far from ordinary as we typically use the word. Epiphany's good news concerns not only Jesus' baptism but also the manifestation of the gospel to the nations. Epiphany is a season that tells the story of a faith that spreads to the globe's four corners.

11

The lesson from the Hebrew Scriptures for today is postexilic. It is a hope-filled text, because for Israel it signals the coming of light after the exile's long darkness. The message also endows Israel with a great responsibility. Israel offers itself as a model of people upon whom God's light has shined. Hence, Israel is to lead others to the light that God offers. Israel is to steward the gift of light that only God can offer the world. By extension, now the church becomes the bearer of God's light.

I heard a speaker once say, "What America does today the world will do tomorrow. This means Americans will have a lot to answer for." In a sense, this is Isaiah's message to the people of Israel. Isaiah tells Israel that "nations shall come to your light." Strictly speaking, of course, "your light" to which the nations and kings are drawn is God's light. But now God, who gave the world its original light (Gen. 1:3–5), gives again the light to Israel. Light therefore becomes a gift of trust. But Israel participates in the gift of light by accepting responsibility for it. Isaiah implies that Israel exchanges its previous existence in darkness for God's light. As Israel shares the light with others, Israel leads the nations toward God's light. Consequently, Israel exercises its stewardship of God's light by modeling what a holy people look like when illuminated by God's light. Perhaps this idea of modeling faith was behind Jesus' words, "Be perfect, therefore, as your heavenly Father is perfect" (Matt. 5:48).

How is Israel a "steward" of the light? To answer such a question we must recognize that the gift of light that Israel receives is not self-generated. Those who employ stewardship never apply stewardship with respect to the things that they own. Rather, stewardship is always a management of another's property. In this case it is God's light given to Israel as a gift to oversee. Accordingly, Isaiah seems to mandate what the people's proper response to the gift shall be. Isaiah writes the command: "You shall see and be radiant; your heart shall thrill and rejoice." Isaiah also seems to mandate the nations'—that is, the Gentiles'—response as well. The prophet writes that "the wealth of the nations shall come to you." Isaiah also adds the kinds of wealth about which he writes: "camels, gold, frankincense" and the proclaiming of "the praise of the Lord."

The gift of light that Isaiah promises Israel is in obvious contrast to the decades of darkness Israel has so long endured. Nevertheless, a new day dawns and Israel is to become a steward of God's gift of light. We Christian believers also manage the gifts that God has given us in Christ. Epiphany is a season in which we can show our neighbors the gifts that came our way this past Christmas: grace, mercy, forgiveness, and the light of Christ. These are God's gifts that we manage as stewards.

Baptism of the Lord
(First Sunday after the Epiphany; Sunday between January 7 and 13)

Matthew 3:13–17   The Stewardship of Baptismal Authority

"It is proper for us in this way to fulfill all righteousness."
(Matt. 3:15)

Perhaps no question is as obvious and ultimately unanswerable as this: Why does Jesus need to be baptized? Matthew 3 focuses entirely on the relationship between John the Baptizer and Jesus. Paul calls both him and his companions "stewards of God's mysteries" (1 Cor. 4:1). We too are stewards of God's mysteries, and this includes the mystery that we know as baptism. Jesus' baptism has long baffled believers, although Matthew is clear that Jesus was adamant about John baptizing him.

Baptism excites Christian sensibilities because often we associate baptism with salvation. Some people are prone to think that baptism is a straightforward transaction, like buying a violin or a vacuum cleaner. This thinking suggests that if a church properly baptizes people, then they enjoy the status of salvation. This view of baptism triggers the same disturbing faith question: Why does John need to baptize Jesus? Does Jesus need salvation? Does the Savior need to be saved?

A second reason baptism fuels our sensibilities is because we often associate baptism with a ritual cleansing. If the waters of baptism cleanse us, then God washes away our sin. We may now ask, "From what is Jesus cleansed? What exactly was Jesus' sin?" Later Christian testimony argues against this thinking. In fact, Hebrews 4:15 candidly states, "We have one who in every respect has been tested as we are, yet without sin." The question remains: Why does Jesus insist on baptism, and why does he need it?

The answer, vital for an understanding of Christian stewardship, seems to address the need to be under authority. Stewards only act out of the authority conferred on them by God. Too often we believe, because of our bent toward individualism, that we each know what is best. Those of us who live and think this way have no use for any authority that is not self-imposed. We think we know it all and can go it alone. However, if there were anyone who could go it alone and not be subject to baptism, it would be Jesus. Why then does Jesus insist on baptism?

The exchange between John and Jesus offers us a clue. Jesus insists on being put under God's authority via baptism. Jesus, fully human and fully divine, in effect says to those who witness his baptism—and this includes John—"If baptism is good enough for you, then baptism is good enough for me." By Jesus' example he implies the reverse as well: "If baptism is good enough for me, then baptism is good enough for you."

Baptism explicitly puts believers under God's authority. As those under God's universal authority, we gather in worship and mission as those authorized to act on behalf of God. God assembles us a community, and baptism initiates us into that community. If baptism is God's work, then our work begins after baptism. Our response to what God has done for us through baptism is our gift back to God. To respond to God's call is to be a disciple and a steward of God's grace. In the sharing of that gift of grace, we each become stewards of the mysteries of God.

Second Sunday after the Epiphany
(Sunday between January 14 and 20 inclusive)

1 Corinthians 1:1–9   Christian Identity: God's Gift to Us

"He will also strengthen you . . . so that you may be blameless."
(1 Cor. 1:8)

Paul begins 1 Corinthians with these words: "To the church of God that is in Corinth, to those who are sanctified in Christ Jesus, called to be saints . . ." At times it is tempting to pass over such introductions and head straight for the content instead. However, Paul's preface to 1 Corinthians is like an arrow, silently cutting the air and hitting us where we live. The "sanctified" are those persons "called to be holy" or "called to be saints." Christian stewards believe in holiness as a gift from God.

Despite this kind of thinking, however, some folks believe that being "sanctified," "holy," or "a saint" leaves them out of the holiness loop. To be a saint is not as limiting for people today any more than it was for people in Corinth. Although separated by twenty centuries and many miles, Corinth and modern America are surprisingly alike. The Corinthians were wealthy, well educated, and prone to what the Bible calls "licentiousness." Regardless, Paul summons the Corinthians to holiness. Our lesson today is a preface to faith issues Paul explores in the whole epistle to Corinth. Stewards of faith today must, like the Corinthian church, confront these same matters.

Paul addresses three chief matters in this letter. The issues are surprisingly similar to modern America's most explosive concerns: disunity, sexuality, and idolatry. Secular people address these topics in assorted ways, but Paul offers another avenue by which believers as stewards may live. This alternative path is by the gift of Christian identity. God furnishes our identity as believers through Christ. Stewards seek holiness by managing God's resources for the benefit of others.

First, Paul confronts disunity. Factions plague the congregation, prompting Paul to write: "Each of you says, 'I belong to Paul,' or 'I belong to Apollos,' or 'I belong to Cephas,' or 'I belong to Christ.' Has Christ been divided? Was Paul crucified for you? Or were you baptized in the name of Paul?" (1:12–13). Sadly, too often in our world it takes a natural calamity such as a tsunami, a mudslide, an avalanche, or a Hurricane Katrina to unite people. Paul's appeal to church unity is straightforward: God called them "into the fellowship of his Son, Jesus Christ."

Second, Paul addresses sexuality and related issues. Such issues have modern-day parallels: Whom should we accept into church leadership? What of sexuality should we teach in public schools? What are accepted standards for behavior in our community? These questions evolve from our discomfort as sexual creatures. Human sexuality pertains to a wide variety of topics: marriage and family, procreation, divorce, reproductive technology, and pregnancy. Paul cuts to the heart of the issues: Does our behavior build up the church, or not?

Third, Paul responds to idolatry. Idolatry means worshiping something other than God. The world too often tries to define us, whether through Madison Avenue or the trends our friends set. As Christian stewards, however, we know that it is God alone who defines the authentic identity of disciples. Paul writes about who we Christians are—then and now. When we step off the path, our way back is plainly to remember who we are. Paul writes to the Corinthians who have outwardly lost their way. They have forgotten that they are God's people. In every era God's gift to stewards is our identity.

Third Sunday after the Epiphany
(Sunday between January 21 and 27 inclusive)

Matthew 4:12–23   An Impulsive Gamble

"Immediately they left their nets and followed him."
(Matt. 4:20)

To be a Christian steward requires a believer to take risks. Outsiders see tithing or giving of time and treasure as hopelessly naive, a waste of resources that prudent people stockpile for survival or enjoyment. Yet a proper theology of stewardship understands that God loaned us all we possess. As believers we recognize that what we have is not really ours.

Those who offer advice about such things recommend that shoppers never go to the grocery store hungry. The reason is that stores employ "shopper psychology." They cleverly place nonessential items in the path of unwary shoppers, believing that innocent shoppers will toss random items into their carts as they move through the store. This strategy translates into impulsive buying. Impulsive behavior generally gets us in trouble, and we are all guilty of it.

The second half of our Gospel lesson involves impulsive behavior on the part of four disciples. Jesus, walking along the Sea of Galilee, sees two fishermen. To these brothers Jesus says, "Follow me." Impulsively and immediately they follow Jesus. Perhaps they had heard about Jesus, but even so what they did was rash. The Bible records no meditation or prayer over the decision. Matthew simply writes, "Immediately they left their nets and followed him." Peter later speaks to Jesus about this decision: "Look, we have left everything and followed you" (Matt. 19:27). For once, Peter gets it exactly right!

Soon after, Jesus summons two other brothers with the same result: "Immediately they left the boat and their father, and followed him." Jesus calls to himself an alternative community that reflects the coming reign of God, what

Matthew regularly calls the kingdom of heaven. The disciples' response is impulsive.

These four followers made an impetuous and colossal decision. Perhaps their decision is difficult for us to understand in the twenty-first century. Like prior generations, these disciples had always been fisher-folk. No doubt, they too expected that their children and their children's children would be fisher-folk. But then along came Jesus, and Jesus transformed all this predictability into a call to ministry: "Follow me." If these disciples had taken a safe, nonimpulsive course of action, history would have forgotten them within a generation. Yet two millennia later we still talk about them and, in our best moments, emulate them.

What if John Wesley had not, on a whim, decided to attend a church meeting on Aldersgate Street in London in 1738? What if Martin Luther had decided to be more cautious and not nailed his Ninety-five Theses to the Wittenberg church door? What if Dietrich Bonhoeffer had not decided to defy the Nazis?

As stewards and followers of Christ, when we contemplate whether to be bold or not, we can simply remember Jesus' promise to his disciples: "Everyone who has left houses or brothers or sisters or father or mother or children or fields, for my name's sake, will receive a hundredfold, and will inherit eternal life" (Matt. 19:29).

On occasion, being impulsive is a good way to practice Christian stewardship.

Fourth Sunday after the Epiphany
(Sunday between January 28 and February 3 inclusive;
if it is the Last Sunday after the Epiphany, see Transfiguration)

Micah 6:1–8   What Does God Want from Us Anyway?

"O my people, what have I done to you? In what have I wearied you?"
(Mic. 6:3)

Very few of us do not have at least an idea of what goes on inside a courthouse. If we have never actually witnessed a trial, we at least have watched a lot of them on TV. Our television viewing habits suggest that the inner workings of justice have regularly fascinated us. Some viewers cut their teeth on *Perry Mason*. Steady audiences from other generations have watched *The Defenders, Matlock,* or *Law and Order*. The most ardent legal voyeurs even watch *Court TV*. For this reason alone, our lesson from the prophet Micah is easy for us to grasp. This staged "courtroom" drama pertains to stewards largely because Micah's prophecy spells out what the Lord really wants from his disciples—the faithful obedient whom God calls to stewardship.

Micah, acting the part of the prosecutor, asks the people on God's behalf, "O my people, what have I done to you? In what have I wearied you? Answer me!" Then the prophet-prosecutor brings out some convincing particulars. He enters into evidence these facts concerning God's faithfulness to the people: (1) "I brought you up from the land of Egypt," (2) "[I] redeemed you from the house of slavery," (3) "I sent before you Moses, Aaron, and Miriam." Micah also drops the name of one from whom the Lord rescued Israel: King Balak of Moab. In addition, the geographical names of Shittim and Gilgal remind the chosen people exactly how far God will go to preserve their nation. The names bid them to "know the saving acts of the LORD."

As in any good trial, however, the accused also has a chance to respond. So Micah enters the people's voice. They ask in distress: "Shall I come before him with burnt offerings, with calves a year old? Will the LORD be pleased with thousands of rams, with ten thousands of rivers of oil? Shall I give my firstborn for my transgression, the fruit of my body for the sin of my soul?" In a nutshell and using good Hebrew hyperbole, these questions plainly suggest that Israel thinks it is finished with its sacrifice. What more can the people do to satisfy their God? Their questions imply Israel has done enough.

But Micah is not finished. The prophet ironically lampoons the people and, from his perspective, their pathetic defense. With one of Scripture's most insightful sentences and bottom-line truths, Micah responds. Micah practically mocks the people by the simplicity of his answer: all the Lord requires from God's people is "to do justice, and to love kindness, and to walk humbly with your God." When believers perform these tasks of mercy and goodness for God's creation, they clearly fulfill any obligations to the divine. They become stewards of God's will.

If Christian believers follow the Lord's precepts of justice, kindness, and humility before Almighty God, then they can claim the name "Christian steward." Of all the households stewards manage or administer on God's behalf, these simple acts of faithful charity surely construct the foundation of righteous living.

Matthew and Luke record Jesus as saying to some opponents that although they may have abided by the law's literal word, they "have neglected the weightier matters of the law: justice and mercy and faith" (Matt. 23:23; Luke 11:42). If we attend to the triad of God's requirements brought forward by Micah, we are stewards. Case closed.

Fifth Sunday after the Epiphany
(Sunday between February 4 and 10 inclusive;
if it is the Last Sunday after the Epiphany, see Transfiguration)

Matthew 5:13–20   Stewards of Light

"You are the light of the world."
(Matt. 5:14)

Jesus tells his listeners that they are the light of the world. Biblically speaking, the contrast of light and dark is a prominent theme and pertinent for stewardship. From Genesis to Revelation, images of light and dark pepper the biblical landscape. For example, in the Letter to the Ephesians the writer tells his audience that "once you were darkness, but now in the Lord you are light." He pushes these believers to "live as children of light—for the fruit of the light is found in all that is good and right and true." He suggests that "everything exposed by the light becomes visible" (Eph. 5:8–13). Stewards are persons who live in the light of Christ.

The Gospel lesson comes from the Sermon on the Mount in Matthew. The text is appropriate for Epiphany, a liturgical season that emphasizes God's light shining in dark places. Previous Epiphany texts from Year A have told readers that for Israel "your light has come" (Isa. 60:1), "the Lord is my light and my salvation" (Ps. 27:1), "the people who walked in darkness have seen a great light" (Isa. 9:2), and "your light shall rise in the darkness" (Isa. 58:10). Thus, light is a major motif for the Epiphany season. But here Jesus tells the crowds that they not only have the light but are themselves "the light of the world." And light never fails to illumine whatever it falls upon.

Jesus teaches those who follow him that wherever they go they will be the light of God in the world—they will shine light on otherwise dark places. Jesus emphasizes stewardship of the light by exhorting the crowds to "let your light shine before others, so that they may see your good works and give glory to your Father in heaven." In this fashion, Christ's light radiates outward in the lives of disciples—like a pebble thrown into a pool. The ripples of gospel light will overcome the world's darkness.

Perhaps this is why in the 1960s, along with "We Shall Overcome," one of the central songs of the civil rights movement was "This Little Light of Mine." Human beings are capable of shining light in dark places, for light exposes the truth. Light becomes a key element in finding something—the contents of an envelope, an object or, especially, the truth. Even at creation light begins the process of life when God separates it from darkness. Moreover, John reminds believers, "The light shines in the darkness, and the darkness did not overcome it" (John 1:5).

For Christian stewards light—either having it or being it—is a remarkable responsibility. We must manage our use of it and the intensity by which we use it. In one church there was a powerful group that did not particularly concern itself with the people living in poverty in the same neighborhood. Yet many church members wanted their church to reach out to its community. A retired pastor suggested, "Bring all the opponents together and shine a light on them." His suggestion was that when the community of faith laid out all the facts, then the gospel's light would expose the opposition. The retired pastor was right. The church voted down the opposition to mission and acted in faithfulness. The church opened a tutoring center for neighborhood children. These church members became bona fide stewards of the light they had—and "the darkness did not overcome it." Jesus reminds us now as then, "You are the light of the world."

Sixth Sunday after the Epiphany
(Sunday between February 11 and 17 inclusive; if it is the Last Sunday after the Epiphany, see Transfiguration)

Deuteronomy 30:15–20   Stewards Manage Decisions

"I have set before you life and death, blessings and curses."
(Deut. 30:19)

Stewards manage their decision about what to do with what God has loaned them. God provides all and loans it to us to build up God's realm. Thus, God and Christian stewards are partners. God provides the wherewithal; stewards handle God's resources. Stewards function likewise as a response to God's goodness. Yet regularly, into a steward's spirit of gratitude, seeps the reverie of a conditional reward, and stewards use God's bounty for another incentive beyond gratefulness to God. What gives rise to this understanding?

The lesson from Deuteronomy offers a partial answer. Deuteronomy through 2 Kings tries to make clear why Israel suffered. Theologians advanced a theological understanding of God and divine punishment to implore Israel back into a proper relationship with God. The thinking went that human disregard of the divine covenant incurred God's wrath. If people live well, this is because God continues to bless them. However, if people suffer, then God has either cursed them or made them vulnerable to evil's penalty. Consequently, the text is stark: "I have set before you today life and prosperity, death and adversity."

One of the prominent features of Deuteronomic theology is that it often establishes a conditional "if-then" formula. Our text gives an excellent example in verse 16: "If you obey the commandments of the LORD . . . then you shall live and become numerous, and the LORD your God will bless you in the land that you are entering to possess." Often, however, part of the condition is merely assumed, so that although the conditions "if-then" are not explicit, they reside below the surface. One example of many is Deuteronomy 6:25: "If we diligently observe this entire commandment before the LORD our God, as he has commanded us, [then] we will be in the right."

In life's logic, the thinking that fashions the Deuteronomic theology makes common sense. "If you do your homework, then you will do well on the test" and "If you spend your time with the right kind of people, then you will stay out of trouble" are guiding examples parents habitually offer children. In most cases this is solid thinking. The quandary arrives when the "if" condition is met, but the "then" conclusion is unmet. As we all know, even the most faithful people suffer, and those who do evil often succeed. Job is one of the Bible's responses to the Deuteronomic theology.

Although stewards expect to reap rewards of faithful living by a generous management of God's resources, there is no guarantee that things will always turn out the way we expect. For faithful stewards, the gift of managing God's resources, regardless of any auxiliary reward, is the end product of righteous living. Jesus himself proved that a life lived to perfection has disastrous consequences from the human point of view. Even so, in God's calculus, the one who lives honorably before God has already received divine compensation. This compensation is a divine love that is always and everywhere unconditional. Sometimes faithful stewards act not because of but despite our outward human circumstances or incentives. We are stewards of the mysteries of God because Jesus is the steward of our souls.

Seventh Sunday after the Epiphany
(Sunday between February 18 and 24 inclusive; if it is the Last Sunday after the Epiphany, see Transfiguration)

Leviticus 19:1–2, 9–18   Guarding Each Person's Pride

"You shall leave [the fallen grapes] for the poor and the alien."
(Lev. 19:10)

When I was preparing for confirmation, for scheduling reasons my father would drop me off at our church several hours before class. While I awaited the pastor and my fellow students, I roamed the church. Often I studied the reproductions of paintings scattered throughout the Sunday school rooms. Warner Sallman's *Head of Christ* drew my attention. I have heard that this print has sold more than 500 million copies. Yet *The Gleaners* by Jean François Millet was my favorite. My Sunday school teacher told the class that this picture was of Ruth working in the fields. He taught us about "gleaning." Later I discovered that the painting was likely not of Ruth, since Millet was a part of the nineteenth-century realism movement and painted contemporary scenes. Still, the painting conveys the biblical concept of gleaning.

Gleaning was one of the social nets that provided for the poor. Those who harvested grapes or barley or other crops did not clear their fields of everything. Rather, they left some "leftovers." In fact, this practice was so central to Israel that they wrote it into the law. An example similar to that found in the Leviticus passage is in Deuteronomy 24:21: "When you gather the grapes of your vineyard, do not glean what is left; it shall be for the alien, the orphan, and the widow." This procedure did two things. First, it provided for those who did not own land, or enough land, to feed their families. Second, it offered dignity to those who gleaned. Indisputably the practice was charity, but it also allowed the beneficiaries an opportunity to work for their gift of food.

In the book of Ruth, gleaning plays a key role in the story. Boaz tells his harvesters about Ruth, "Let her glean even among the standing sheaves, and do not reproach her. You must also pull out some handfuls for her from the bundles, and leave them for her to glean, and do not rebuke her" (Ruth 2:15–16). Ruth's family was essentially destitute. But Boaz, a wealthy landowner, had compassion. He allowed Ruth to glean after his harvest. As the story unfolds, we learn that Boaz may have had designs on Ruth. But through his actions Boaz reveals the intent of Israel's agricultural laws that provided for the hungry.

The church can learn something from what Leviticus discloses. Our lesson offers several ordinances the Lord reveals to Moses—"You shall not steal," "You shall not defraud your neighbor," "You shall not render an unjust judgment," and "You shall not take vengeance"—yet regulations concerning gleaning in particular teach sensible stewards an essential lesson.

Most of us want to help the poor among us, and we want to do "the right thing." We want to follow Jesus' admonition to "show kindness to [the poor] whenever you wish" (Mark 14:7). Why do we want to do these things? Because God commanded it. Treating the poor generously is the right thing to do. But Leviticus unveils perhaps the most important reason. We live a certain way because, as Moses tells the people, "You shall be holy, for I the LORD your God am holy."

When we give to others, would it not be wise for us to allow their dignity to remain intact? If we are to be stewards of God's gifts loaned to us, then would we not do better to offer others God's providence in ways that make them grateful to God? Gleaning was a legal practice that permitted this dignity. In this way, today's stewards might learn how to guard each person's pride.

Eighth Sunday after the Epiphany
(Sunday between February 25 and 29 inclusive; if it is the Last Sunday after the Epiphany, see Transfiguration)

1 Corinthians 4:1–5   Stewards as Imitators of Paul

"It is required of stewards that they be found trustworthy."
(1 Cor. 4:2)

Paul is dealing with a thorny situation in Corinth. The fledgling church has many problems. We can deduce some of these troubles from the questions that Paul poses, and then answers, in 1 and 2 Corinthians. What is of interest to this commentary is Paul's reference to himself and Apollos as "servants of Christ and stewards of God's mysteries." What does this mean for Christian stewards?

In the text that follows this lesson, Paul employs "kingly" imagery. Paul writes to this congregation, "You have become kings! Indeed, I wish that you had become kings, so that we might be kings with you!" (4:8). Yet Paul has described himself and Apollos as "servants" and "stewards." Thus, for Paul the contrast for believers is marked. At once Paul wishes the Corinthian believers to be kinglike, while he describes himself and Apollos as servants. Clearly a dialectic of identity is at work here, even more so when we read a few verses later, "I appeal to you, then, be imitators of me" (4:16). So which is it for believers— sovereignty or servanthood?

If these were the only descriptions Paul used for himself and believers, then it would be easier to ferret out Paul's meaning. However, Paul tells the Corinthians that he and Apollos are also "as though sentenced to death," "fools," "weak," "in disrepute," "hungry and thirsty," "poorly clothed and beaten and homeless." The crowning self-deprecation appears when Paul reveals that he and Apollos are "like the rubbish of the world, the dregs of all things" (4:9–13). Why does Paul write these things? What is the rhetorical purpose of this hyperhumility?

The key is within the congregation at Corinth. As the saying goes, "All theology is local." Thus, Paul addresses the congregation's specific circumstance. Divisions exist within the congregation. Some individuals think too highly of themselves and put themselves in a superior position with regard to the rest of the congregation. Thus, Paul pulls these arrogant believers back into their relative place—"so that none of you will be puffed up in favor of one against another" (4:6).

Genuine stewards are those who imitate Paul. Apollos, the other apostles, and Paul are those who may, if indeed anyone can, claim pride of place in the early church. But Paul makes it obvious that he wants the Corinthian believers to "think of us in this way, as servants of Christ and stewards of God's mysteries." In a subtle argument, Paul wants the arrogant to recognize that it is not their place to judge others, or even to rank believers in some sort of "pecking order" of faithfulness. As Paul asserts, judgment is solely God's task. We might even suggest that God alone evaluates, measures, and judges Christian stewardship. Therefore, the only thing that concerns believers, from Paul's perspective, is that God finds stewards trustworthy.

Stewards, above all else, are individuals who think of themselves as *doulos*, or "slaves." Humility and meekness are qualities that mark dependable disciples. In fact, Paul seems to think that it is in our humility as disciples and stewards that we will find our sovereignty as God's people. This is Paul's aim and why he urges his followers to "be imitators of me" (4:16).

Transfiguration Sunday
(Last Sunday after the Epiphany)

2 Peter 1:16–21   Right Living and Being Stewards of Scripture

"No prophecy ever came by human will, but . . . by the Holy Spirit."
(2 Pet. 1:21)

Transfiguration Sunday is the capstone Sunday of the liturgical season of Epiphany. This season of worship expresses in many and various ways God's power coming to dwell in human life. Epiphany includes the story of Jesus' baptism and bears witness to the light of God's Messiah that illumines human existence. For stewards, the ways we manage the power of God and God's revelation are part and parcel of Epiphany.

Many people crave a guarantee. In Christian circles we have a guarantee we call "the assurance of faith." Although we speak of faith virtually every day, life has a way of undermining every certainty to which we cling. It is in this search for meaning that we worship and study the Bible. The epistle text offers insight into the authority of those who teach Scripture in the church. The assurance of Scripture, as well as our stewardship of its teaching, comprises our lesson.

Some scholars think that 2 Peter's author was approaching death and wished to leave a sort of last will and testament. The epistle includes provisos by which Christians might live. It judges that right living in community is a priority for those worthy of Christ's kingdom. The letter gravely urges—in fact, insists—that the faithful not fall away from the apostolic teaching. The church had waited several generations for the return of Christ, and the faith of some believers had begun to wane. As 2 Peter is a late document, perhaps it has a word for us as a settled church, one that also waits for the Lord's return.

Second Peter attempts to encourage Christians, to offer an assurance of faith in God's power, and to rekindle hope. In addition, it supplies some meaning to suffering and offers guidance as to how these believers can nurture one another as a congregation.

How does the author of 2 Peter make the argument? First, he confesses that he is not a fancy public speaker: "We did not follow cleverly devised myths," as celebrated first-century rhetoricians did. The author rather evokes the faith community's memory: "We made known to you the power and coming of our Lord." Further, the author alludes to having been an eyewitness to the transfiguration, in which God fully revealed Jesus to Peter, James, and John.

Second, the author reminds his readers that they will do well to be dutiful to this disclosure as "a lamp shining in a dark place, until the day dawns and the morning star rises in your hearts." The lamp shining in a dark place refers, no doubt, to the radiance of Jesus' life against the world's dreary background.

Third, the author affirms that Scripture is not any individual's possession. It is community property. The author appears to debate with those who believe they have cornered the market on truth. Second Peter reminds the church about its responsibility for Scripture and its interpretation. Accordingly, the church protects itself from falsehood by keeping close to the stories of Jesus and protecting Scripture's sacredness. When we do this, we become faithful stewards of God's revelation of truth for all people everywhere. Each Christian is a steward and guardian of Scripture that reveals Christ's incarnation.

Lent

Ash Wednesday
[See Year B]

First Sunday in Lent

Matthew 4:1–11   Giving Ourselves Up for Lent

"One does not live by bread alone."
(Matt. 4:4)

I recently received a note from a congregant. In essence it read, "I am giving up something for Lent, but my coworkers either think it silly or believe I am desecrating Lent by trivializing it." Curious, I asked him what he had given up. As it turned out, he had given up chocolate. The meaning of Lent for many modern people turns on a proper understanding of this time-honored ritual of "giving something up" for Lent. I told this congregant that although giving up chocolate to commemorate Jesus' sacrifice on the cross seems trivial to some, perhaps it is at least a minor beginning. Maybe someday he can offer a more costly sacrifice.

To be a Christian steward means to live sacrificially each day. We give to God and the church as a response to our faith and trust in God. As King David once suggested, "I will not offer burnt offerings to the LORD my God that cost me nothing" (2 Sam. 24:24). As God's stewards, our giving and "giving up" usually cost something if we are making an appropriate sacrifice. Matthew recounts high drama in the desert at Lent's beginning. Jesus' encounter with the devil reveals much about us.

All three of the temptations point to *the* temptation of life: to be as God. The temptation to act like God (stones to bread) came early in the human experience. In depicting Jesus' human struggle with temptation, Matthew merely puts a fine point on the Genesis temptation story. There the serpent suggests to the woman, "you will be like God, knowing good and evil" (Gen. 3:5). This is a story for every generation.

Perhaps for Lent we believers might give up the idea of playing God. We decide at every turn what is good for us and for others. We put many idols in God's place: our reputations, our careers, our income-generating abilities, our stock portfolios, our nation, our children, our winter or summer cottages, our self-assertions that we presume will bring us contented self-realization. Matthew can give us pause. With heavenly words ringing in Jesus' ears, "This is my Son, the Beloved, with whom I am well pleased," Matthew relates that "Jesus was led up by the Spirit into the wilderness to be tempted by the devil" (Matt. 3:17; 4:1). If we are Jesus' disciples, then what does this say to us?

Perhaps Matthew's story tells us that those who suggest that our life in Christ will make life easier are lying to us—as surely as the serpent lied to the woman. If we presume that when we come to Jesus we will leave the heartache and misery of our former life behind, then we lie to ourselves. Being the stewards God calls us to be makes life more difficult rather than trouble free.

Reliable Christian stewards sacrifice the notion that we call the shots and make the decisions that pertain to the good life. Instead, we lean toward Jesus' prompting—the Jesus who "emptied himself, taking the form of a slave . . . [and] humbled himself" (Phil. 2:7–8). When we come to ourselves with this knowledge of God, offering ourselves as stewards to God's world, then we know that we do not "live by bread alone." Rather, we live into Christ's promise that life has a more ultimate meaning for us and others. As stewards, in a sense, we give up ourselves for Lent.

Second Sunday in Lent

John 3:1–17   Exploring Discipleship

"Nicodemus, a leader of the Jews . . . came to Jesus by night."
(John 3:1–2)

In the middle of the Sermon on the Mount Jesus praises secrecy as a virtue: "When you give alms, do not let your left hand know what your right hand is doing, so that your alms may be done in secret" (Matt. 6:3–4). Jesus is drawing a contrast with what the "hypocrites do in the synagogues and in the streets, so that they may be praised by others." It is God who rewards true giving, not other people.

The Gospel lesson from John reveals the "secret" character of Nicodemus, who comes to Jesus "by night." Under the cover of darkness this exceptional layperson and member of the Jewish Sanhedrin avoids drawing undue attention to himself by his association with Jesus. John's Gospel at times uses the term "night" to identify an ominous occasion. For example, John tells readers that "after receiving the piece of bread, [Judas] immediately went out. And it was night" (John 13:30). John here contrasts the evil in Judas' heart with Jesus as the Word. Early in his Gospel the evangelist writes of Jesus: "The light shines in the darkness, and the darkness did not overcome it" (John 1:5). So why does Nicodemus come to Jesus by night?

Uneducated and ordinary followers, such as the Twelve, gladly heard Jesus' good news. Yet for those in positions of influence and power, such as Nicodemus, being in Jesus' company posed a threat. Nicodemus spent a lifetime establishing his status. He was no doubt a person of wealth, which may account for his standing in the community. Not only did he possess means, but he was doubtlessly well-educated and probably had a good family name. Over the years he had worked hard to become well connected among the elite religious community in Palestine. Weighing the risk to his reputation against his innate religious curiosity, Nicodemus approaches Jesus—by night.

To become a disciple, to become a faithful steward, all believers come to a moment of decision. We must, each of us, decide whether or not following Jesus as Messiah is worth the termination of human associations and lifestyles that are incompatible with Christ. We may say that Jesus speaks hyperbolically when he says, "Blessed are you when people hate you, and when they exclude you, revile you, and defame you on account of the Son of Man" (Luke 6:22). Yet the words are still on the biblical page; we find them difficult to explain away. When Jesus says, "Whoever comes to me and does not hate father and mother, wife and children, brothers and sisters, yes, and even life itself, cannot be my disciple" (Luke 14:26), it gives the most earnest of us pause. Like Nicodemus, often we too make sure that we are counting the cost.

Nevertheless, within the veil of all our caution, we stewards must choose this day whom we shall serve: either the Messiah of God or our self-generated lives of power and prestige. Few of us have as much to surrender as did Nicodemus. The Gospels tell us little about what happened to him. Yet after Jesus dies, John does drop something of a footnote: "Nicodemus, who had at first come to Jesus by night, also came" (John 19:39). Evidently over time, Nicodemus made his choice of whom to serve.

Third Sunday in Lent

Romans 5:1–11   On Boasting

"We boast in our hope of sharing the glory of God."
(Rom. 5:2)

We church folk are deep into Lent. The lectionary offers us several robust preaching choices on this Sunday. Exodus 17:1–7 is the story of a crisis in the desert: "The people thirsted there for water; and the people complained against Moses and said, 'Why did you bring us out of Egypt, to kill us and our children and livestock with thirst?' " Ironically, the Gospel lesson, John 4:5–42, is the story of Jesus and the woman at the well and his offer to her of "living water." Jesus tells the woman, "Everyone who drinks of this water will be thirsty again, but those who drink of the water that I will give them will never be thirsty. The water that I will give will become in them a spring of water gushing up to eternal life" (John 4:13–14).

For those with stewardship interests, however, we look to Paul's reflection regarding a believer's sole reason for boasting. Generally, boasting is a term Paul uses to allude to human pride, usually by fulfilling the ritual law. In Romans, for example, Paul writes, "But if you call yourself a Jew and rely on the law and boast of your relation to God and know his will and determine what is best because you are instructed in the law . . . " (Rom. 2:17–18). Paul then completes the idea with examples of teaching one thing and doing another. He implies that all boasting leads to hypocrisy and, thus, to sin. At the diatribe's conclusion Paul asks a critical question: "You that boast in the law, do you dishonor God by breaking the law?" (2:23). Yet Paul also writes, as if in opposition, "We boast in our hope of sharing the glory of God." Why?

In the earlier citations "boasting" pertains to human achievement in striving to fulfill the law's requirements. Yet in today's lesson Paul confirms that for Christians it is God who establishes our foundation for boasting. In the first part of Paul's tightly reasoned exposition, he reminds believers that (1) faith in God justifies humans, (2) we have peace with God, (3) Jesus Christ is the ground of that peace, (4) we obtain access to God's grace, and (5) we boast in our hope. Both the KJV and NIV translate as "rejoice" what the NRSV translates as "boast." Surely overlap occurs in the word's shades of meaning, but Paul uses what God does for believers as our lone source of boasting. Thus, if something is of God, we boast; if something is of human origin, then our boasting is misguided. This is the difference. Paul ends by telling his readers that "we even boast in God through our Lord Jesus Christ, through whom we have now received reconciliation."

Many people give to the church's ministries, often as humble servants. However, creeping into some minds and hearts is a temptation to surrender to a presumptuous pride. It whispers, "I did something holy and right and good." For Paul, our giving is not a ground for boasting any more than is our faith. Rather, God offers us the heart to give, as the heart to believe, as gifts for us to use as stewards. Christians give only as they receive. Faithful stewards know that what they give to God is a measure of their true devotion. It is true that one may give without believing, but one cannot believe without giving. Christians also know that the Holy Spirit powers our desire and ability to give.

Thus, if we must boast, may we boast only about what God has given us. May "we boast in our hope of sharing the glory of God." We give that others may hear the gospel.

Fourth Sunday in Lent

1 Samuel 16:1–13   What Does God See?

"The LORD does not see as mortals . . . but the LORD looks on the heart."
(1 Sam. 16:7)

The Hebrew Scripture lesson details one story about David becoming Israel's king. From the standpoint of stewardship we will explore the statement "The LORD does not see as mortals see; they look on the outward appearance, but the LORD looks on the heart." What does this phrase teach modern believers called to be stewards about the nature of God?

Our text begins with Israel in a crisis condition. I am told that in Chinese, two characters make up the word *crisis*. One Chinese character symbolizes "danger," while the other character signifies "opportunity." It is clear from the subsequent history of the people of God that Israel has a glorious opportunity for leadership from a person who will go on to become arguably Israel's finest leader. Yet this opportunity also spells danger. That Samuel senses this danger is evident by his timid response to the Lord's request: "I will send you to Jesse the Bethlehemite, for I have provided for myself a king among his sons."

Samuel knows that if he begins searching for another king, he may arouse the ire of the incumbent king. For this reason, Samuel responds to the Lord, "How can I go? If Saul hears of it, he will kill me." By a divine ruse, the Lord works out a suitable scenario for Samuel's journey to Jesse's house. Samuel is to tell the people that he has come "to sacrifice to the LORD." At the moment this subterfuge seems to placate all the nervous elders of Bethlehem, and they gather for sacrifice.

At the sacrifice Samuel looks over the sons of Jesse. They appear in order from the first to the (almost) last—Eliab, Abinadab, and Shammah pass by Samuel.

Each time the Lord tells Samuel, "This is not the one." Finally, after all the sons have passed by, Samuel asks Jesse, "Are all your sons here?" Jesse then recollects David. Samuel says in a most dramatic fashion, "Bring him; for we will not sit down until he comes here."

In one of the Bible's most ironic moments the text reads, "Now [David] was ruddy, and had beautiful eyes, and was handsome." Only a short time before, we learned that "the LORD does not see as mortals see; they look on the outward appearance, but the LORD looks on the heart." Despite this irony, the Lord tells Samuel, "Rise and anoint him; for this is the one."

A key to understanding this text is to note when the Lord tells Samuel that "the LORD does not see as mortals see." The Lord speaks these words to Samuel as he looks upon the first son of Jesse, Eliab. He thinks to himself, "Surely the LORD's anointed is now before the LORD." Samuel is no mere mortal; he is a seer of Israel—and a prophet and judge to boot! Yet the teller of this splendid story recounts events in this way that reveal even Israel's most discerning leader can get it wrong. Samuel has already missed the mark with Saul as king, choosing Saul, albeit reluctantly. Without the Lord's guidance Samuel seems bent on making another "kingly mistake."

This story teaches stewards that although we may have discerning spirits, the disciple's true wisdom comes from the God revealed in Christ Jesus. If the old sage Samuel fails to see as God sees, then how can we properly see? Stewards' prayers would do well to include petitions for the humble discernment to follow God's will.

Fifth Sunday in Lent

Ezekiel 37:1–14   Sharing Hope as Stewards

"You shall live; and you shall know that I am the LORD."
(Ezek. 37:6)

As one might expect on this fifth Sunday in Lent, our readings pertain to human mortality and God's ability to give new life. The Gospel lesson is the raising of Lazarus story. Included in this extended account of one of Jesus' many miracles is one of Jesus' "I am" sayings. Jesus tells Martha, "I am the resurrection and the life. Those who believe in me, even though they die, will live, and everyone who lives and believes in me will never die" (John 11:25–26). The Epistle lesson conveys for believers Paul's witness about life and death. Paul writes to the Roman church, "To set the mind on the flesh is death, but to set the mind on the Spirit is life and peace" (Rom. 8:6). But for stewardship reflection, we turn to the Hebrew prophet Ezekiel.

Perhaps we live in a death-denying culture as some social critics imply. Yet to be human means coming to terms with the last enemy, as Paul describes death (1 Cor. 15:26). The Lord brings Ezekiel to a place that appears, smells, tastes, and feels like death itself. The site is a valley "full of bones . . . and they were very dry." The text paints a scene like a lunar landscape—it is the essence of death. Except for the prophet, the scenery has no living thing present. Hopeless and barren are descriptions that come to mind. Then the Lords asks, "Mortal, can these bones live?"

From the human point of view, the realistic answer would be a resounding no. Yet in this valley of death, the life-giving spirit of God blossoms. Further, because of the spirit's presence, Jesus' later spoken words have a deeper import: "For mortals it is impossible, but for God all things are possible" (Matt. 19:26 and parallels).

Out of hopeless circumstances God's promise remains steadfast. Whether God blesses the closed womb of one of Israel's ancestors (Gen. 30:22; 1 Sam. 1:5) or rescues Israel from certain death at the Red Sea (Exod. 14:15–18), God nevertheless makes good on divine promises. For Ezekiel, whose nation stares despair in the eye, God again comes to reinitiate the promises made to the ancestors and to the little nation of Israel—God's chosen people. At the historic moment in which Ezekiel prophesies, Israel believes it has lost everything. The nation has (it thinks) no future—no more land, no more monarchy, no more nation, and no more temple. Yet like the valley of bones that God rouses, Israel's forsaken status is not fatal.

A retired minister friend of mine lived through one of the most agonizing experiences a parent can face—the suicide of a son or daughter. Few of us can think of an event more heartrending—a literal valley of dry bones. The raw pain of this tragedy has never departed my friend. He confessed that not a day goes by when the remembrance of it fails to haunt him. Yet out of my friend's valley of despondency has come a considerable ministry to parents who have lost children to death. No human pain is as deeply felt as a parent's grief endured over a child's death.

My friend has taken death's sting and converted his pain into a healing miracle for others. Could we say he is a steward of his emotional pain? Perhaps. Stewards are believers who share with others what they have been given. In this case, a deeply loyal person shares his painful experience and the glimpses of hope recovered with those who cannot yet grasp hope's possibility. Whether we stewards stand in a valley covered with dry bones or beside an empty grave, we share the hope God offers. After all, the God we worship and glorify knows something of losing a child.

Passion/Palm Sunday
(Sixth Sunday in Lent)

Psalm 118:1–2, 19–29 (Liturgy of the Palms)   Biblical Success

"O LORD, we beseech you, give us success!"
(Ps. 118:25)

Churchill surely was on to something when he quipped, "Success is the ability to go from one failure to another with no loss of enthusiasm." But just as true is what Tennessee Williams said: "Success and failure are equally disastrous."

As Christian stewards it may be necessary to debunk the current ideal of success as the only target at which people aim their lives. For some people, success is merely one more elusive aspiration. These folks simply give up and have no long- or even short-range life goals. Generally, most modern individuals agree that success is good. We strive for it. We work for it. We dream of it. Even the psalm extols success (Ps. 118:25). This psalm is a communal hymn of praise in which Israel offers thanks to God for all that God accomplishes among them. It also petitions God to "give us success!" What success, no doubt, depends upon the one who prays it.

Despite all the positive aspects of success, however, Christians are obliged to recognize and explore success from faith's viewpoint. Nothing stewards think or do should be thought or done in a vacuum. Rather, Scripture reminds us that we have "the mind of Christ" (1 Cor. 2:16). A quandary success brings is that it is so seductive. Success breeds more responsibility, and thus more success. Success is like a merry-go-round that we can never jump off. As Henry Kissinger remarked, "Each success only buys an admission ticket to a more difficult problem." Thus, the issue for us today is simply, "How can we be successful and Christian stewards simultaneously?" It is worth noting that by worldly standards Elvis Presley, Howard Hughes, and J. Paul Getty had successful lives. Yet these individuals' biographies read more like tragedies.

When Psalm 118 sings of success, it reflects life's success of a different order than cars or houses or prestige and all the modern images success conjures. Success from a biblical point of view means the same thing as faithfulness. It means trusting God to provide for us. It means that God grants us success in our life of faith. Biblically, success means something completely different from our autonomous, Western, capitalist, American ideas of achievement. A danger in living in contemporary America is that success may seduce us away from God. Do you want to live in a world where all knowledge, insight, and experience is self-generated?

Recently I preached in a church where thirty choir members sang in the chancel. They sounded beautiful and looked joyful. The pastor lamented to me later, "Why doesn't this happen on Sunday?" I suppose he meant that his choir would support special church events, but the more mundane and week-to-week faithfulness they lacked. Role models help influence others and help them come to faith by living the Christian life each and every day. Our success or effectiveness as Christians is a day-to-day calling—one we extend to others. If you really want to be successful as a Christian, then help someone come to faith. Maybe stewards help others come to faith by singing in choir or by mentoring young people. But stewards need to do something. Christian stewards habitually succeed in the small, seemingly mundane, things of life.

Do you remember when the children of Israel left Egypt for the land of promise? Everyone went. Not some, but all. The ironic thing about a Christian steward's success is that we seldom succeed unless those around us also succeed. We need one another, and we need to reach out to others. This is what real stewardship success is all about. In today's psalm notice the intentional wording: "Save us, we beseech you, O LORD. . . . Give us success!" (Ps. 118:25). For Christian stewards, discipleship defines success.

Holy Thursday
[See Year C]

Good Friday (A, B, and C)

John 18:1–19:42   What Manner of Steward?

"Pilate asked him, 'So you are a king?' "
(John 18:37)

This passage's length makes it unwieldy for preaching, even if many church traditions read the entire text on Good Friday. Wise preachers will carefully choose parts of this text to preach. For stewardship reflection, John offers two themes for exposition.

First, John narrates the world's dismissal of Jesus. The Fourth Evangelist often uses the term "the world" in a negative sense, breaking this tendency only occasionally. By and large, "the world" opposes Jesus. Jesus even admits that the world opposes his teaching, although he speaks "openly to the world" (John 18:20). Where Jesus goes and preaches, he creates divided opinions among the people of the world.

A second major theme in this lesson is that even the illogical horror of Jesus' crucifixion is part of God's redemptive plan. God glorifies Jesus on the cross. When reading the exchange between Jesus and Pilate, we sense some of what we might describe as the "powerlessness of the powerful." Pilate seems frustrated in his conversation with Jesus, even though Pilate's power in Palestine was beyond question. However, Jesus, the poor itinerant prophet, appears to baffle the Roman procurator. We recognize Pilate's annoyance when he asks Jesus, "Do you not know that I have power to release you, and power to crucify you?" (John 19:10). Of course, Jesus has an answer.

In "the world's" big picture, money is power. In Pilate's day, with the Roman military backing him up, military might made one powerful. Either by way of naked force or money, power is persuasive. Still, with power also comes responsibility. Rome boasted that everyone living within the boundaries of its authority was due justice. In our lesson today the falsity of that claim is too evident even to point out.

Some political utilitarian ethicists might suggest that Pilate's decision regarding Jesus served a greater good. Perhaps in Jesus' sacrifice the Roman military machine spared many other Palestinians. This suggestion echoes Caiaphas's observation regarding Lazarus (which foreshadows Jesus' death): "You do not understand that it is better for you to have one man die for the people than to have the whole nation destroyed" (John 11:50). However one understands Pilate's actions, the issue of why Jesus died by crucifixion may raise more theological questions than it answers. Still, in God's inscrutable wisdom, Jesus' crucifixion offers humankind redemption.

Christian stewardship reflects the truth that how we do something may be as important as what we do. The Christian faith is not utilitarian, in other words. We do not merely look at the bottom line; we look at how we arrived at the bottom line. This means for a steward that "the means to an end result" are as important as the end itself. Perhaps God could have thundered humankind into salvation, but God used Jesus' self-sacrifice for divine purposes. Accordingly, the Christian faith makes little sense to our managed, linear, logical, rational ways of doing business with the world. Maybe this is why the world rejects Jesus. God's means to the end just don't make human sense.

In our world of efficiency and utility, the gospel reminds stewards that how we offer ourselves and our talents to God and others is often as crucial as our offering the gifts and talents in the first place. The way we give food and drink to strangers at our door says a lot about how we exercise power and authority with those who have little.

Easter

Easter Day

Colossians 3:1–4   Looking in the Right Place

"Seek the things that are above."
(Col. 3:1)

Easter Day confidently gathers the church as no other day can. This is a source of invariable clergy cynicism, yet we might also interpret Easter attendance as a signal of hope. We live in a culture that for the most part pays lip service to the church. Nevertheless, people still make their semiannual trek to sanctuaries of every conceivable denomination because the church still offers the outside possibility that it has what people want—and more importantly, need. To preach about stewardship on such a day is not clerical insanity. Rather, preaching about stewardship on Easter Sunday offers people the hope that their self-perceived "little piddling" lives may make a difference after all. This, at least, is the attendee's hope.

Although Colossians remains on the disputed list of authentic Pauline epistles, the seminal theological ideas are derivative of Paul's thinking. For the sake of convenience, I will refer to the author as "Paul." Paul appears to be encouraging a congregation to remain steadfast to Christ. At the epistle's beginning Paul exhorts the congregation "to endure everything with patience, while joyfully giving thanks to the Father, who . . . has rescued us from the power of darkness" (Col. 1:11–13). Paul also writes of "thrones or dominions or rulers or powers" as if these may rival the living God of Jesus Christ (Col. 1:16). These textual clues indicate that the Colossians were either losing faith's hope or being seduced to other objects of worship. If this is true, then the Colossians resembled other early Christian communities.

Paul offers the congregation, via this letter, reasons for faith in Christ. He also expresses concern for the church at Colossae and shares how new life in Christ makes a difference. There is much discussion about moral applications of the faith and a warning against false teachers. Then Paul uses a conditional phrase: "So if you have been raised with Christ." This phrase lays the foundation for much that Paul writes in the letter's balance. "So if you have been raised with Christ" primarily signals two things. First, if these believers are not so convinced that they have been raised (by God) with Christ, then all else Paul writes will be chaff in the wind. Second, if they do believe, then Paul wants them to extend themselves. God extends them as believers stretched by faith as people of Christ.

Our modern culture tends to mire us believers in the sludge of the world. Our Easter attendees work and scrimp, trying in many cases to eke out a living for themselves and their families. We take evidence for success from a formula that the world judges us all. Education, income, and other entrapments of successful living chain us. We hunker down, pushing and pulling our way through our culture, which resembles in some ways what Jesus' protagonist faced in the parable of the Prodigal Son. There the truth freed the prodigal "when he came to himself" (Luke 15:17). Another way of saying this might be "when he looked up from his pig sty" or as Paul suggests, "Set your minds on things that are above, not on things that are on earth." This is why people attend church on Easter!

Even people in the twenty-first century need a purpose for life that transcends "making ends meet." God created us to live and share with others. The chief function of a steward is to pass along the gifts, talents, and time that God offers us as a loan. When we look toward God to define our "success" in life, then we have looked in a proper direction.

Second Sunday of Easter

John 20:19–31   You Want Proof?

"Put your finger here and see my hands."
(John 20:27)

The foundation for Christian stewardship is confidence: that God is both creator and provider. Thus, God provides the stuff of abundant life. If we believe this article of faith, then we can trust and believe in God. Yet many modern people live in a different world. We are wary of truth claims until someone proves them to our satisfaction. Thomas might have understood this stance.

Few of us want to give to a cause or institution that fails to instill confidence. Bad publicity casts a shadow on relief groups when they mismanage funds. Public trust wanes. We humans want to support worthy causes. When we feel that we have poured our money down a "rat hole," our confidence erodes. We want assurance that our labor is not in vain. Thomas seeks a faith guarantee, and he seeks assurance.

The Gospel lesson for this Sunday addresses an all-too-human issue of which churches reluctantly speak—doubt. It often seems as if the church asks people to check their doubt at the door along with their hat and coat. John's lesson addresses the skeptics among us, a story to which many of us can relate. At times critical thinking or skepticism have their good points. Many of us test for truth everything we read or hear. Often the matters are weighty, but we question the mundane as well—phone messages or directions, for example. We ask, "Is this number right?" or "Is this the best way to get from here to there?" Our loved ones tell us that a born skeptic can drive others mad.

Maybe deep down we feel a kinship to Thomas. Perhaps when we read Thomas's words, we think they sound like something we might say. Traditionally the church has regulated Thomas to a rank beneath that of other disciples—Peter, James, John, and Andrew. Still, to the rank-and-file "skeptical Christians," Thomas reacts to the news about Jesus' appearance much as we might. To those trained in questioning everything, can we doubt that someone might question the authenticity of Jesus' appearance to the eleven?

Yet Jesus does not leave Thomas on the unbeliever's hook. Jesus returns to put the finishing touches on Thomas's skeptical faith. Jesus comes again and says, "Put your finger here and see my hands. . . . Do not doubt but believe." Subsequently, Thomas deserts skepticism and embraces faith. The philosopher John C. Sherwood wrote, "Even for the most skeptical, belief is an absolute necessity for practical experience. . . . Without belief, action would be paralyzed; we should never know what to do in a given situation."*

Stewards know that we are never in greater danger of error than when we are

---

*John C. Sherwood, "Introduction to Logic," in *Readings for Writers*, 10th ed., ed. Jo Ray McCuen and Anthony C. Winkler (Fort Worth: Harcourt College Publishers, 2001), 555.

absolutely certain that we are absolutely right. To be a little uncertain is to be human—and humane. The gospel word for today's modern skeptics is that you do not have to be absolutely sure in order to be right. But despite this, trust in Jesus' words offers us an assurance of acting in faith, despite our protest of "nonetheless."

There are occasions in life where faith as belief and trust is not merely an alternative—it is the only alternative for a full, abundant, and meaningful life. Stewards know that at some point we must set aside our skepticism and embrace faith as Thomas did. The proof resides in the life, death, and appearance of Jesus in our lives.

Third Sunday of Easter

Acts 2:14a, 36–41   Do Something!

"Save yourselves from this corrupt generation."
(Acts 2:40)

The book of Acts recounts the stories of the apostles traveling about the Mediterranean world. Many sermons, sometimes called speeches, punctuate these apostolic journeys. Accordingly, Marion L. Soards discusses various ways scholars count these Acts' speeches: "M. Dibelius recognizes twenty-four speeches," while G. A. Kennedy, "who is interested in the rhetorical dimensions of the speeches, discusses twenty-five speeches; but several of the speeches are not exactly the same as those cited by Dibelius." Soards then lists thirty-six speeches (or sermons) as authentically from Acts.* Regardless of how we count, Acts has a lot of speeches, and our lesson for today includes part of Peter's most prominent sermon.

For the purpose of stewardship, Peter's speech offers us a key insight. For modern culture, the Christian faith seems ethereal and vague. Much theological language sounds slippery to those wanting concrete handles by which to understand life or rules by which to live. Peter's Acts 2 sermon achieves things that effective sermons can do: it confronts the world's idols, it leads to hearers' self-reflection, it calls for confession, and it offers words of gracious forgiveness and pardon. But Peter's sermon offers a crucial feature for its listeners—it calls for a response. Good preaching begins in careful listening: to the biblical text and to the community of faith. No doubt Peter heard the cry, "What should we do?" Peter has a ready answer. Peter calls for a positive response to the gospel: "Repent, and be baptized." But Peter also identifies from what they need salvation: "Save yourselves from this corrupt generation."

Stewardship is a faithful response to God's gifts of time, talent, and treasure. On the positive side, stewards use what God has loaned them to assist in the

*Marion L. Soards, *The Speeches in Acts* (Louisville, KY: Westminster John Knox Press, 1994), 18–22.

building up of God's realm on earth. Negatively, our response to the gospel is to eschew the very forces that try to usurp God's claim on us. These claims function for modern people as idols did in Israel's day. Whenever we elevate nation, family, lust for material possessions, or unhealthy attachments to working for our daily bread, then we replace God with an idol. Whether our graven images are dressed for modernity or not, they still remain idols.

Commonly, Christian believers are not indifferent to sharing gifts and graces with God through their gifts to their congregation. Rather, when people do not know what to do, they tend to do nothing. Offering people ways to respond to the gospel is not only helpful, but it is the essence of good preaching. Peter accomplishes this preaching aim when he suggests that those who hear him stand in need of repentance and baptism. In addition to living fully in God's realm, these believers also need to flee from the world's definition of authentic life. Peter puts it like this: "Save yourselves from this corrupt generation."

We pastors know that our people are willing and able to respond to God. But people won't give if no one asks. If we can take Peter's lead, then perhaps we too can help guide congregations toward responses that will extend the gospel's connection to a hurting world. If we preachers can do such things, then we will not only be good preaching stewards—we will be "servants of the word" (Luke 1:2).

Fourth Sunday of Easter

Acts 2:42–47   Togetherness in All Things

"All who believed were together and had all things in common."
(Acts 2:44)

In my formative years, people lambasted communism and socialism and Marxism with all their might. When Joseph McCarthy and his ilk threw suspicion upon many persons in the 1950s, all they did was suggest a person seemed a "little pink" to them. Yet after five decades we capitalists have said goodbye to most communist governments; Marx may have been wiser than we freely admit. Life does appear to come down to dollars and cents.

Our lesson today from Acts reminds us that just a few days removed from the marvelous Pentecost experience (perhaps merely hours distant), those in the church found themselves in the realm of economics. The apostles initiated a rough organizational plan to act out the life of Christ in community. Luke offers the readers a "job description" for the nascent church: "They devoted themselves to the apostles' teaching and fellowship, to the breaking of bread and the prayers." In other words, the four chief tasks of the early church consisted of preaching, *koinonia*, communal worship, and cultivating the life of prayer. This practice allowed the apostles, with the steering hand of God guiding the action, to perform "many wonders and signs." As Luke tells the story, the people became awestruck.

Near the beginning the church had to confront the idea of property. What belongs to my family and me and what should I share with others? Naturally, because those in the early church believed that Jesus' return was imminent, they threw all their resources together. Not only this, but they had genuine love and devotion for one another. Acts 2 tells the story about many who came to Jerusalem for Pentecost religious festivities. Could it be that the influx of new believers put pressure on the apostles and the church in Jerusalem to help provide food and lodging for these out-of-town believers? No one knows, but necessity sometimes fosters creativity. However the early church under apostolic leadership lived, we do know from Acts that they had "all things in common." It is a fundamental principle of the Christian life—we share with one another and help those in need.

There are a number of faithful reasons for being Christian stewards. Maybe one of the best reasons is to advocate for the kind of values we believe lead to divine living on earth. The society in which we live has its own values. If we follow the church as depicted in Acts 2, then we can become a community that believes abundant life is found in giving, not in getting.

"From each according to ability; to each according to need" rephrases the socialist mantra. Our American culture cultivates, maybe even indoctrinates, us into deeming this mantra a next-door neighbor to death itself. Yet, in a perfect world, it would press us to argue against the notion's humanity. Fundamentally this is precisely what the church summons from stewards. The church is like a large family that we all volunteered to be a part of. Whether or not we enjoy the specific details of our family life, we share and care for one another. Family defines and completes us. The church is no different. It is a community such as this that Luke tells us, "Day by day the Lord added to their number."

Fifth Sunday of Easter

1 Peter 2:2–10   Stewards Grow in Grace

"Long for the pure, spiritual milk, so that by it you may grow."
(1 Pet. 2:2)

Growth is a key fact of life. The ancients, like people now, survived on nature's usual cycles for agricultural success. Jesus knew this well, so he taught via parables about growth and harvest. Jesus repeatedly used agrarian figures of speech. Addressing anxiety, he asked, "Why do you worry about clothing?" By way of a nature image, he then told listeners, "Consider the lilies of the field, how they grow; they neither toil nor spin" (Matt. 6:28).

An older and wiser colleague once said to a group of us gathered for coffee, "A church is either growing or it is dying." Perhaps this same sentiment is also true for individuals. Perhaps it is true for believers and for faithful stewards. Of course, there are many kinds of growth. When we speak of our economy, for example, we talk about it getting bigger and stronger. Bigger and stronger is how most of us conceive growth. Yet from the biblical perspective, growth may signify something a little different.

Growth and harvest are both metaphors that Jesus uses to describe the kingdom of God. He goes so far as to say that "the harvest is the end of the age" (Matt. 13:39). Harvest is a metaphor for the final fulfillment of God's purposes for the world that God created. Harvest is repeatedly apocalyptic and, in the wrong hands, can scare the dickens out of people. Still, the Epistle lesson reminds us that there is both a beginning to life, suggested by the phrase "newborn infants," and an end that becomes life's terminal point. In between, stewards grow as things in nature grow.

Last week I saw a colt that was fifteen minutes old. Within just a few hours the colt was under his mother seeking not the "spiritual milk" of which 1 Peter speaks, but rather the fluid that offers life and staves off death. When 1 Peter speaks of spiritual milk, it speaks of that which nurtures and sustains believers. It is the stuff that makes growth possible.

However, after two verses 1 Peter alters the metaphor and speaks about the "living stone," Jesus—"the stone that the builders rejected." It is from Jesus that we build our "spiritual house." It is this house that fashions "a holy priesthood" and through which we "offer spiritual sacrifices acceptable to God." Thus, whether the image is one of building or of growth, God somehow works in us to make something of us. Whether organic or material, 1 Peter alerts us that God works in us "in order that you may proclaim the mighty acts of him who called you out of darkness into his marvelous light."

Today we hear and read many statistics and appraisals about "church growth." By and large, "church growth" involves how the church promotes itself to a culture mired in buying and selling. Yet authentic stewardship as discipleship is what we might describe as "growth in grace." Growing in grace means that believers—and stewards—continue on in their faith journey that ends in sanctification. Sanctification, "being made perfect in love in this life," is the proper aim for all believers. We continuously grow in faith and its fruits until we die. Sanctification grows believers from the inside out. God wills our growth so that we can mature into what God created us to be in the first place. God provides our milk.

Sixth Sunday of Easter

Acts 17:22–31　　　　　　　　　　　　　　Does God Need Anything?

"The God who made the world and everything in it . . . "
(Acts 17:24)

This may be the only speech/sermon delivered to a strictly pagan audience in the entire Bible. For this reason, preachers will want to note how Paul handles such an audience. Many of the people we preach to today take their living cues from the culture rather than the church. In terms of stewardship, our culture does not generally speak about compassionate care for the down and out. Rather, our culture offers us tips on how to obtain and preserve whatever we can. For stewardship preaching, Paul offers insights that can help today's disciples know the gospel's truth.

Paul waits for his companions to join him in Athens. Paul and Silas had been in Thessalonica, where Paul preached in the synagogue for three Sabbath days. But, as good preaching sometimes does, Paul created bad feeling among the religious authorities there. A riot ensued, and "that very night the believers sent Paul and Silas off to Beroea; and when they arrived, they went to the Jewish synagogue" (Acts 17:10). They continued preaching there, but eventually the same rabble-rousers from Thessalonica caught up with them in Beroea and began "to stir up and incite the crowds" (Acts 17:13). The believers at Beroea took Paul to the coast and on to Athens, but Silas and Timothy remained behind with instructions to join Paul later. Luke tells this complicated story to account for Paul's being in Athens alone.

While in Athens Paul roams the city. In due course, he preaches in both the Athenian synagogue and the marketplace. Paul's listeners then invite him to speak further and take him to the Areopagus. This is where our text begins.

Paul tells the audience that he sees "how extremely religious you are in every way." By doing so, Paul curries favor with his listeners, although earlier he had been "distressed to see that the city was full of idols" (Acts 17:16). As Paul's sermon unfolds, he gently confronts one of paganism's most glaring defects. He suggests that the God of which he speaks "does not live in shrines made by human hands, nor is he served by human hands, as though he needed anything." Pagans believe they must appease—or even bribe—their gods to get in good stead with them. Paul says his God needs none of this. Why? Because the God of which Paul speaks is the God who gives "mortals life and breath." Thus, Paul's God does not need anything at all from human beings. This point of view separates Christian believers from generic pagans.

Sometimes when we hear appeals to give as Christian stewards, we hear people suggest that we are giving to God. Yet we do not give to God because God needs anything, but rather we need to give to ground us in our confession that God gives to us. God has loaned the divine possessions to stewards to manage and care for. Our confession of faith, by our lives and our purses, is how we show our allegiance to God. When we confirm such allegiance, then we are worthy of the moniker "Christian."

Modern people fall prey to the idea that unless we give to God, then God's work cannot be carried on without our gifts. When Paul preaches to pagans at the Areopagus, Paul puts this theological error to rest. God does not need us, but God does want us to become part of God's "kingdom people." We pledge our allegiance to God's realm when we freely and earnestly offer back what God has already given to us as God's people. We do this through the ministries of the church, the body of Christ. Good stewards know that the materials we handle are not ours; they are only a loan from God Almighty.

Ascension of the Lord
[See Year B]

Seventh Sunday of Easter

Acts 1:1–14   The Sanity of Mundane Stewardship

"Then they returned to Jerusalem from the mount called Olivet."
(Acts 1:12)

Luke/Acts swings on an ascension hinge. Luke not only ends his Gospel with Jesus' ascension, but he also begins Acts with an ascension story. For Luke, Jesus' ascension signifies the last time Jesus is physically present to the disciples. In place of Jesus' bodily presence, however, the divinely appointed Holy Spirit accompanies believers. Perhaps these ascension accounts offer clues to modern disciples who function as stewards without Jesus' physical presence. God decisively designated Jesus as Messiah via Jesus' bodily resurrection. It is to these clues concerning stewardship we now turn.

In the lesson today, Jesus gathers "the apostles whom he had chosen." They ask him an eschatological question: "Lord, is this the time when you will restore the kingdom to Israel?" Jesus sidesteps their question. Even so, he offers his apostles both a promise and a task. Jesus tells them, "You will receive power when the Holy Spirit has come upon you; and you will be my witnesses in Jerusalem, in all Judea and Samaria, and to the ends of the earth." The gift of the Holy Spirit is the substance of the promise. The apostolic task is witnessing, beginning in Jerusalem and continuing "to the ends of the earth." It is not accidental that for Luke this outlines the apostles' Acts ministry. As Luke 24:49 suggests, they will be "clothed with power from on high." Believers wear the Spirit like "the whole armor of God" (Eph. 6:11, 13).

The full encounter with Jesus was no doubt a heady one for the apostles. Yet for faithful people, reality dictates that we return from such mountaintop events to the valley of mundane human service. Luke from time to time suggests such a theme. After the transfiguration story (Luke 9:28–36), he writes, "On the next day, when they had come down from the mountain . . . ," and then he describes how Jesus heals a demon-possessed child (Luke 9:37–43). Luke indicates that despite our high and holy moments apart with Jesus, God continues to draw God's disciples and stewards back into the rough-and-tumble world of human need.

Following both of his ascension stories, Luke implies this commonplace element of practical theology. Luke's Gospel tells us that after Jesus' ascension the disciples "worshiped him, and returned to Jerusalem with great joy; and they were continually in the temple blessing God" (Luke 24:52–53). In Acts after Jesus' ascension, we read that "they returned to Jerusalem" and "were constantly devoting themselves to prayer." In other words, the apostles returned to the ordinary duties of Jesus' faithful followers. The difference, however, is that Jesus has promised that soon they will be "clothed with power from on high."

Stewardship derives its power from God mediated through Jesus' life, death, and resurrection, while the Holy Spirit sustains that power. In life's nickels and dimes, God empowers us to discover value and meaning in the life that Jesus offers us. The Spirit is Jesus' abiding presence in our lives. The Spirit's presence encourages us and counsels us as we share God's gifts, which have been loaned to us. Reliable stewards recognize that whatever good we do as faithful disciples, we do only by a power beyond us. Stewards offer time, talent, and treasure to God's realm, driven by the engine of the Holy Spirit. Routine life offers us countless opportunities to offer God's gifts to the world.

Pentecost

Day of Pentecost

Acts 2:1–21   On Working Together

"At this sound the crowd gathered and was bewildered."
(Acts 2:6)

A good question for stewards to ponder is "Why did God call the church into existence?" Because the church has existed, more or less intact, for nearly two millennia, one suspects the hand of God provides the church's foundation. The story of the church's birth, the first lesson for the day of Pentecost, speaks to the mighty hand of God. God empowers the gathered community in this story via the agency of the Holy Spirit. What does this miraculous story have to teach Christian stewards?

At the beginning of Acts, Jesus appears to the apostles just prior to his ascension. In the course of Jesus' last teaching, he promises the apostles, "John baptized with water, but you will be baptized with the Holy Spirit not many days from now" (Acts

1:5). Our lesson today carries out Jesus' promise. Interestingly, the apostles had gathered in one place as the Spirit began to fill the house where they were sitting. Most Bible readers know the part of the story where "there came a sound like the rush of a violent wind." These apostles "were filled with the Holy Spirit and began to speak in other languages, as the Spirit gave them ability." This spectacle drew a crowd. Luke tells us that this phenomenon of the Holy Spirit bewildered those gathered "because each one heard them speaking in the native language of each."

The Holy Spirit supplies power. Yet the Holy Spirit pours out the power on all those gathered as one. Therefore, the power is not simply for two or three random individuals. The power of the Spirit empowers the whole collection of believers. We all know the truth of the old saying, "Many hands lighten the load." It is much easier for six pallbearers to carry a casket than it is for two funeral directors. Together as a community of faith we are much stronger—and more effective—when we work in concert.

Picture a church fellowship hall after a covered-dish dinner. The room needs clearing for a later event. If two or three people break down tables and fold the chairs, this work will take some time. Yet if a host of people all pitch in and help clear the room, they can accomplish the task in minutes. The power of a congregation is evident where and when believers work together.

This shared work is a principle behind stewardship in a local church. When many people, prompted to generosity by the Holy Spirit, give liberally, then the church can accomplish substantive ministry. If a congregation relies on only a few "big givers," then that church effectively compromises its mission outreach.

It is no accident that God chose to pour out the Holy Spirit on many. The tongues of fire representing the Spirit "rested on each of them." Many received the Holy Spirit, and they, as a result, became stewards of that Spirit. Together they became strong. The Pentecost story exhibits the quintessential team concept.

In Acts, a crowd brings Jason before the Thessalonian authorities. They accuse him with shouts that he and other believers "have been turning the world upside down" (Acts 17:6). In essence, this is why God sends the Holy Spirit's power upon us—to turn the world upside down. We do this by simply managing the stewardship households God gives to the church. If a church works as one for the shared goal of God's realm, then nothing can hinder its potency.

Trinity Sunday
(First Sunday after Pentecost)

Psalm 8   Mandate to Manage Creation

"You have given them dominion over the works of your hands."
(Ps. 8:6)

The Psalm for Trinity Sunday supplements the reading from the Hebrew Scripture. Each reading celebrates creation's wonder and glory. These balanced lessons uphold the human obligation/privilege of "dominion over the works of your hands" (Ps. 8:6) and "dominion over the fish of the sea and over the birds of the air and over every living thing that moves upon the earth" (Gen. 1:28). God offers no greater duty to people than having dominion over creation (Gen. 1:26). From the beginning, God created human beings as stewards—and this is one of the church's vital missions.

Trinity Sunday is a liturgical day conceived to help people put an understanding of God into proper perspective. How do the various parts of the God-head—Father, Son, and Holy Spirit, or Creator, Redeemer, and Counselor—relate to one another? We try to answer these kinds of questions analogically, all the while knowing that human articulation of such deeply profound truths is doomed from the start. Yet we do our best, using our limited reason and faltering tongues to make sense of what is for most of us nonsensical—or at least, ultimately unknowable.

Psalm 8 brings us on Trinity Sunday to something of a paradox. While on this liturgical day we try to explain God and put God in proper perspective, in reality this psalm puts us in our proper place. Psalm 8 reminds us of our place in God's grand design. Speaking of what God has done in the creation of people, Psalm 8 says that God has made humans "a little lower than God, and crowned them with glory and honor." Psalm 8 also charges human beings with the task of having "dominion over the works of your hands." God has "put all things under their feet, all sheep and oxen, and also the beasts of the field, the birds of the air, and the fish of the sea, whatever passes along the paths of the seas." This task is a tall order for believers. It calls forth the best ecological stewardship we can muster. God puts it all under our feet!

Three or four decades ago, we Christians used to talk a lot about recycling, the environment, planting trees, and finding alternatives to fossil fuels. Pockets of believers still speak of such matters, but our custodians of ecological stewardship seem rarer and rarer. In fact, our culture's discussions about preserving natural resources appear aimed at economic agendas rather than at the preservation of the earth's natural wherewithal. Yet we stewards are the descendants of the first humans, whom God placed in the garden of Eden to "till it and keep it" (Gen. 2:14–15).

If we Christian stewards acknowledge that stewardship requires responsible management of all our God-given resources, then care for the earth is no doubt part of that management. Psalm 8 begins and ends with the exaltation of God's sovereignty of all the earth: "O LORD, our Sovereign, how majestic is your name in all the earth!" However, God in God's wisdom has given us dominion over God's creation. How we exercise control over what God has loaned us goes far in defining our effectiveness as stewards.

Perhaps it is time again for the Christian church to reassert itself as a community of advocacy. Can we speak out for the defense of the earth and its inhabitants, both human and animal? To exercise this voice will have implications for our witness that our earth is a blessed gift from God. It will also mark us as those who steward creation.

Sunday between May 29 and June 4 inclusive
(if after Trinity Sunday)

Romans 1:16–17; 3:22b–28 (29–31)   Grace as God's Underpinning
for Stewards

"They are now justified by his grace as a gift."
(Rom. 3:24)

The Epistle lesson oddly begins with Paul's assertion that "I am not ashamed of the gospel." Why does Paul say this? We may read the statement as ironic. Perhaps Paul writes to the Roman church so that he can boast in the gospel—borne out by verse 3:27, which asks, "Then what becomes of boasting?" Boasting, the way Paul uses it, draws attention to the pride that people have in their possessions or abilities.

Yet Paul wipes out every pretension of human pride by reminding believers that everything they have and everything they are is from God's gracious benevolence. One of these possessions for believers is the state of salvation that God offers. The power for human salvation comes directly from God. God does for us what we cannot do for ourselves. For this reason, the gospel as efficacious for salvation may seem like high comedy to nonbelievers. After all, Jesus is crucified as a common criminal. If nothing else, this crucifixion would occasion shame and not boasting. Still, Paul reminds his readers that God gives this salvation as a gift. We do not occasion our salvation; rather, God gives it as a bequest. What then are the theological implications for stewardship?

A cardinal rule of stewardship is that God has dominion over everything. Believers presume this theological principle because our creator God controls and sustains all creation. When we employ any part of creation, our gifts and talents included, then we recognize God gives these functions for our management. Although we may control the exercise of such gifts, they are genuinely God's good gift to us.

When my children were younger, I often gave them money, such as on the occasion of my birthday, so that they could buy me a birthday present. They had no means of earning the money, yet I wanted them to feel a part of our family by buying me a birthday present. Without parental help they would have been spectators and not participants in our family's birthday ritual.

In a like manner, we as stewards do not manage that which we own. Stewardship by definition is the management of another's property. Hence, Paul reminds those in the Roman church that the salvation in which they stand is a gift from God. They did not earn it; it is a pure gift from God. Thus, those who receive the gift merely use it until God recalls it at our time of death. Until then, however, the loaned gifts from God are ours to use—and to manage.

Paul offers the theological basis upon which we stewards respond. When he roughly quotes Habakkuk 2:4, "The one who is righteous will live by faith," Paul provides stewards a foundation for a righteous life of faith. Because, as Paul writes, "all have sinned," then the only means by which we can be justified is by God's good gift. Through this gift we may live righteously before God.

When a conscientious farmer leases land from another property owner to farm, he or she will turn the land back in better condition than it was before. In God's realm, this is what we stewards do with the gifts and graces that God loans to us as those who live in righteousness. It is not boasting if it is fact.

Sunday between June 5 and 11 inclusive
(if after Trinity Sunday)

Genesis 12:1–9   A Steward's Response

"So Abram went, as the LORD had told him."
(Gen. 12:4)

We preachers are given to hyperbole. It comes with the territory. The promise of God to humankind is to "outsiders" and is one of the more grandiose claims that a human being can make. Thus, to nonbelievers we can only ask pardon for our claims that seem to the uninitiated as something akin to exaggerated overstatement. But this is how the Bible reads. Yet of all the Bible's extraordinary stories, the Genesis text today is among the most amazing. It also guides stewards in the management of what God calls us to be—and likewise what we are to do as a response to the divine summons.

Genesis 12 begins with God appearing to a wandering sojourner named Abram. If there is some "getting-to-know-you chit-chat" at the beginning of God's monologue, then the biblical writer does not reveal it. Rather, God gets down to business by giving Abram a command and polishes off this first encounter with a series of promises. God tells Abram that God will make a great nation of him. God will also bless Abram and give him as a blessing to "all the families of the earth."

After this opening scene we find one of the most remarkable three-word responses in Scripture: "So Abram went." No argument, no questions for clarification, no quibbling—Abram simply went. It is little wonder that Paul later writes of Abraham's faith (Rom. 4:16), as does the writer of Hebrews (Heb. 11:8, 17). In marked contrast to Moses, who argues with God for some two and a half chapters in Exodus about Moses' call, Abram doesn't utter a word of protest. Abram just goes. Later, after God and Abraham get to know one another better, there are heated negotiations (Gen. 18:22–33), but for now Abram is plainly obedient.

We live in a world that often misunderstands the blessings of God. A sportscaster once interviewed a basketball player after he made a fifty-five-foot shot with time running out. The goal allowed this player's team to advance in the NCAA basketball tournament. When the sportscaster asked him how he felt about being a hero, he replied, "God blessed me to allow our team to win, and that is why God helped me make that shot."

Aside from the unlikelihood that God follows "March Madness," or whether God cares that one specific university wins a basketball game or not, believers must raise a theological question about this mindset. Does God bless us to win games, or be successful in business, or in school, or in our chosen fields of pursuit?

Any Christian steward worth her or his salt knows that the reason God blesses people is no different today than it was when God blessed Abram several thousand years ago. God was unequivocal with Abram: "I will bless you, and make your name great, so that you will be a blessing." The well-worn Christian aphorism puts it, "We are blessed to be a blessing." In an honest theological measure of Christian stewardship, authentic stewards recognize in God's promise to Abram two small words. God offers the promise to Abram *so that* Abram will be a blessing. Similar to what God does for humanity in Jesus, God does with Abram's blessing. Through one person God blesses all people. God could have done otherwise, but God did not. God uses human agents to pass on divine blessings. Today we might even call them "stewards."

Sunday between June 12 and 18 inclusive
(if after Trinity Sunday)

Genesis 18:1–15   The Gift of Hospitality

"Do not pass by your servant."
(Gen. 18:3)

In today's church there is a troubling aspect of stewardship that is nothing less than a colossal theological error. This error suggests that Christian stewardship only pertains to money. Although stewardship does involve a person's purse, the term has a much wider application. The Genesis lesson teaches stewards much about managing the resources God has loaned us, one of which is offering hospitality—a gift of welcome.

The story begins with the Lord's appearance to Abraham as "he sat at the entrance of his tent in the heat of the day." Three men abruptly appear to Abraham, almost as if from out of nowhere. Abraham then does something that no self-respecting patriarch would do—he runs to meet them. No one in the ancient world who commanded respect would ever condescend to running. Running is strictly the province of children. Yet as a sign of respect and hospitality, Abraham runs to greet them. Abraham also extends welcome by bowing down and suggesting to them that he "bring a little bread, that you may refresh yourselves." Embedded in these gestures of welcome to his desert guests, Abraham offers the stewardship of hospitality.

In the late 1970s I lived in Liberia. Liberia has existed at the poverty level for many years, even as in 1847 it became the first African democracy. Today's morning newspaper reports that Liberia's unemployment rate sits at 85 percent. Yet my Liberian year amply taught me about the stewardship of hospitality and welcome.

When my African students took me to preach at their "bush churches," the people received us Americans as if we were part of a royal family. Each hut in the village expected us to dine with them—and sumptuously, at that. I have never eaten so much food in my life. The remarkable part of these weekends was that the people offered us so much, yet they possessed so little. I learned that even if a person has little to share, the gift of hospitality and welcome is a gift that is always at hand.

We sometimes think that the only important church members are the "people of means." Few would ever speak such nonsense out loud, but we habitually function as if this fallacy were true. This myth suggests that "big givers" call the shots and make the decisions. This absurd attitude plainly belies Jesus' attitude about a believer's gifts. For example, Jesus taught regarding the poor widow's donation, "All of them [the rich] have contributed out of their abundance, but she out of her poverty has put in all she had to live on" (Luke 21:1–4).

The Liberians had little to give, but they offered strangers what they had. Each of us can offer the gift of hospitality, even if it is the only thing we have. Our evangelistic work hinges on the hospitality that churches offer. Whether by "thought, word, or deed," how many church guests receive hostility rather than hospitality when they first visit? "You are sitting in my pew," is voiced too often to be an anomaly.

Today people still seek salvation. One way the church can help those who seek salvation is to offer hospitable welcome through common relationships. We church folk foster relationships; it is our stock and trade. We can only lead people toward salvation via the relationships that our hospitality first advances. As Hebrews 13:2 reminds us, "Do not neglect to show hospitality to strangers, for by doing that some have entertained angels without knowing it." For those with nothing to give, offer hospitality. Can you recognize an angel? Abraham afterward recognized the Lord in three strangers.

Sunday between June 19 and 25 inclusive
(if after Trinity Sunday)

Matthew 10:24–39   Finders Weepers, Losers Keepers

"Those who lose their life for my sake will find it."
(Matt. 10:39)

The context of today's Gospel lesson is the call of the disciples and warnings about awaiting persecution. In terms of stewardship, on occasion the persons closest to us are most resistant to our living the biblical mandate "It is more blessed to give than to receive" (Acts 20:35). It is no little irony that when Jesus said, "Get behind me, Satan" (Matt. 16:23), he was speaking to his closest friend. There will always be opposition to believers who try to live the good news of Jesus Christ.

I remember one of those mundane days of endless student sermons in preaching class. Perhaps they seem interminable because the student preachers hold forth in a classroom and not in a sanctuary. Perhaps listening to student sermons seems ceaseless because the preachers are, well, novices. Yet for those who have ears to hear, the gospel sneaks in and catches us unaware. An apprentice preacher let me in on a little-pondered piece of human psychology that helped me understand why the gospel is so difficult to live in our world. When Jesus spoke a parable about a sower, he said, "The cares of the world and the lure of wealth choke the word, and it yields nothing" (Matt. 13:22). My young preaching student shed light for me on the gospel's difficulty.

At first the student droned on and on, with words like "ought" and "should" abundantly sprinkled throughout. Doubtless he merely mimicked what he had heard countless times. Then he spoke personally. Having earlier wanted to become a police officer, he needed to straighten out his life. This "straightening" meant that he needed to stop drinking. This decision cost him many of his intimate friendships. Then he remarked that although he did not have trouble living a sober life, his friends had severe problems trying to relate to the "new" him. This was a profound insight.

For many who acknowledge Jesus before others, Jesus will acknowledge them before God. This is the positive side of discipleship. Yet a negative side reveals how others fail to adjust to our "newness of life" as disciples. We become a "new" someone else, but our old relationships suffer because we are no longer who our friends (or father or mother or son or daughter) know us to be. Jesus may convert us to faith, but all the other intimates will have to adapt to us if we are to keep our relationships. This is a troubling aspect of coming to faith. Stewards in time come to this awareness as disciples.

To lose one's life in this world simply means shedding the ingrained, and perhaps even natural, inclination to go along with the crowd. Most people want to fit in and not be considered odd by those whom they respect. Yet when Jesus enters our lives as "Lord and Savior," as 2 Peter uses the term (2 Pet. 1:11; 2:20; 3:2, 18), then every part of life changes—including relationships with those whom we most cherish.

When we claim Jesus by faith, then we eschew our culture's measurement of successful life. Rather, we take the standard that God establishes in Christ as the measure of authentic life. This is the Christ who tells disciples, "This is my blood of the covenant, which is poured out for many for the forgiveness of sins" (Matt. 26:28). When believers become bona fide stewards, they are not the only ones who will adjust accordingly. Sometimes it is those we love who must change as well.

Sunday between June 26 and July 2 inclusive

Psalm 13   The Bottom Line

"I will sing to the LORD, because he has dealt bountifully with me."
(Ps. 13:6)

Stewards are faithful in giving and managing the talents God loans to us, regardless of the outward success of the mission. Too often we church folk deplore wasting vital resources on people and projects that seem doomed from the start. In every church we try new ministries to reach people, and sometimes they fail. We lament that our best efforts do not seem to cultivate the same level of commitment among those people we try to help. Perhaps because we really struggle, our efforts taste like ashes in our mouths. However, a reflective truth of reliable faith is plainly that first-rate stewards, just as nonstewards, suffer life's adversity. Stewardship does not protect believers against disillusionment. If anything, good stewardship merely increases the pain of failure.

We all know what it means for others to forget us. I have a friend who treasures his birthdays. He does so because as a child his family always made him "king for a day." His wife planned a big party for one of his major birthdays, but it was a surprise. She invited many of his old friends from high school and college. She went to a lot of work putting the whole thing together, but no one so much as mentioned his birthday; it was a surprise, after all. But he mentioned it. He whined and complained. He groused and moaned about how his family forgot his birthday. His lack of trust embarrassed him when the day of the big party came.

Psalm 13 speaks to the psalmist's glum plight. The lament begins by asking a series of barbed questions: "How long, O LORD? Will you forget me forever? How long will you hide your face from me? How long must I bear pain in my soul, and have sorrow in my heart all day long? How long shall my enemy be exalted over me?" These questions reveal the psalmist's deepest feeling that the Lord has forgotten him. As "dis-graceful" as this psalm sounds, it does reveal a key truth about the writer's relationship with God.

The psalmist's questions expose a tenacious and dogged relationship between the one who laments and God. A truism of human life is that people rarely clash over things that matter little to them. Conversely, people go to extremes when fighting for what they stalwartly believe in. For the reason of absolute conviction, religious allegiance and patriotic devotion become exceedingly dangerous. Those who fight for religion or nation stop at nothing to see their will done.

Thus, when the psalmist critiques God's treatment with such passion, readers sense the enduring trust that underlies all the human reproving of God. Psalm 13, although stark in its calling God to task, is nonetheless a confession of faith. It is a confession of faith in the sense that this writer hopes to move God to action. Not only this, but this psalmist has confidence that this (nearly) spiteful tirade will have a stirring effect on the Lord. Perhaps the psalm's words will move God to action.

If readers stopped reading at verse 5, then we would miss a final word of affirmation: "I will sing to the LORD, because he has dealt bountifully with me." This confession suggests that in the midst of the psalmist's theological temper tantrum, God is the foundation of the psalmist's life. Stewards remember that even when our best efforts appear to fail, God supports them with an everlasting love. When all is said and done, God remains steadfast to our gifts and graces, despite all evidence to the contrary.

Sunday between July 3 and 9 inclusive

Matthew 11:16–19, 25–30   The Gospel's Odd Logic

"For my yoke is easy, and my burden is light."
(Matt. 11:30)

Stewards have supreme trust in God and confidence that what they do will build up God's realm. If stewards did not have this confident assurance of God's providence, then giving to the church's ministries would be like pouring money down the proverbial rat hole. Trust in God is vital to stewardship. The lesson from last week's Hebrew Scripture (Gen. 22:1–14) is a case in point. Abraham had supreme trust in God—without substantial proof beyond God's promise! That trust sustained his service to God.

Maintaining trust is easier said than done, however, when those around a steward find fault with everything that a trustworthy steward attempts to do. Today's lesson addresses this fault-finding tendency in human beings. For example, a woman I know takes great delight in taking her red pen and circling every typographical error, every misspelled word, and every sentence fragment in the material she receives from her church. Whether it is the worship guide, the church newsletter, or merely a letter from her pastor, she marches into her church office and announces, "Well, I found you have not taken care of your English this week!" As my children say, "She needs a life."

The Gospel lesson from Matthew takes up this issue. Jesus begins the lesson by comparing "this generation" to children in the marketplace. They neither play nor weep when appropriate. It is a sort of parable on life—even modern life. Jesus uses John as an example of this contrariness on the part of people. When John comes "neither eating nor drinking," some say that "he has a demon." When the Son of Man comes "eating and drinking," and here Jesus refers to himself, the same people say, " Look, a glutton and a drunkard, a friend of tax collectors and sinners." But Jesus counters this negativity: "Wisdom is vindicated by her deeds." By using this common image, Jesus puts the cynics in their place. Stewards must recognize that no matter what good we try to do through sincere stewardship efforts, there will be those who critique the effort.

The final part of the text, however, offers hope. Jesus speaks to those who are weary from "carrying heavy burdens." Jesus offers them rest. In fact, Jesus tells them, "You will find rest for your souls." How does being a Christian steward help us find rest?

Something always measures us in life. Our culture measures us by success in business, or by educational degrees, or by status in a corporation or institution. People judge us by achievement, not for who we are. Yet we will never measure up. There is always another hurdle, another wall to climb, another mountain to ascend. As we scale the final and highest peak, hundreds more come into view. We are on a treadmill off of which we cannot exit.

Yet in faith God promises us rest. Jesus and his cross completes all our striving to measure up. By faith in Jesus, God allows us to exit the treadmill. God furnishes our human validation on the cross. Hebrews 4:3 puts it this way: "For we who have believed enter that rest, just as God has said." God built our rest into the Ten Commandments (Exod. 20; Deut. 5).

To find rest in Jesus means that we manage what God loans us and we do the best we faithfully can. The final outcome for the world—for our lives—does not rest on our shoulders but rather on the shoulders of Jesus. We simply do what we can do. But as we do our best in stewardship, even in the midst of criticism, we know that God blesses the work of our hands. God not only blesses our gifts, but God also blesses the givers.

Sunday between July 10 and 16 inclusive

Matthew 13:1–9, 18–23   The Hope of Good Soil

"What was sown on good soil, this is the one who hears the word."
(Matt. 13:23)

My teenaged son recently told me how we could easily mitigate the disappointment that comes with unmet expectations. He suggested that we simply lower our expectations. His attempt at humor unfortunately is precisely the approach that many adults use to address the problem of thwarted expectations. For stewards, a realistic vision and discernment of expectations is vital to stewardship's fulfillment.

Most people cradle idealistic goals and expectations at some point during their lives. Yet after one disappointment or another, we often settle for our second- or third-best goal, hopeful that this will satisfy our deepest hunger for meaning. We function like a frontier marksman who shoots first and then draws a target around the bullet hole. Perhaps we too amend our goals after our efforts, rather than before.

In the parable of the Sower, Jesus acknowledges that expectations enjoy different degrees of reasonableness. The interpretive verses of the parable (18–23) picture Jesus referring to "the word of the kingdom." Jesus' analogy suggests that the sower slings the word of the kingdom similar to the way in which a farmer arbitrarily flings seed. The farmer takes a handful of seed and throws it to the four winds. He flings seed repeatedly. Of course, this method disperses the seed rapidly, but it is plainly not the most efficient means. The best farming technique is to plant seeds in furrows. Yet Jesus' point moves beyond mere farming practice. Jesus speaks about broadcasting seed, I have often wondered if broadcasting seed—that is, throwing it to the north, east, west, and south—is the source of the word "news."

Broadcasting the seed of God's word in this fashion, therefore, is to scatter seed in multiple directions. Because this distribution of the seed is random, some of it necessarily lands in inhospitable places. Jesus tells the listeners that some of the seed will land on paths, rocky ground, or among the thorns. Nevertheless, some of the seed will find itself in good soil. It is in the good soil that the harvest will yield "grain, some a hundredfold, some sixty, some thirty." Jesus' method may be a gamble, but for God's realm this is the way to get "the word" out. When God broadcasts the gospel in this fashion, we understand what to expect—not all the seed lands on good soil. We are free to keep our expectations in proper perspective.

Today we expect low voter turnout in elections. Elections are an exercise of citizenship. We who believe in democratic principles can become easily disappointed at these low numbers. The church is little different. Many churches expect low attendance during the summer months and thus plan accordingly. Expect nothing, get nothing.

Nonetheless, and from time to time, God turns our nominal expectation on its head. For example, our congregation offered a Bible study titled "Vacation Bible School for Adults." Attendance, in the middle of July no less, staggered our leaders' ever-so-slight expectations.

Stewards of God's word live expectantly. Our realism about the ways that God works among us tempers our occasional and often minimal expectations, for sometimes the seed falls on good soil—even when we least expect it.

Sunday between July 17 and 23 inclusive

Romans 8:12–25   Stewards of a Great Debt

"So then, brothers and sisters, we are debtors."
(Rom. 8:12)

A bumper sticker I saw once read, "I owe, I owe, so it's off to work I go." The life of debt is a common fact for many modern people. Between house and car payments and the like, almost all people exist under debt's cloud. For this reason Paul's use of *opheiletes* ("debtor") becomes a transitional key. This word closes Paul's discussion about how God's Spirit enables believers to live in the spirit and shun life in the flesh. Thus, Paul helps us appreciate that we are no longer debtors to the flesh; rather, our debt to the Spirit frees us to remember that "we are children of God."

Paul varies the metaphor of "debt," substituting images of believers being adopted and becoming heirs of God, beginning with verse 14. Yet being debtors proves a powerful concept in Paul's transition. One can either be in debt to the flesh or be in debt to the spirit. If in debt to the former, then one can anticipate the consequence, which is death. If one is God's debtor, then the result is life. Here Paul writes of life in the sense that Jesus speaks of life: "Anyone who hears my word and believes him who sent me has eternal life, and does not come under judgment, but has passed from death to life" (John 5:24).

For modern people debt is a concept that needs little explanation. Consequently, as a theological notion, indebtedness resonates with us. We, of course, commonly understand debt as a monetary concept, but debt can involve owing something to someone else. Whether our debt is owed to a teacher, coach, parent, or pastor, believers who honestly look at their lives conclude quickly that their gain is a result of other people's interest in them. Few piano players learned to play the piano on their own. Most of our surpassing achievements we accomplish because someone guided us.

Paul wants believers to recognize that we have a clear choice, because one way or another, we will always be in debt to someone or something. For Paul the choice is between life in the flesh and life in the spirit. Life in the flesh insinuates that our passions and whims control us. However, life in the spirit suggests that God and God's Spirit control a person's actions. Life in the flesh leads to death; life in the spirit leads to life, and life that is abundant.

This text from Romans (beginning at 8:5) is unusual in that it offers ethical teaching in a part of Romans that mainly concentrates on theology. Paul occasionally inserts moral exhortations in the first eleven chapters, and this is one example. Paul suggests that those who live by the spirit will live in particular ways. The ways of living indicate whether one lives by the spirit or by the flesh.

Being in debt means that one is under an obligation to repay the debt. Good stewards are faithful managers, whether this means managing our talents or our money. But the question arises: How does one repay a debt to God? Paul might answer this question by saying that the most faithful way to put one's account straight with God is by passing along to others what God has already given one as a gift. Thus, for good stewards the gifts of mercy, forgiveness, and the love of Christ become methods of repayment. Stewards can only manage what God has first given to them. Vis-à-vis the debt of love, 1 John 4:19 puts it nicely: "We love because he first loved us."

Sunday between July 24 and 30 inclusive

Matthew 13:31–33, 44–52   The Kingdom of Heaven's Definitive Value

"The kingdom of heaven is like treasure [or] . . . fine pearls."
(Matt. 13:44–45)

Jesus tells these two one-sentence parables, and they seem simple enough. Yet within these few words Jesus shows the value of "the kingdom of heaven," or what we might also call "the realm of God." In fact the lesson from Matthew's Gospel is a series of short parables. These parables have the cumulative effect of a boxer's jabs. Separately they may cause minor damage, but collectively they pack quite a wallop. The metaphors are short and direct but taken together give many images of Jesus' message concerning God's kingdom. These images include a mustard seed, yeast, treasure in a field, a pearl, and a net. I will concentrate on the treasure hidden in a field and the merchant in search of fine pearls.

In some respects the parables of the treasure hidden in a field and the merchant in search of fine pearls reveal similarities. Each describes the kingdom of heaven, but they also show us that people will offer all they have to possess these prizes.

There are differences as well. In the first, the one who finds this treasure does so quite by accident. Evidently, as a farmer plows a field, he hits something; this is not unusual, as farmers regularly scrape rocks or hidden tree stumps. We might assume the one who plows is plowing in another person's field. Perhaps the farmer has leased it to put in the crop. But upon stumbling onto this treasure, the farmer immediately surrenders all he possesses to purchase the field. Thus, we imagine that the one who plows is a common day laborer who simply, in today's vernacular, wins the lottery.

Conversely, a merchant in search of fine pearls is a person who has undoubtedly already amassed some wealth. The merchant intentionally searches for fine merchandise, trading presumably in other finery besides pearls. Diamonds, gold, and other precious commodities may make up the list of trade wares. What makes his circumstance similar to the one who plows is that the merchant also sells all to obtain the pearl of great price.

One of the characters is relatively poor, while the other is affluent. One intentionally seeks that which has great value while the other simply trips over it. But in both cases, the individuals sell everything to attain the object of unsurpassable worth.

What would you give for the kingdom of heaven? In today's world there is a philosophy that suggests that we must "give to get." In theological circles, at least in some churches' theological understandings, we often express this mentality as "the prosperity gospel." This gospel teaches people that if they give in abundance, then they will prosper—perhaps even get rich. This is not the subject of which Jesus speaks here.

Jesus teaches that the greatest value in human life, lived in obedience to God, is the kingdom of heaven. This "kingdom" or "realm" differs from the realm of everyday life, the realm of buying and selling. Rather, the shrewd or wise person recognizes, whether sought out or accidentally stumbled upon in this realm, that occasionally we will discover an objective that brings exceeding joy. When we recognize this object, good stewards know that everything else is worth sacrificing for this end. Indeed, the kingdom of heaven is not simply an external objective reality, although Jesus uses these words to describe it. The evangelist recalls Jesus' words: "The kingdom of God is among you" (Luke 17:21).

Sunday between July 31 and August 6 inclusive

Genesis 32:22–31   The Gift of a New Name

"You shall no longer be called Jacob, but Israel, for you have striven with God and with humans, and have prevailed."

(Gen. 32:28)

Faithful stewards generously give to God and others because they recognize what they are and what they have do not belong to them. Instead, a steward's talents or possessions are gifts from God. Not only are talents and possessions simply gifts from God either. Rather, good stewards sense that God loans these "households to manage." We use these stewardship households to further God's will in the world. To manage these gifts and possessions, as if we have finally seen them in the proper light of faith, is to become stewards who offer the abundance of our lives with renewed gratitude.

A car dealership in a small West Texas town provides financing under the motto "Fresh Start Financing." The dealership offers a finance program for people who want to buy a car but may not have adequate credit. The fresh start idea reveals the dealership's willingness to offer people with poor credit the ability to begin all over again. In a strict monetary sense, it is a fiscal risk for the owners. Yet the offer furnishes hope for those with poor credit.

In our lesson from Genesis, God offers Jacob a new name and start. Behind this text is the fact that our "hero" Jacob is a person of conflict. Jacob created conflict with his brother Esau after he shrewdly tricked Esau out of his birthright. In ancient times the birthright was the portion of the family inheritance that went to the firstborn. Today the family inheritance is usually divided in more equitable ways. In biblical times, however, the birthright was an important privilege of family life. A birthright represented security, affluence, fruitfulness, and property.

Not only did Jacob seize Esau's birthright, but he also tricked Isaac, their father, out of the blessing that the patriarch bequeathed to the eldest son. Thus, Jacob had not only created a lethal enemy in Esau, but he deceived his father. Genesis 32 offers a glimpse of Jacob's last night prior to facing his deceived brother, which was a night of struggle.

Jacob obtains a new name in his encounter with the "man" with whom he wrestles. The name "Jacob" means "he who supplants" or "he who takes by the heel." We know from all the stories of Jacob that the description "heel" certainly fits his character. Now, however, the nocturnal visitor gives him a new name, "Israel," meaning "the one who strives with God." Like Cephas/Peter or Saul/Paul, a name change reveals a shift in character.

On the playground, when youngsters playing baseball have a close play and cannot decide among themselves whether the runner is out or safe, they decide to have a "do-over." In the church at times people will consult the pastor and say, "I lost my job. For the time being we must cut back our giving to the church." Sometimes the reason is health issues or some other domestic problem. However, when people do get back on their feet, this becomes a perfect time for a do-over. People can take advantage of the "fresh start" idea. Now that they have had a close look at what it is "to be in want," these believers have, at this instant, an occasion to give abundantly to the church as both stewards and grateful people.

Sometimes we are at our best after life has humbled us. Jacob now meets life with a new sense of humility. After an intense night of wrestling—in which Jacob not only was humbled but also was given a chance to start over—Israel can begin again. God gives us all a second opportunity to claim our name.

Sunday between August 7 and 13 inclusive

Psalm 105:1–6, 16–22, 45b   The Ruler of Possessions

"He made him lord of his house, and ruler of all his possessions."
(Ps. 105:21)

What tethers stewards to God is God's promise that we discover in Scripture. Of course, God made the divine promise to people long ago in faraway places. Yet as people of faith we too partake of these promises as "heirs of God and joint heirs with Christ" (Rom. 8:17). Not only this, but Paul also writes, "If you belong to Christ, then you are Abraham's offspring, heirs according to the promise" (Gal. 3:29). Our lesson from the Psalter today recounts Israel's story. This psalm narrates Israel's story from the time of Abraham through the nation's settlement of the land of promise.

God's promise to Israel, originally delivered to the patriarchs and the matriarchs, entails possessions—the land, descendants, and a relationship with God (see Gen. 17:8). Thus, there is a quite tangible aspect to the promise that God made to our forbears. Land, progeny, and a relationship with the God who was later revealed in Christ—these are certainly concrete signs of God's promise to God's people.

Psalm 105:16–22 recollects the story of Joseph. Joseph is of interest to stewards because he came into possession of the storehouse of Egypt in order not only to preserve the Egyptian people but also to care for his kindred as well. It is the story of a faithful steward who shrewdly manages what bounty God provides in order to save many people from a worldwide famine. Joseph understood the foundational principle of stewardship: everything belongs to God!

What we have is not our own but is rather a loan from God. We use our gifts until God calls them back at death. As Jesus said, "From everyone to whom much has been given, much will be required; and from the one to whom much has been entrusted, even more will be demanded" (Luke 12:48). People never steward the things that they own; they can only manage property belonging to another. If we believe that God owns everything, then how we use God's possessions becomes the measure of our faithful stewardship. Good stewards understand that God allows us to manage God's largess until God recalls God's possessions back for an accounting.

In Joseph's circumstance, "the ruler of the peoples set him free" and made him "lord of his house, and ruler of all his possessions." Pharaoh was no doubt one of the wealthiest individuals alive during the time described by Genesis. Yet those who read the Bible with care recognize that behind Pharaoh's wealth the mighty and omnipotent hand of God operates. As the Genesis story reminds us, revisited by Psalm 105:16–22, behind the scenes of human history God moves on behalf of God's people.

Joseph's example is applicable to Christian stewards today. Joseph, presumably led by the dreams God sent him and later by shrewd management (see Gen. 41), was able to secure enough food to save Egypt and his own people from starvation. If the church could shrewdly pool its resources as stewards, then it would be hard to imagine the impact we could have on a hungry world. In Joseph one person made the difference in the lives of countless people. Stewards have such opportunities even today.

Sunday between August 14 and 20 inclusive

Romans 11:1–2a, 29–31   The Enduring Gifts and Calling of God

"For the gifts and the calling of God are irrevocable."
(Rom. 11:29)

"Has God rejected his people?" This is a searing rhetorical question that Paul asks. Who among us has not wondered whether or not we will be accepted back by our family after bringing some shame or another upon our family's good name? This question haunts the younger brother as he makes his weary way home from the far country in Jesus' parable of the Prodigal Son. This wasteful child rehearses the speech he wants to make for his awaiting father at home. He is certain that there will be a heavy price to pay for his prodigality. Paul here wonders out loud if God has abandoned Israel.

There are times when all of us feel that our parents may reject us for "behavior unbecoming" to the family's name. For good reason, parenting images (usually masculine, but not always; see Isa. 66:13, Luke 13:34) abound in Scripture when writers grope for metaphors describing the divine-human relationship.

The most crucial of all parental attributes is a total devotion to children through unconditional love. We see unconditional love plainly in a story relating the tragic hostilities between King David and his son Absalom. Absalom fought and chased David, trying to wrest the kingdom from his father. Absalom threatened the kingdom and his own father's life on multiple occasions. Despite Absalom's behavior, David loved Absalom more than his own life. In fact, when David hears news of his enemy son's death, David responds out of love: "The king was deeply moved, and went up to the chamber over the gate, and wept; and as he went, he said, 'O my son Absalom, my son, my son Absalom! Would I had died instead of you, O Absalom, my son, my son!' " (2 Sam. 18:33).

Like the love of a parent, God's love never forsakes God's children. This very love of God is what binds God to God's children—even in our waywardness. Paul writes that "the gifts and the calling of God are irrevocable." Once God gives a gift, God does not rescind it. We may think that our actions will put the gift of God in jeopardy. Likewise, we may think that immoral behavior will put our parents' love for us in question. Yet when parents practice "unconditional love," they respond to their primal nature as parents. Paul tells believers that God never forsakes God's people.

Stewardship means, "to manage someone's property that has been loaned as a sacred trust." As Christian parents understand children as God's gifts, so too do stewards understand God's gifts and calling as sacred matters to administer. In Paul's assurance of these two things, gifts and calling, Paul gives believers confidence that God really intends for us to steward or manage them. If we are always "looking over our shoulder," wondering whether in our ineptitude God will remove our stewardship, then we can never keep our focus on managing our gifts and graces.

God means for us to be partners in God's creation. As such, God does not randomly or cavalierly eliminate our stewardship responsibility. The father of the prodigal as well as David as Absalom's father loved their children despite the latter's conduct. God has granted us gifts and graces—talents, if you will—in order for us to use them as partners in creation. Some of us will take longer than others to exercise proper stewardship. But then, God can wait. God is, after all, "the alpha and omega."

Sunday between August 21 and 27 inclusive

Romans 12:1–8   Worship Primes the Gift Pump

"We have gifts that differ according to the grace given to us."
(Rom. 12:6)

A 1958 Christmas song features lyrics that describe a poor shepherd who gives the newborn king a fine gift. But because he is poor he can only play his little drum for the baby—and, as it turns out, his gift is sufficient. I suppose nearly all Christians—except those who suffer from the sin of arrogance—feel like the best they have to offer Christ is never good enough. But when Paul dips his quill into the darkest ink he can find, Paul reassures the Roman church that "we have gifts that differ according to the grace given to us." Paul implies that all believers as stewards have some gift worthy of offering. One's gifts may differ from another person's, but we all have gifts to offer. It is often in worship that we come to receive what John Wesley called "the means of grace."

In Romans 12–15 Paul concentrates on exhortation. He urges people to live the implications of the gospel outlined in Romans 1–11. Some scholars divide the theology (Romans 1–11) and the ethics (12–15), even though moral counsel can be found earlier in the letter (6:12–14 and 8:5–13, for example). But in the main, Romans' final chapters reveal how Christians can live out their faith in tangible ways. Naturally, one way believers live out faith is through divine worship, although Paul goes beyond this minimal requirement. Paul believes that all church tasks are important.

Often in local churches people think that only a few selected tasks are truly vital. This kind of thinking suggests that the remaining tasks merely give the rest of the congregation something to do. From Paul's point of view, nothing could be further from the truth.

In one of the churches where I was pastor, our church council distributed a "time and talent survey." The goal of the survey was to unveil gifts that members possessed. It so happened that at this time our church required three persons for the personnel committee and twenty-seven adults to teach Sunday school classes. There was no little irony that twenty-seven people signed up to serve on the personnel committee while only three signed up to serve as Sunday school teachers. What greater service could a Christian steward render than to teach, encourage, and shape young people's faith? Still, many members preferred to make the "big" decisions of hiring and setting salaries. We diminish Christ's work among us when we forget the importance of the "behind the scenes" ministries.

Paul recognizes that each person has a gift to offer. But when he begins writing about the different kinds of gifts, he first roots the believer's offering of gifts in worship. Paul instructs the Romans "to present your bodies as a living sacrifice, holy and acceptable to God." In addition, he draws a distinction between the way the world does business and the way that Christian stewards can "renew their minds." Perhaps he makes use of the Christ hymn in Philippians 2. There he urges "the same mind be in you that was in Christ Jesus" (Phil. 2:5). Worship is a place where Christians examine weekly their minds and hearts to measure their Christlike quality. Worship is where Christians gather, sing, pray, and seek the grace of spiritual discernment. Our gifts to God are entrenched in worship. We offer our gifts and talents as a response to what God has already done for us in Jesus Christ. We are God's smorgasbord of talents and gifts waiting to be served up on behalf of God's world. Stewardship begins in worship and ends at our neighbor's needs.

Sunday between August 28 and September 3 inclusive

Matthew 16:21–28   Authentic Life in Jesus

"What will it profit them if they gain the whole world but forfeit their life?"
(Matt. 16:26)

There are several questions that haunt people today: "Why am I here?" and "What is the purpose of my life?" Yet these questions have also beset people throughout human history. Matthew allows Jesus to weigh in on the matter. Jesus asks, "For what will it profit them if they gain the whole world but forfeit their life? Or what will they give in return for their life?" In essence, Jesus' inquiry concerns the meaning of life.

The Gospel reading puts Jesus and the disciples on their fateful journey to Jerusalem. There, of course, Jesus will live out his destiny. But on the way to Jerusalem, Jesus teaches the disciples what he hopes they will carry with them to the end of their days. These days of journey are among the last days that Jesus spends with the disciples.

Jesus' teaching here includes what will happen to him as he enters Jerusalem. After Jesus outlines his great suffering, death, and resurrection on the third day, Peter speaks (perhaps during Jesus' censure Peter wishes he had kept his thoughts to himself): "God forbid it, Lord! This must never happen to you." Could it be that Peter really means, "God forbid it, Lord! This must never happen to *us*"? We can never know, but stewardship understood as discipleship means heeding Jesus' call of "Follow me" (Matt. 4:19; 8:22; 9:9; 16:24; etc.).

The heart of the Christian message is that those who believe that Jesus is the Messiah, and thereby God's anointed, obey this call to follow. At times, following is easy and meets our natural inclination to be useful, kind people. Yet far too often we find following Jesus goes against our sense of survival and need for safety. We chafe under the yoke of our crosses. Occasionally, following Jesus produces anxiety and moves us out from the umbrella of comfort and security we have spent a lifetime assembling.

In Matthew's story Jesus addresses this anxiety by asking rhetorical questions: "For what will it profit them if they gain the whole world but forfeit their life? Or what will they give in return for their life?" In other words, Jesus attempts to put life into a larger envelope than simply keeping safe and clinging to our self-generated security. In these questions of life and its meaning, Jesus forces believers to determine what is really essential and what is merely of relative consequence.

A saying goes that a person at death's door will not say with regret, "I wish I had spent more time at the office." For stewards, the decisions made over time in "the nickels and dimes of life" are the consistent, important decisions. Our earthly time and the way we choose to spend our days are the markers by which we can best judge life. It is not "the one with the most toys at the end who wins," as some have suggested. Instead, the measure of our lives as those who believe in

Christ inheres in the small ways we manage what God has given us. These small things make us stewards.

The best way to be a faithful steward is to follow the Christ who offers us the real and authentic meaning of life—sharing with others what he has first shared with us.

Sunday between September 4 and 10 inclusive

Exodus 12:1–14   Stewards of Sacred Memory

"This day shall be a day of remembrance for you."
(Exod. 12:14)

When people gather to swap stories of past experiences, at a family reunion or a class reunion, for example, someone may say to a storyteller, "I think your memory is playing tricks on you." As a former parishioner once confessed, "The older I get, the better high school athlete I become." Memory is an odd thing. It can be a tool for self-aggrandizement, or it can honor relationships and formative experiences. Because we live in a culture that tends to dismiss the past, it is all the more important that believers grow as stewards of sacred memory. The church is a vital site for remembrance. Consequently, believers have a stake in preserving sacred memory.

The body of Christ comes by its mandate to remember honestly. Yet sacred memory has never been the church's unique territory. As early as the covenant with Noah, God emphasized remembering. God tells Noah, "I will remember my covenant. . . . When the bow is in the clouds, I will see it and remember the everlasting covenant" (Gen. 9:15–16). Strangely, the bow is for the purpose of reminding God and not people about the covenant promise. To remember signifies a sacred task. Later God also calls the chosen people to remember. The Decalogue includes the commandment "Remember the sabbath day" (Exod. 20:8). Deuteronomy offers even a more compelling basis for Sabbath observance: "Remember that you were a slave in the land of Egypt . . . ; therefore the LORD your God commanded you to keep the sabbath day" (Deut. 5:15). Sacred memory even unites Jews and Christians in a common history.

Various Protestant churches employ what the Methodist family of denominations calls the "Wesleyan Quadrilateral." Four criteria test whether or not a particular theological statement is true to Christian doctrine. The four measures are Scripture, tradition, reason, and experience. A most vital function of the church is to pass along its sacred memory (or tradition) to subsequent generations. We do this through Scripture, but in other ways too. Judaism in part transfers its sacred memory through its Seder meal. Christians transmit tradition by sharing a meal with Jesus' words, as related by Paul: "This is my body that is for you. Do this in remembrance of me" (1 Cor. 11:24). Accordingly, whenever we celebrate the Eucharist, we remember together.

A crucial role today's church plays is to steward the historic faith. We are faith's caretakers. We do so by linking contemporary believers to Christian tradition. New expressions for faith in Christ arise constantly. Yet it is imperative for modern people to remember that we did not formulate the faith. Rather, we have inherited the faith as a sacred trust both through the centuries and from believers around the world. As stewards of the living God, we make available both the context and the content of faith for new Jesus followers. Each hymn, each creed, each understanding of God whom Jesus revealed was a previous generation's response to its explicit circumstances. Collectively, these incarnations of our faith represent a rich and diverse tradition that tells us who God is—and also who we are before God.

When a family gathers to eat a holiday meal, often a member of the oldest generation tells about that family's "olden days." By doing so, this person passes along the lore and tradition of that family. In the Christian faith, we steward God's story by telling Israel's story and "the new Israel's" story. We are stewards of our tradition. It is important work.

Sunday between September 11 and 17 inclusive

Matthew 18:21–35   Generous Forgiveness

"How often should I forgive?"
(Matt. 18:21)

Quantification is at work in this Gospel lesson. Peter asks Jesus, "Lord, if another member of the church sins against me, how often should I forgive? As many as seven times?" Jesus offers Peter a fundamentally incalculable number of "seventy-seven" times. Jesus then tells the parable of the Unforgiving Servant to reinforce the teaching.

The idea that a person may deny forgiveness implies that forgiveness is a stewardship household that believers manage. Forgiveness is something we can offer, or not offer, according to our will. No doubt, Peter assumes that to forgive someone up to seven times signals a deep generosity. Before Jesus concluded the parable, the original audience might have laughed heartily. The listeners' own lack of compassion might also have convicted them, however, as the parable unfolded.

The basis for laughter would have been in Jesus' exaggerated demands for forgiveness. To suggest forgiving someone seventy-seven times essentially suggests that no one can ever exhaust forgiveness toward another. Forgiveness in this teaching is essentially infinite. Jesus says in effect, "When it comes to forgiveness, you need not bother counting. True forgiveness does not keep score." We cannot forgive enough.

The parable stresses this point by its designation of the first servant's forgiven debt of ten thousand talents, a debt so colossal that no one in the first century could have repaid it. Thus, Jesus' listeners would have been more than amused by a person who could "ingeniously" rack up that kind of debt—the equivalent of about a billion dollars in today's reckoning. Yet this same servant turns out to be less than generous when he declines to forgive another individual who owed him a measly "hundred denarii." One implication is that in order to receive forgiveness, one must be willing to extend forgiveness. Hence, the first servant comes across as a person entirely devoid of sympathy. In his refusal to extend a "tiny" forgiveness, he betrays the fact that he has benefited from a "huge" forgiveness.

In Hebrew Scripture, David says, "I will not offer burnt offerings to the LORD my God that cost me nothing" (2 Sam. 24:24, and a near parallel in 1 Chr. 21:24). Ironically, in terms of stewardship and giving, forgiveness is something we disciples and stewards can offer our sisters and brothers that costs us little—if we can but swallow our pride. No great reserve of materials or money is necessary to offer forgiveness to another. Certainly some offenses are more difficult to forgive than others; we do not trivialize offenses against persons. Yet forgiveness, from Jesus' point of view, is an act that those who follow the Messiah can offer lavishly.

God's forgiveness of human sin rekindles the bond linking the human and the divine. Forgiveness among believers reestablishes a foundation upon which people may begin anew in a formerly ruptured relationship. To forgive another person is a gift that says, "Let us begin again." Forgiveness does not keep score; it allows a fresh relationship to flourish. However difficult, forgiveness is a gift that begins a healing process.

For Matthew, forgiveness is so essential to community life that Jesus' parable ends ominously: "If you do not forgive . . . " Stewards of forgiveness need not worry about this threat, for those who prize forgiveness also realize that God has forgiven us.

Sunday between September 18 and 24 inclusive

Matthew 20:1–16   God's Enigmatic Openhandedness

"Am I not allowed to do what I choose with what belongs to me?"
(Matt. 20:15)

Of all Jesus' parables that challenge the minds and lives of modern people, the parable of the Laborers in the Vineyard surely ranks near the top. It unmistakably runs counter to the ways our teachers teach us. It contests everything about the work ethic our parents tried to instill in us. Undeniably, many honest and hardworking church folk never get past the parable's offense. To not get beyond the offense is to fail to hear Jesus' message. This parable addresses our labor and God's stewardship.

The manner in which God functions with respect to creation is in part what Jesus' parable tackles. The line from Isaiah, "For my thoughts are not your thoughts, nor are your ways my ways" (Isa. 55:8), has perhaps never been better illustrated than in this parable. One thing the parable suggests is that while we often allude to the relationship between God and people as similar to human relationships, it is not so. The Psalter tells us, "As a father has compassion for his children, so the LORD has compassion for those who fear him" (Ps. 103:13), and God in Isaiah says, "As a mother comforts her child, so I will comfort you" (Isa. 66:13). We regularly draw on these types of family metaphors to express our relationship with God. Perhaps these ways of speaking make our parable so difficult to grasp. But when speaking of the inexpressible God, we grasp at human words.

Thus, when we arrive at this parable, one which describes God's relationship with God's creatures, we recognize that our relationship with God is an association distinct from our commonplace human interactions. Jesus' master in the parable offers a gift to everyone who accepts it. Customary relations between employers and employees and between teachers and students do not hold here. Typically in human interaction we take for granted a give and take. Alas, in this parable we see little negotiation but instead a pure gift. The danger lurks in that the workers are tolerant until they begin to compare what they receive with what the "less deserving" others receive. Resentment now sets in. The "all-day" workers grumble when they discover that they receive the same pay as the "one-hour" workers. The master then says to one of them, "Friend, I am doing you no wrong; did you not agree with me for the usual daily wage? Take what belongs to you and go; I choose to give to this last the same as I give to you. Am I not allowed to do what I choose with what belongs to me? Or are you envious because I am generous?" The parable discloses that God's generosity falls equally on all. We "faithful working stewards" need not bargain, bribe, or wheedle some gracious gift from God. God gives to us willingly.

We might describe this parable as a somewhat negative stewardship lesson— but a lesson that many modern believers need to learn. We stewards do not offer our lives to God, nor do we disciples give God tithes and offerings in order to attain some sort of divine insurance policy. Rather, we present our gifts to God as our response to God's loving-kindness. To maneuver God into giving us what we think we have earned is no less foolish than children trying to win the love of a parent—yet we human creatures do it incessantly. God's link with us is different.

The result of this parable for stewards is that God gives to all God's children as God chooses. We may not approve of God's heaping divine grace on the "wrong" people. Nonetheless, the Lord of the universe retains a prerogative to govern creation in the manner he sees fit. Are we envious because God is generous?

Sunday between September 25 and October 1 inclusive

Matthew 21:23–32   Saying "Yes" and Living It

"Which of the two did the will of his father?"
(Matt. 21:31)

In every group of people assembled to hear a speaker, there are always those who arrive with a skeptical attitude, who want to trip up the preacher. The Gospel lesson today tells us about some in the crowd that Jesus taught: "the chief priests and the elders of the people." Some of these, no doubt, came with receptive spirits. But Matthew also notes that the religious establishment questioned Jesus "by what authority" he taught. These were not likely innocent questions. Those who questioned Jesus had an agenda.

Jesus, in excellent rhetorical fashion, answers the authority question with a counterquestion: "Did the baptism of John come from heaven, or was it of human origin?" The chief priests and the elders knew that any answer they offered would expose their agenda. They also were "afraid of the crowd." Thus, the matter passed.

The subsequent parable speaks to Christian stewardship in a peculiarly modern way. After the rhetorical stalemate Jesus presses on and relates the parable of the Two Sons. The basic gist of the parable is a father who asks his sons to work in a vineyard. One son says he will not but later changes his mind and goes to work. The other son says he will go but fails to appear for work. Jesus then asks, "Which of the two did the will of his father?" The answer, as related by the religious authorities, is the son who initially said no, but later yielded and went to work. Then Jesus teaches about God's nature. According to Jesus, God welcomes those who have had less than ethical lives but who have repented and desired the goodness of God and God's realm.

Today various people presume that something auxiliary to faith in the God revealed in the life, death, and resurrection of Jesus makes them true believers. Some folk consider a proper grasp of and ability to articulate theories of Christian dogma qualifies one for God's realm. Others may say that they have deep faith in God but live life in a fashion that promotes faith in a "gospel of moral rectitude." Some trust an explicit denomination, a specific way of interpreting Scripture, a proper "Christian" economic doctrine, or an unambiguous type of experiential conversion—complete with date, time, and place of the experience. Despite these secondary aspects of authentic faith, however, those who put their faith in something other than God's grace may become distracted from the heart of the gospel if they fail to live out God's mandate to "love your neighbor as yourself" (Lev. 19:18).

The journey we stewards call the Christian life is to remember who we are. The chief priests and the elders remembered how to say who they were, but they forgot to perform according to God's will. Conversely, those persons represented by the tax collectors and the prostitutes may have had difficulty articulating that they were sons and daughters of God, but Jesus honors them in the parable. Why? Perhaps because they found out who they were by living the good news as they heard it.

We stewards today have a fourth option. This fourth scenario is to be faithful stewards who say "Yes, I will go," and then go. Our choice, according to Jesus' parable, is to say yes, and fail to go, or to say no, and then repent and go. A steward's faithful response to God's gracious invitation is to simply say yes and then go. In faithfulness our yes can be counted on. In so doing, we stewards serve the master.

Sunday between October 2 and 8 inclusive

Exodus 20:1–4, 7–9, 12–20   Stewards Live in Contentment

"You shall have no other gods before me."
(Exod. 20:3)

The Ten Commandments, one of the most recognized parts of our Bible, has recently been the focus of a controversy. Alabama Supreme Court judge Roy Moore "staunchly defends his right to display the Ten Commandments in his courtroom," reports John C. Holbert. "Such displays, [his supporters] say, will somehow make the world a better place. . . . Just seeing them, reading them, or reciting them would somehow improve the moral fiber of the nation."* Of course, not every American practices Judaism or Christianity. But for Jews and Christians the Decalogue reminds authentic stewards about their life before God and in community.

There are many ways to get at the meaning of these words presumably spoken to Moses. One way is to suggest that some of the commandments address the relationship between the human and the divine. The balance of the remaining commandments, therefore, pertains to the relations between people in the community of faith. In the way the lectionary falls, verses 1–4 and 7–9 address the divine-human relationship, while verses 12–20 speak to human concerns.

In the divine-human section of the Decalogue we could place all the issues under the rubric of "avoiding idolatry." As the Hebrews lived and practiced faith, they did so in the midst of numerous tribal groups that practiced one type or another of pagan worship. Thus, the Decalogue was an attempt to "place a hedge" around those who worshiped the Lord. Therefore, commands to "have no other gods," not to construct idols, not to use the Lord's name to no purpose, and to hallow the Sabbath were each intended to observe covenant keeping. These commands also kept the human-divine relationship squarely before the people. If the people remember who their God is, then it is likely they will remember who they are as people created in God's image.

*John C. Holbert, *The Ten Commandments* (Nashville: Abingdon Press, 2002), 7.

People who live in community must necessarily live in a disposition of trust and interdependence. Some scholars disparage the Decalogue's negative decrees. However, social groups—that is, nations, clubs, institutions, and the like—often render legal documents in this negative mode. The prohibitions simply provide the boundary within which the community may live its life in trust and inter-dependence.

One topic that the Decalogue addresses in several ways is the human trait of greed manifested in theft. God instructs us not to take another's life, another's spouse, or another's possessions. At times, greed originates in a person's desire to care for self and family. Often, however, self-care devolves into excessive self-centeredness, even self-indulgence. What begins in a desire for security morphs into pure greed—and greedy people rarely enjoy happiness. Perhaps a reason for unhappiness is that the greedy person can never get enough. Paul counsels about this when he writes, "There is great gain in godliness combined with content-ment" (1 Tim. 6:6).

Stewards value the Lord's mandates because they direct community life. These guides to life help us learn contentment. Jesus assures us with this word: "Strive first for the kingdom of God and . . . these things will be given to you as well" (Matt. 6:33).

Sunday between October 9 and 15 inclusive

Matthew 22:1–14   The Steward's Robes of Righteousness

"Friend, how did you get in here without a wedding robe?"
(Matt. 22:12)

Human customs seem to swing from one extreme to another. If old enough we may remember the "old line, main line" church culture in which no self-respecting male over ten years old attended worship without a tie. Women's church fashion was commensurate. Denominational officials time and again counseled their young male counterparts then (and in the main they were male) that "reverends always preach better in a white shirt." Those days seem long past. Obviously, today we can visit these same sorts of churches and see few ties in the crowd. Because our Gospel lesson appears to ponder what we might call a "dress code," we may ask what a wedding robe could have to do with stewardship.

Matthew alerts us about Jesus' form of teaching when he writes, "Once more Jesus spoke to them in parables." This parable, like all of Jesus' parables, attends to an event in life to which everyone in his audience could relate. Weddings and the attendant feasts were exceptional social events that broke the commonplace toil of earning one's daily bread. People would periodically gather for a neighbor's or relative's wedding. These festive occasions functioned as major communal events for people who had few social outlets. In some ways they served as giant family/community reunions.

Jesus used the wedding banquet as a metaphor for the kingdom of God. The parable begins as a king sends out invitations for his son's wedding—no doubt a liberal summons. However, those who receive the king's generous request "made light of it" and "seized his slaves, mistreated them, and killed them." The heretofore hospitable king responds by destroying the murderers and burning their city. Then the king charges his slaves to invite anyone to the banquet they come across. In an allegorical reading, Jesus teaches about God's invitation to God's realm. Everyone gets an invitation.

Ironically, when the king greets the guests and we remember that his instruction is to invite "both good and bad," the king sees one lacking a wedding robe. We hardly imagine that when inviting everyone that all would be appropriately dressed. But the king addresses the one without proper attire, "Friend, how did you get in here without a wedding robe?" The ill-clad attendee is mute. The king then has him tossed out. In an apocalyptic fanfare Jesus concludes the parable with these menacing words: "Bind him hand and foot, and throw him into the outer darkness." What kind of warning is this?

In the history of the interpretation of this parable many observers have put forth proposals regarding this unfortunate and underdressed wedding guest. Such is the multivalent nature of a parable. In this parable the person lacking a wedding robe oddly suffers much the same fate as did those who initially refused the king's invitation. Perhaps Jesus' point is that although the invitation to God's realm is open to all, it nevertheless rests upon the invited to respond appropriately. Plainly he was invited, but he also exhibited a degree of impertinence in not wearing proper attire.

Disciples who aspire to faithful stewardship recognize that when we respond to God's invitation, we do so with a proper bearing. We do not buy our way into God's realm. Yet God's gracious invitation obliges our response by more than merely showing up. The capacities with which God endows us are a robe of integrity that Christ places upon on us. When we arrive at God's banquet, we approach as those ready to share in the festivities, and we offer our lives to serve those for whom Christ died.

Sunday between October 16 and 22 inclusive

Matthew 22:15–22   What Is God's, Exactly?

"Give therefore to the emperor the things that are the emperor's."
(Matt. 22:21)

The four Gospels include several incidents similar to the one found in the lesson for today. Matthew's account begins with some religious authorities who "plotted to entrap him [Jesus] in what he said." Jesus' swelling status among the common people prompts religious factions such as the Pharisees and the Herodians uncharacteristically to collaborate to thwart Jesus' popularity among the people.

Luke subtly alludes to a similar phenomenon of "strange bedfellows" by writing about a budding relationship between Herod and Pilate, who "became friends with each other; before this they had been enemies" (Luke 23:12). The Pharisees and the Herodians aim to commit Jesus to either betraying God by saying yes to Roman taxes or to expose his disloyalty to Rome by leading him to commit sedition by saying no to state taxes. Jesus deftly extricates himself from this logic trap. In addition, he offers a fine lesson on stewardship.

Jesus uses a "coin trick" to avoid the trap. It is important to note that when the religious authorities asked the question about taxes, they were standing within the confines of the temple (Matt. 21:23). Jesus, in response to the question, says, "Show me the coin used for the tax." Apparently, one of the questioners extracts a denarius from his pocket. Because Jewish law prohibited Roman coins within the temple precincts (hence the necessity of money changers), the one who produced the coin also defied Hebrew law. Accordingly, Jesus exposes his questioners as the hypocrites that Matthew has already revealed by his notation that Jesus was "aware of their malice."

After exposing the Herodians and the Pharisees, Jesus puts the finishing touches on the public undressing of their hypocrisy by requiring them to name the image on the coin, which is the emperor's. They have condemned themselves by their own words. Jesus completes the lesson by giving the true answer to the question concerning taxes: "Give therefore to the emperor the things that are the emperor's, and to God the things that are God's." It is little wonder that Matthew finishes the scene with this observation, "When they heard this, they were amazed; and they left him and went away."

In the modern church-state debate, Jesus leaves the choice to believers. We try to decide from among situations which circumstances are secular and which are sacred. It is as easy to sort out this question as it is to answer the question: "Why do the innocent suffer?" But Jesus' answer offers a clue. When Jesus said to give to the state the things that are the state's, and to God the things that are God's, Jesus voiced the first principle of Christian stewardship. The principle plainly concedes that *everything is God's*. Matthew's lesson about Caesar and God pertains to our stewardship awareness. All believers possess is simply God-given, with regard to the state and/or with regard to Christ's dominion lived out in the body of Christ. What we have is not our own but is God's loan to us. We employ our borrowed gifts until God recalls them at death.

Whether stewards operate in the state realm of voting or paying taxes, and whether stewards function spiritually by praying or sharing bread with others, in all cases we operate within the veil of God's creation. Thus, because God owns all, we are merely stewards of God's provisions. To Jesus, there is no God or Caesar. There is only God.

Sunday between October 23 and 29 inclusive

1 Thessalonians 2:1–8   Sharing Is Timeless

"Our coming to you was not in vain."
(1 Thess. 2:1)

Paul writes that "our coming to you was not in vain." In this little phrase we see the economy of the steward's way of life. In Paul's confession to the Thessalonians, Paul reveals much about a believer's, and therefore a steward's, approach to the life of faith.

Our culture specializes in trivial pursuits. Whether whiling away precious time watching inane television, surfing the World Wide Web, playing video games, or reading trifling, indulgent "literature," our society dedicates itself to passing time by what the Bible might call vain interests. Vanity, or actions that belie the vain, are simply things that have no value. We suffer from the temptations of vanity in ways our forbears did not, simply because we do not live life today chasing our next meal or working full-time merely to survive. However, perhaps we have made an idol of idle time.

The title of the magazine *Vanity Fair* comes from an allusion in John Bunyan's classic novel *Pilgrim's Progress*. In Bunyan's book, a town named Vanity conducts a perpetual fair that is the epitome of lavish frivolity. Perhaps many modern folk know exactly where this town exists. "Vanity presses" prey on authors so engrossed in getting published that they willingly pay for the privilege—and handsomely. From the point of view of faith, this kind of approach to life is, in a word, prodigal. Thus, when Paul writes that he and his companions did not come to Thessalonica "in vain," he simply affirms that they came with a steadfast purpose. This purpose is in keeping with God's economy. When God creates, the creation has a profound intention behind it. As Proverbs 16:4 says, "The LORD has made everything for its purpose." This attitude of faith has implications for disciples who are God's stewards.

In this section of the epistle, Paul outlines his and his companions' deeper objective for engaging the Thessalonian church. Despite great opposition, Paul acknowledges that through much suffering he mustered the courage to speak the gospel to this church. Paul did so because, as he writes in retrospect, "you have become very dear to us." Paul's desire is not only to share the gospel with those he loves but also to share the lives of Paul's fellow workers with the people. This is the deep purpose for which Paul comes.

Too often we in the church overuse the word "love." Yet for Paul, this is the ultimate motive for all that he is and all that he does. The love of Christ compels Paul "to share with you not only the gospel of God but also our own selves." Love too is the steward's motive.

Stewards discern the value of time and, so, redeem it. Stewards recognize that God fashions all things for a purpose and that our life's end is to honor God with our time and treasure. Our generation will, no doubt, finally draw near nihilism when we discover that the days of shopping or watching television sports are little likely to give life meaning or value. Like the Preacher, we too may intone, "I hated life, because what is done under the sun was grievous to me; for all is vanity and a chasing after wind" (Eccl. 2:17). Faithful stewards understand that to fulfill God's purpose is to share ourselves, and in doing so, we also share the gospel. Sharing is timeless.

Sunday between October 30 and November 5 inclusive

Matthew 23:1–12   Not as I Do . . .

> *"Do whatever they teach you . . . but do not do as they do."*
> (Matt. 23:3)

Being a parent is often hard work. Parents must be on guard lest they engage in some activity or another that they have explicitly instructed their children to avoid. How many parents who smoke have received stern lectures from their child about the health hazards of smoking? It is a tough pill to swallow from your own offspring. Believers willingly abide by the counsel or guidance that they impart on those whom they lead.

A nice woman in one of my churches, with a martini in one hand and a cigarette in the other, once told me she wished modern pastors were more "spiritual." This made me want to respond that perhaps it was the company we kept. People who make professions of faith are by definition stewards and disciples. Yet those who aspire to lead others in a congregation must be ever vigilant about being stewards over the very leadership they exercise.

The Gospel lesson addresses this idea of being a steward of leadership. There is a deep sense (that all pastors will instantly recognize) that when one vaults into a position of leadership, then one is no longer a free person. Rather, that person becomes a part of what we might call "the public domain." If you do not believe me, ask Bill Clinton or Tom DeLay. These public leaders have had their critics scrutinize their actions from every conceivable angle. Likewise, Jesus sees the lives of leaders like the scribes and the Pharisees as fair game.

Jesus begins his critique of the scribes and the Pharisees by noting their place of leadership as those who "sit on Moses' seat.". "Moses seat" simply designates a position of authority in Israel's religious life. However, although these leaders had rights assured them by their office, they failed in their leadership responsibilities. Rights without responsibility seems unreasonable from Jesus' point of view. For this reason Jesus teaches the crowd and the disciples to "do whatever they teach you and follow it; but do not do as they do, for they do not practice what they teach." Jesus effectively characterizes their leadership as hypocritical.

Jesus seems to say that although the scribes and Pharisees offer sound teaching, they fall short of leadership expectations by not following the very advice that they dish out. Hence, Jesus says, "They tie up heavy burdens, hard to bear, and lay them on the shoulders of others; but they themselves are unwilling to lift a finger to move them."

The essence of leadership recognizes that leaders must constantly be willing to live by the standards they set for others. When the church calls some of its members to leadership positions, these "called out" leaders value their followers' expectations. Too many churches have people on the finance committee who fail to offer much financial support for their mission work. How many people on a congregation's worship committee have worship attendance that we could at best describe as lukewarm? Those who exercise leadership in Christ's ministry need to remember that they belong to the church's rank and file believers. In other words, leaders become public people—those called to set an example. Anything less is hypocrisy.

A wise pastor once told me, "Giving leadership is leadership giving." We always measure stewards by the standards of truth and integrity.

All Saints'
(November 1, or may be used on the first Sunday in November)

Revelation 7:9–17   Before God's Throne

"These are they who have come out of the great ordeal."
(Rev. 7:14)

Revelation's author, known to Christian tradition as Saint John the Divine, finds himself in the heavenly throne room. To this point in the Apocalypse, John has been earthbound, but now John finds himself transported to the throne of God. John writes, "At once I was in the spirit, and there in heaven stood a throne" (Rev. 4:2). Today's text furnishes a description of but one of the many things John sees in the throne room. Among the visions is "a great multitude." When John suggests that these are those "who have come out of the great ordeal," John implies those who have been faithful to Christ's ministry with their lives—that is, martyrs. In this sense, they are the convincing stewards. These stewards have offered everything to God's realm.

All Saints' Sunday is the day that the church celebrates those believers who have died in Christ. It is a day of remembrance. On occasion believers ask, "How does a person become a saint?" All Saints' Day and Revelation bring this sort of question to mind. Revelation 6 details the opening of six of seven seals. In the prophecy of the seals are warhorses, God's altar, and natural disasters that plague the earth. After the sixth seal's opening, Revelation furnishes an interlude. Perhaps readers need a respite after the horrors of the first six seals. The sealing of the 144,000 begins chapter 7. This image is of the church militant, that is, the church struggling for life among earth's principalities and powers. John's next image is of the church triumphant—the community of those who rest from their earthly labors.

Chapter 7 provides strangely contrasting visions of the church militant and the church triumphant. First, there is a specifically calculated throng of 144,000 contrasted to "a great multitude that no one could count." Second, John contrasts the twelve tribes of Israel to "a multitude from every nation." Third, John describes the church militant as a company prepared for threatening peril and distinguishes it from the victorious and secure counted in the church triumphant. Whatever this chapter wants to impart, above all, it is John's attempt to describe a vision of heaven.

Over the centuries the concept of heaven has fueled much speculation. A cartoon once appeared in the *New Yorker* that showed a group of heavenbound saints lined up just outside the heavenly gates. Peter stood at a podium, reading off the answers to the most frequently asked questions on earth, now finally and decisively answered in heaven: "# 48, true; # 49, false; # 50, William Shatner; # 51, yes; # 52, the Ponderosa; # 53 , every other Tuesday . . ." People have inquiring minds and want to know. John's heavenly apocalyptic vision offers us one such image.

"How does a person become a saint?" For stewards this is a controlling question, for we all believe that our response to God offers us a just "reward." But however we conceive of heaven, John writes at least this much: heaven is the place where saints or believers—they amount to the same thing—commune with God.

Our efforts do not make us saints. Rather, we become saints when God confers on us "gifts and graces" to handle as stewards. When we use God's resources for shaping God's realm, then God develops us into true saints. God bestows sainthood at the point where God's grace encounters our stewardship. There we find God and God's saints.

Sunday between November 6 and 12 inclusive

Matthew 25:1–13   People Get Ready

"Keep awake . . . for you know neither the day nor the hour."
(Matt. 25:13)

Jesus' parable of the bridesmaids addresses the stewardship theme of being alert and ready. This is Matthew's final parable that addresses the abruptness of the kingdom's coming. Jesus uses the backdrop of a wedding feast in order to make the point. In the first century, a wedding feast often lasted for more than a week. Jesus used this familiar wedding image to emphasize the long wait for the actual consummation of the wedding vows. The parable pertains to the watchfulness of stewards, who are primed to offer their God-given gifts to the realm of God. The Boy Scout motto nicely summarizes the parable's theme: "Be prepared."

Jesus' parable teaches that the bridegroom's arrival is the moment of truth. Five maidens are ready with the oil they have stored for this moment. This preparation has made them wise. Five maidens have not done what was necessary to secure the oil. Their failure has made them foolish. A steward is either ready or is not, and this detail is the parable's gist.

Stewards prepare for life's decisive moments. The trouble with the bridesmaids who lack oil is that they have waited too long to prepare. As the English poet Edward Young says, "Procrastination is the thief of time." Some interpreters consider the bridegroom's arrival to represent the time when God's reign on earth will begin. Accordingly, the parable's determining image is that God— and God's Messiah—provides wedding feasts. Consequently, when God is ready for the feast, then it is time to start. The bridegroom initiates the feast, not the guests. The bridegroom is delayed, but when he arrives it is too late to begin the preparation.

A story recounted in an unpublished sermon of Thomas Lane Butts Jr. illustrates the stewardship principle of preparedness. A man driving late one night along an isolated road pulls over when his engine stops. Seeing no other cars, he believes he is stranded for the night. Happily, an hour later another car approaches. The affable motorist removes a rope from his car's trunk and tows the stalled auto nearly forty miles to a garage. The first man offers the motorist money, but he refuses to take it. He also declines an offer of a tank full of gas. Frustrated because he feels grateful and wants to express this in some way, he insists on repaying the man. The stranger replies, "If you really want to show your gratitude, buy a rope and always carry it in your car."

The parable's good news for stewards is that today's preparation enables our gifts to be used by others tomorrow. To those who save for a rainy day or those who would give to God's kingdom rather than prodigally waste resources, this parable offers hope. Perhaps this parable suggests ways to spend one's time and effort on significant things. A steward's decisions today prepare for a later day when God's realm comes upon us suddenly. "Keep awake therefore, for you know neither the day nor the hour."

In the long run, it is not the arrival of the bridegroom that makes some wise and others foolish; the bridegroom's return simply reveals which are which.

Sunday between November 13 and 19 inclusive

Matthew 25:14–30   If I Had Only Known

"For to all those who have . . . they will have an abundance."
(Matt. 25:29)

This familiar parable comes from Matthew and occurs in a series of Jesus' teachings that address discipleship, waiting, and preparation. As a result, this commentary's last several weeks have highlighted Matthew. Stewardship teaching and parables pervade this section of Matthew's Gospel.

Briefly, Jesus' parable teaches that a wealthy man goes on a journey and entrusts his slaves with talents, a financial entity. To the three slaves he gives five, two, and one talent, respectively. The first two slaves double what the master loaned them, but the third buries his solitary talent. His explanation to his master is inventive, if not a social blunder of the first order: "Master, I knew that you were a harsh man, reaping where you did not sow, and gathering where you did not scatter seed; so I was afraid, and I went and hid your talent in the ground. Here you have what is yours." He seals his own fate with his words.

We can infer several lessons from this explicit stewardship parable. First, those who risk what they have been given please their master. The two enterprising slaves gratify their master, but the master responds to the fearful slave, "As for this worthless slave, throw him into the outer darkness, where there will be weeping and gnashing of teeth." A third and perhaps more allegorical meaning detects Jesus' parable as teaching that risk takers, those creative with the master's talents, are useful to the building up of God's kingdom. The noncreative slave simply lacks value in God's work. Perhaps this parable suggests that stewards must gamble their talents for God's realm.

The parable's context also helps disclose its meaning. The prior text is Matthew 25:1–12, the parable of the Ten Bridesmaids. This parable teaches that preparation is the watchword for stewards, and Jesus ends it by reminding listeners to "keep awake therefore" (25:13). The parable of the Judgment of the Nations follows today's parable. The most remarkable detail about this parable is the declaration of both the righteous and unrighteous: "Lord, when was it that we saw you hungry and gave you food, or thirsty and gave you something to drink?" (25:37, 44). This parable endorses the idea that authentic disciples do the righteous thing without regard to reward. Their faithfulness simply beckons them to care for those in need. This parable speaks to the essence of stewardship.

Accordingly, when we align Matthew's three parables in chapter 25, we bring to light a sequence: preparation, industriousness with God's possessions, and serving the master through charitable acts toward others. Matthew's narrating these parables in this particular order is intentional. Matthew reveals that true discipleship resides in stewardship.

Jesus never asks stewards to do more than we can do, but he does ask us to do something. No one can tell us what to do. Yet God can lead us as stewards if we are willing to take creative risks for God's realm. God often nudges us in the right direction. Whether they have five talents, or two talents, or a single talent, stewards will let God show them how to risk. A steward is one who is creative and useful in the building up of God's kingdom. That is all God or anyone else can ask of us.

Christ the King/Reign of Christ
(Sunday between November 20 and 26 inclusive)

Matthew 25:31–46   Seeing Others from the End

"When was it that we saw you?"
(Matt. 25:38, 39, 44)

Augustine wrote that when Christians borrow from pagans for God's purposes, it is similar to the Israelites "plunder[ing] the Egyptians" (Exod. 3:22). As Israel takes the best "jewelry of silver and gold," we "begin with the end in mind," to borrow Stephen Covey's second habit.* The church's word for what Covey describes is "judgment." To begin with the end in mind is to start an undertaking from a perspective of its conclusion. Jesus' parable offers stewards a glimpse of what faithfulness to God looks like at its conclusion.

Judgment is a chief theme of today's parable, which Jesus told the last week of his life according to Matthew. The word "judgment" in Greek is *krisis*. *Krisis* means "deciding time," and this is our parable's point. Jesus does not ask what the sheep or the goats have done with their lives. Rather, he tells them what they have done. The crisis resolution hangs on how they treated the hungry, the thirsty, the naked, the foreigners, the sick, and the prisoners in their midst.

In this parable, Jesus does not seem to care about confession, and he never asks either group what they think about him. All present are believers. Jesus' basis for division is simply how each group treated the last, the lost, and the least. According to Matthew, salvation belongs not automatically to those who have faith, but rather to those who *do* faith. In this parable, *everyone* is surprised. Perhaps Matthew wants readers to understand that Jesus is judge because Jesus sees things as God sees them.

In a 1991 film called "Defending Your Life," Albert Brooks plays the role of Daniel Miller, an insecure but likable "whiner" who is killed in a head-on automobile collision at the film's beginning. Subsequently, Daniel arrives in Judgment City, which looks very much like the world he left behind—only nicer. As it turns out, Judgment City evaluates people's lives to determine whether they should move forward to the next level of existence or go back to earth and have another crack at living. The entire movie and its premise offers us pause for reflection. Each moment of life God plays on a large screen in front of all our friends, family, coworkers, and perfect strangers. No one edits our film. It plays in the video screening room just as it happened, both in its good parts and in its bad. Imagine seeing your life in this fashion.

Fortunately for us, God does not see the story of our lives as we see the story of our lives. God sees as God sees. This becomes our saving grace. When we think about judgment, we can appreciate beginning with the end in mind. When we

---

*Stephen Covey, *The 7 Habits of Highly Effective People* (New York: Simon & Schuster, 1989), 95ff.

begin with the end in mind, we visualize life's process in which we stand in the middle. In the midst of a forest, it is difficult to see the trees. When we are in the midst of life, we have difficulty seeing life and its purpose clearly. This is why judgment is not so much a negative force with which we must contend but rather an opportunity to see the purposes for which God created us.

For stewards this perspective reminds us that as we live out our faith, the small kindnesses we show others are part of the reason "we live and move and have our being" (Acts 17:28). God created us for community. In community we do not extend comfort to others for the good we will receive in return. Rather, we offer to comfort others, for this is the way God intended people to live. Thinking about our end helps us thrive in the present.

Thanksgiving Day

Deuteronomy 8:7–18   Give Credit Where Credit Is Due

"Do not exalt yourself, forgetting the LORD your God."
(Deut. 8:14)

Two primary principles of Christian stewardship mandate that everything belongs to God and that God includes people as partners in creation. Most stewards recognize and even uphold these principles. But given the human propensity to be prideful, it is often easy to forget what we profess to believe. One of the hallmarks of Deuteronomy is its presentation of Moses' last testament. As Israel prepares to enter the land of promise and as Moses' leadership begins to wane, the prophet/lawgiver/liberator addresses the wilderness sojourners with his wise words. Today's lesson contains what looks like a sermon. Moses preaches about the good that God offers the people and their requisite response—remembrance and deference to the Lord. Although Moses preached this sermon to people long ago and far away, nonetheless its words speak to the issue of Christian stewardship even today.

I have a pastor friend who told me of a time when one of his church members, a bank officer, invited him to bless the opening of a new bank. Such a request astounded my pastor friend. He pressed the bank officer as to why he had asked him to bless this new business. The officer replied, "We want our bank to be one that truly honors and glorifies the Lord." Clearly this was to be banking of a different sort. The officer's appeal did, however, imply much that Deuteronomy suggests. Moses tells the people: "Take care that you do not forget the LORD your God, by failing to keep his commandments, his ordinances, and his statutes, which I am commanding you today." To honor God in this case means first to remember God and then obey God's teaching.

Thanksgiving is a national holiday that encourages Americans to celebrate what the church celebrates on a weekly basis. We pause and offer our gratitude to God. Stewardship is simply a response of gratitude to God for the gifts and talents God has loaned us. We did not create our talents, nor are they really ours in any substantive sense. Genuine stewards know that they are merely caretakers of God's assets offered to us for the building up and maintaining of God's world.

Moses' sermon begins by cataloging all the benefits God has poured upon the people. Included are productive lands with "olive trees and honey, a land where you may eat bread without scarcity, where you will lack nothing." Hills where the people may mine copper God throws in for good measure. They shall eat their fill—no mean promise in a time when the next meal was always a prevailing concern.

But Moses foresees the people's character. Earlier Moses warned the people about a tendency to "become complacent in the land" (Deut. 4:25). In order to avoid such attitudes, Moses reminds the people to "take care that you do not forget the LORD your God." Indeed, after they have enjoyed the Lord's largesse, they are not to exalt themselves, "forgetting the LORD your God, who brought you out of the land of Egypt, out of the house of slavery." Perhaps this is a wise word to twenty-first-century people too.

If nothing else, Thanksgiving offers stewards an occasion to acknowledge the God from whom all blessings flow. In gratitude we remember who we are and how we arrived where we are. In addition, Thanksgiving Day also provides a moment of reflection about our relationship to God and the obedience we offer the Lord of the universe. Believers know that we should be more thankful. Stewards reflect their heartfelt thanks to God by recalling their blessings and obediently sharing them with others.

YEAR B

Advent and Christmas

First Sunday of Advent

1 Corinthians 1:3–9   Giving Thanks as an Act of Stewardship

"I give thanks to my God always for you."
(1 Cor. 1:4)

I received a thank-you note recently that was not really addressed to me at all, but rather to my congregation. Eight years ago a young woman had left the congregation as a regular worshiper in order to begin her long term of study for the ministry. She worked in various churches, which prevented her from worshiping with her home church. Now as she approached her ordination, she sent a note to our church. The note simply thanked the congregation for nurturing her in the faith, which enabled her call to ministry. The note was a splendid example of the stewardship of thanksgiving.

Paul, too, knew the value of thanksgiving. In this Corinthian passage, he thanks God for the people with whom he works. In Romans 16:3–4, Paul thanks

Prisca and Aquila "who risked their necks for my life, to whom not only I give thanks, but also all the churches of the Gentiles." Good stewards are always thankful believers.

The situation in Corinth was as complicated as it was difficult. Evidently several members of the church fired off letters to Paul asking his advice on local church conflicts that had surfaced. For one example, Paul addresses the thorny issue of sexual immorality: "a man is living with his father's wife" (1 Cor. 5:1). Of course, there were many less spectacular, but no less troubling, issues that congregants asked Paul to weigh in on. However, before he begins to sort through the Corinthians' troubles—sometimes encouraging, often chastising—he pauses and gives thanks to God. Paul's thanksgiving for the congregation is no mere rhetorical ploy. He genuinely holds deep affection for these church folk. He also knows that what he must write to them out of an authentic concern will trouble many of them. Therefore, he reminds the church at the outset just how precious his relationship with them is. He even encourages them by telling them that they may overcome their conflicts because they "are not lacking in any spiritual gift." In other words, this congregation has the resources to glorify God and resume being the church that God created it to be.

Thanksgiving for others is plainly one of the households that stewards manage. Offering a token of gratitude takes so little effort, and the fruit of such stewardship in personal relationships is gratifying to all concerned.

Perhaps one of the most treasured gifts one individual can offer another is simply to say thank you. We often regard stewardship as offering our gifts to God, but it is just as true that offering ourselves to others is a noble form of managing our relationships with them. During Advent we may fret over the perfect gift for someone, yet saying thanks is always appropriate. A judicious pastor once advised me, "When you are in a tight spot and don't know what to say, simply say, 'Thank you.'"

Second Sunday of Advent

2 Peter 3:8–15a   In the Meantime . . .

"Therefore, beloved, while you are waiting for these things . . ."
(2 Pet. 3:14)

One feature of Advent worship often pushes the conflict buttons between typical laypeople and the "guardians of worship correctness" (read here: clergy and church musicians). This is Advent hymns. The church has a superb array of meaningful Advent hymns. Yet many otherwise discerning believers do not want to wait until the season of Christmas to sing Christmas hymns. Many in the church want Christmas and its attendant hymns sooner rather than later.

Of course, church folks cherish the minor-keyed hymns such as "Savior of the Nations, Come" or "To a Maid Engaged to Joseph." Not in a minor key but often described by detractors as "dirgelike" is "In the Bleak Midwinter." But as an old axiom suggests, "There's no accounting for taste." Perhaps this conflict over Advent music signals a deeper issue, an issue of interest to Christian stewards. The issue concerns our waiting for God's time.

In today's Epistle text, 2 Peter offers insight into two prominent Advent themes. The first theme concerns the Parousia, or the second coming of Jesus. Jesus' return is imminent from the perspective of early New Testament texts. Yet as time progressed and as God evidently delayed Jesus' return, the writers rein-terpreted this divine deferment. Second Peter tells readers that "with the Lord one day is like a thousand years, and a thousand years are like one day." How-ever, the writer gives assurance that God's promise "is not . . . as some think of slowness." Second Peter is in accord with Jesus' words: "It is not for you to know the times or periods that the Father has set by his own authority" (Acts 1:7). Thus, God sets the divine timetable.

Second Peter addresses a second theme as well by posing the question "What are believers to do as they wait for the Lord's return?" By way of this implied ques-tion the writer speaks to stewards and what we do while we wait. The writer explicitly asks those who wait for the Lord's return, "What sort of persons ought you to be in leading lives of holiness and godliness?" The epistle's answer suggests that stewards as disciples wait "where righteousness is at home." The writer also admonishes his audience to wait and strive "to be found by him at peace" and to "regard the patience of our Lord as salvation."

For stewards, waiting for the Lord can be a painful exercise. Regarding even our worship, many of us are prone to move too quickly to the "good news" of Christmas. We dislike the pain of waiting through Advent, or for that matter, Lent. Patiently waiting for the Lord's coming becomes a test of faith. Yet what are the faithful to do? As stewards, God in Christ calls us to the tasks of ministry until Christ comes in final victory. We are to do as Jesus' parable instructs: "Be dressed for action and have your lamps lit; be like those who are waiting for their master to return from the wedding banquet, so that they may open the door for him as soon as he comes and knocks" (Luke 12:35–36). Waiting is difficult for most of us. Yet waiting for God's time is a mark of faith.

Waiting in expectation and waiting by being busy with Jesus' ministry, these are what God counts on from us. Feeding and clothing the hungry are each tasks that take on special meaning during Advent. Churches that focus on mission at Advent are churches that understand faithful waiting. Stewards manage the households of time and compassion as they wait for the Lord's return. That is cer-tainly something to sing about.

Third Sunday of Advent

Psalm 126:1–6   What Joy Provokes

"The LORD has done great things for us, and we rejoiced."
(Ps. 126:3)

Few times of the year offer as much hope and joy as does the season of Advent. We feel better, act more charitably, worship more enthusiastically at Advent than at virtually any other time of the year. Consequently, today's Psalter lesson speaks not so much to us as for us. Psalm 126 shouts out in adoration, "Our mouth was filled with laughter, and our tongue with shouts of joy." The origin and motive for all Christian stewardship derives from the joy we experience when we recognize that God restores our fortunes as the Lord restored the fortunes of Zion.

Those who compiled the Revised Common Lectionary likely selected Psalm 126 as attendant to the Hebrew Scripture text, Isaiah 61:1–4, 8–11. Each reading relates the return from exile. This interpretation embodies the joy expressed in each text. These exiles had much over which to be thankful and joyful. Joy and thanksgiving go hand in hand.

Ironically, joy is an emotion that many contemporary Christians have difficulty in expressing. Often we members of old-line, mainline denominations are at a loss when we try to express the joy of our faith. Perhaps these returning Hebrew exiles can help us find our way.

Some scholars divide Psalm 126 into two distinct parts, but each part addresses the subject of joy. The first three verses address a joy experienced— that is, the joy of the past—as when God restored the fortunes of Zion. Verses 4–6 address anticipated joy. Consequently, Christian stewards may celebrate by employing Psalm 126. After all, exultant joy is one of the keynotes of our lives in the risen Christ. If and when we believers embrace the magnitude of God's saving acts, then perhaps we can also embrace the joy in our gift of God's salvation.

A hallmark of early American frontier Christianity was its emphasis on "felt" religion. People not only talked about God; they also had a deep desire to experience God. Presbyterians, Methodists, and others commonly subscribed to four fundamental sources by which they thought about theology: Scripture, tradition, reason, and experience. Experience puts working clothes on the other three sources of revelation.

For the reason of living out faith, Christian stewards become persons who so deeply sense the gospel's warmth that they feel stimulated, even passionate, about sharing their experience with others. In so doing, stewards reevaluate their relationship to their possessions. In this reevaluation, stewards become compelled to distribute what may rightfully be their own possessions among others.

Advent is a time when our whole way of life puts an emphasis on giving. Gift giving at Advent and Christmas focuses our lives and experiences on the joy of seeing others receive. Biblically, our response arises from what God offers us as a gift. The Hebrews' gifts inhere in liberation and torah. Christian gifts fix on God's revealed love found in Christ's life, death, and resurrection.

To paraphrase 1 John 4:19: "We give because he first gave to us." The hub of giving is joy, and those who truly experience joy desire to give. An old maxim puts it, "One may give without loving, but one cannot love without giving."

Fourth Sunday of Advent

Luke 1:47–55   God's Preference for the Poor

"He has filled the hungry with good things, and sent the rich away empty."
(Luke 1:53)

As a seminary student I first heard the venerated Carlyle Marney's admission, "Some accuse me of being a communist, but I am simply a New Testament scholar." Luke's "Song of Mary" is a text that provides some context for Marney's claim.

A foundational stewardship standard is that God owns everything. In other words, we do not own anything that we possess; God gives us all our stuff as a sacred trust. Bible readers find ample textual evidence for this theological thinking regarding possessions. Deuteronomy 8:18 puts it this way: "Remember the LORD your God, for it is he who gives you power to get wealth," and Psalm 24:1 reads, "The earth is the LORD's and all that is in it, the world, and those who live in it." A third example is Haggai 2:9: "In this place I will give prosperity, says the LORD of hosts."

Despite the Scripture's clear stance on God's ownership, however, too many modern people live as if they owned their possessions. Since the English publication of Gustavo Gutiérrez's *A Theology of Liberation*, theologians of emancipation from poverty have used the phrase "God's preferential option for the poor." In his groundbreaking book, Gutiérrez writes, "In the Bible poverty is a scandalous condition inimical to human dignity and therefore contrary to the will of God."* Appropriately, Gutiérrez's theology orbits around the poles of God's universal love for all people and God's concern for the poor. The Song of Mary in today's text offers a rationale for such radical thinking. Christian stewardship functions best when it takes its cue from Mary's song.

When mainline preachers use the phrase "God's preferential option for the poor," no doubt many middle-American congregants will throw the word "radical" around after the service. In part, this reaction is based on our idol-making of property and money. There is much anecdotal evidence to support the contention that churches are more willing to forgive clergy sexual indiscretions than they are to forgive sins against the church's bank account. Yet Mary sings that God "has brought down the powerful from their thrones, and lifted up the lowly."

*Gustavo Gutiérrez, *A Theology of Liberation* (Maryknoll, NY: Orbis Books, 1973), 291.

Too often, even the church uses theology to laud the poor without moving to remedy their situation: "Has not God chosen the poor in the world to be rich in faith and to be heirs of the kingdom?" (Jas. 2:5). Another text used to this dubious end is when the church cites Jesus' words, out of context, "For you always have the poor with you" (Matt. 26:11). Far too many Christians use such thinking to protect their idols.

At Advent we rejoice in the Messiah's coming. We hope for a different and better world. We expect that in Jesus God will allow the world to begin anew. Therefore, some of Scripture's most radical words Mary sings in her Magnificat. She sings that God's "mercy is for those who fear him from generation to generation." She sings that God "has scattered the proud in the thoughts of their hearts." We may not like to hear words concerning God's preferential option for the poor. Yet Mary's jubilant song concerns this essential aspect of the good news.

Good stewards recognize that too habitually our possessions possess us. Faithful response to God's good news compels us to open our hearts and our hands to the poor. Of course, the poor are always with us, but that does not mean that we forget them.

Christmas Eve
[See Year A]

Christmas Day (A, B, and C)

Isaiah 52:7–10   Announcing the Good News

"Your sentinels lift up their voices."
(Isa. 52:8)

Many churches offer limited preaching opportunities for Christmas Day. Indeed, in 2005 when Christmas fell on Sunday, many megachurches around the United States canceled worship services because, as they said, "We want people to be with their families on this day." This rationale brings to mind what my then six-year-old son said when Christmas fell on Sunday: "Dad, do we have to go to church today? Church ruins Christmas."

If it is difficult to get people to church on Christmas Day, then what of preaching on a stewardship theme? Yet the text for the day does offer insight pertaining to the management of the stewardship household we could call proclamation. We often assume that the only person who proclaims the faith is the preacher. However, the old cliché that goes, "I would rather see a sermon than hear one," does have an element of truth to it. How stewards live their confession of faith publicly is one way we manage the household we call faith.

Outside the obvious case of Easter Sunday, it would be difficult to conceive a more triumphal day than Christmas. On Christmas Day Christians celebrate not only the arrival of the Messiah but also the appearance of creation's king. It is a day of joy and jubilation. The Isaiah text announces salvation; Israel's elation involves "the return of the LORD to Zion."

Again like Easter, Christmas Day announces the good news that God has offered a way of life to people who thought themselves dead. The prophet offers a blessing upon "the messenger who announces peace" in verse 7. This peace is indeed a peace in two senses. First, a return to Jerusalem gives a peace that only genuine homecoming offers. Second, the exiles' return points to a peace with God that God offers by way of affirmation. As God acts on the divine promise, God affirms the promise to the patriarchs. As the people return to the land of promise, they recognize the hand of God. It is as if the people have moved from death to life. Jesus' words in John 5:24 are suggestive: "Anyone who hears my word and believes him who sent me has eternal life, and does not come under judgment, but has passed from death to life."

Although today's text comes from the Hebrew Bible, it rings true for Christians on Christmas morning. When Isaiah writes, "Break forth together into singing, you ruins of Jerusalem; for the LORD has comforted his people, he has redeemed Jerusalem," the prophet gives a task. Isaiah not only gives stewards a task but also provides a reason for such joy. We sing because we are happy—and saved from death by the birth of the Messiah.

How can a Christian steward become one "who announces peace, who brings good news, who announces salvation"? Perhaps we can best answer such a question by considering the state of our world. God came to liberate the Hebrew people, and no less, God comes today to unfetter us. Whether our affliction is poverty, abuse of human beings, avarice, an absence of meaning, or a failure to protect the environment, we believers accept the role of steward. We announce by our lives that God has come in Jesus Christ. Our lives witness daily to the potency of our profession.

First Sunday after Christmas Day

Galatians 4:4–7   God as Adoptive Parent

"You are no longer a slave but a child."
(Gal. 4:7)

Slavery is an odd subject for the season of Christmastide. Yet slavery forms the hub of the reading for today. Paul uses slavery as a metaphor for the human-divine relationship that existed before God's incarnational intrusion into human flesh.

On this day most church attendees will expect little more than a sentimental sermon on a predictable text, such as the Gospel lesson. Luke's text is unquestionably a magnificent one, and most appropriate for Christmas. For stewardship, however, we find in Paul's Galatian epistle a fine place to explore our relationship to God. All stewardship, as astute stewards recognize, begins in relationship with God.

The Galatian text is both brief and intense. It offers much to ponder while it connects with many other biblical texts and ideas. The first prominent idea Paul presents is the one that speaks of "the fullness of time." Paul here employs the concept of *kairos* time, as distinct from *chronos* time. *Kairos* time signals that the time is ripe for something to happen, for example, crops to be harvested or a child to be born. We cannot schedule *kairos* time. It simply happens. *Chronos* time, on the other hand, suggests "clock time" or "calendar time." *Chronos* time occurs on a predetermined date or at a set time. Paul suggests that in the Christ event the time (*kairos*) is ripe for God to act.

Paul describes God's act in this way: "God sent his Son, born of a woman, born under the law, in order to redeem those who were under the law." In Paul references to the earthly Jesus are rare. "Under the law" implies that Jesus and his parents lived under the Mosaic law, adhering to Hebrew tradition, as Luke's Gospel lesson so well expresses.

The heart of Paul's argument, however, pertains to the slave/child distinction found in other New Testament texts. Paul uses a slave/child analogy and points to God's gift in Christ. By this gift God transfers people's status from being "under the law" into a new relationship. This new relationship now qualifies us as "a child [and] then also an heir." The ancient world divided itself into a multitude of categories, each of which had an explicit and hierarchical social rank. We see this earlier in Galatians when Paul writes that Christ obliterates human categories: "no longer Jew or Greek, there is no longer slave or free, there is no longer male and female" (Gal. 3:28).

To be a child of God, rather than a slave, indicates the highest status for which believers might aspire. Parents (and grandparents) love children and grandchildren in ways few relationships rival. These connections are utterly unique. The Bible, from beginning to end, recognizes this. Although Jacob's blessing is upon his grandchildren, Hebrews notes this near familial relationship: "By faith Jacob, when dying, blessed each of the sons of Joseph" (Heb. 11:21). To move from the status of slave to child and then on to being an heir is simply a believer's remarkable good fortune. By God's gift we now thrive as heirs of God's promises—not as slaves or servants.

A lovely aspect of children is the pleasure they derive from receiving gifts. A quesion familiar in many households with children is "What did you bring me?" What would life look like if all we ever did was ask others, "What did you bring me?" Without givers there are no gifts. Stewards give out of gratitude; we appreciate that God decided to adopt us. In our thankfulness, we extend our gifts on to others.

January 1–New Year
[See Year C]

Epiphany

Epiphany of the Lord
[See Year A]

Baptism of the Lord
(First Sunday after the Epiphany; Sunday between January 7 and 13)

Mark 1:4–11   God's Call to the Common Believer

"You are my Son, the Beloved; with you I am well pleased."
(Mark 1:11)

One of the greatest psychological stumbling blocks to stewardship comes from people who think they do not have "the right stuff" to be stewards. Of course, this is the opposite perspective of those who in pride or ignorance believe they have no need of God. Sometimes people think that their inadequacy dismisses their responsibility. When they think this way, then they are guilty of turning their backs on one of God's greatest gifts to us—our time, treasure, and talent. We all possess these and have something to offer.

Perhaps this lack of confidence in our talents arises from the overestimation of who Jesus is for us. We see paintings of Jesus with a halo's glow around his head. Or we remember our Sunday school stories about Jesus' miracles. But when Jesus came to his baptism, he was a common enough man. No one, at least to this point of his life, had witnessed any miracles. No one had detected any out-of-the-ordinary behavior from Jesus, who was about thirty years of age.

At the beginning of this text, the character who rivets our attention is John. He has just come from the wilderness and preaches in a way that peels the paint right off the walls of village houses. Mark reveals John's attraction by writing that "all the people of Jerusalem were going out to him" and "confessing their sins." John's garb of "camel's hair, with a leather belt around his waist" and his diet of "locusts and wild honey" send the message that this prophet is not one to be trifled with.

Yet, traditionally, perhaps we have emphasized the Baptizer's words from John's Gospel. The evangelist writes that the Baptizer states plainly, "He [Jesus] must increase, but I must decrease" (John 3:30). But we do ourselves and Jesus a disservice when we forget that prior to Jesus' baptism, he no doubt waited in the baptismal line with all the others. Mark's story suggests that Jesus was a common carpenter. He describes no miraculous birth, no magi, and no songs, as Luke's Gospel includes from Zechariah, Mary, or Simeon. We might think of Jesus as just a regular person, at least the way Mark writes the story.

However, a voice from on high announces who this Jesus is: "You are my Son, the Beloved; with you I am well pleased." What had Jesus done to merit this divine approval? Perhaps, simply put, Jesus was faithful to his religious heritage and fulfilled his obligations in obedience. Perhaps Jesus was an honorable craftsman and a trustworthy businessperson who acted honorably in all his dealings. Until the moment of Jesus' baptism his call to faithfulness had been like that of other, what we might call more ordinary and common, people.

Mark provides an important insight for the stewardship of our God-given gifts and talents. God does not wait for us to develop special skills or knowledge to call us into faithfulness. Rather, God's desire is for faithfulness from all disciples from the moment we discern the will of God working in our lives. For people who believe that they have nothing to offer God's realm, God implies that these excuses discount the marvelous gifts God has conferred. If Jesus is faithful in dispatching mundane duties around a carpenter's shop, then surely we can be faithful to God where we serve.

Second Sunday after the Epiphany
(Sunday between January 14 and 20 inclusive)

1 Samuel 3:1–10 (11–20)   Deep Listening Is Stewardship

"Speak, for your servant is listening."
(1 Sam. 3:10)

Stewards respond to God's realm by managing God's households, which have been offered to us as a loan. Consequently, stewards put what they have into God's service from the gifts and talents loaned from God. How are we to discern what God asks of us? Where and when do we employ our graces and gifts for ministry in God's realm? These are questions with which each steward must grapple. To discern God's call is a fundamental discipleship necessity for all believers.

Today's text from the Hebrew Bible is the story of Samuel's call from God. Samuel's mother, Hannah, is barren but prays fervently to the Lord for a child. She asks in her prayers that the "LORD of hosts . . . remember me, and . . . give to your servant a male child, then I will set him before you" (1 Sam. 1:11). The Lord grants Hannah's prayer, and when the boy is of age, she delivers Samuel to Eli, "to the house of the LORD at Shiloh" (1:24). Until the day that our text describes, Samuel was too young to perform the duties for which the Lord had set him apart. But on the night our text relates, Samuel receives his call from the Lord.

The lesson for today describes the call of Samuel. In order to discern the call, which comes four times in the text, Samuel needs guidance from Eli. Eli is the priest of the temple in Shiloh, and the text reveals him to be a good man—with bad children. In fact, Eli's sons, Hophni and Phinehas, are so wicked that the text suggests Samuel will carry on Eli's work as a type of surrogate son.

As stewards we can look to the way that God called Samuel to discern the ways God may call us. Three times Samuel receives the call from the Lord, and three times the youngster thinks the summons comes from Eli. Samuel and Eli are not unwise, but they act in accord with the fact that "the word of the LORD was rare in those days; visions were not widespread." People who expect little generally get little. Samuel and Eli did not anticipate the Lord to speak.

Eli, however, finally recognizes that the call may be coming from the Lord. His action now becomes an important link in the story. Eli tells Samuel what to answer the next time the summons comes. Thus, as the Lord calls yet again—a fourth time—Samuel answers as Eli has directed him: "Speak, for your servant is listening."

Part of the task of a steward is to handle the households that God has given us to manage. We manage households of faith, love, hope, service, prayer, and so forth. Deep listening is an act of stewardship. Listening is not easy, especially when we try to listen for the voice of the Lord. We must filter out all other competing voices in order to hear the voice of the One who creates and sustains us. Eli, in a sense, helps Samuel listen for and discern God's call. Eli also helps Samuel understand the faithful response that God apparently is looking for from the child.

Often when we think of stewardship, we think in terms of action or doing some task or another. Yet here Eli helps Samuel understand that prior to any response is the discipline of focused living. A great deal of human prayer involves not so much our telling what we want or need, but rather listening for God's direction in our lives. Those who manage the deep listening for God's voice are those who become authentic stewards.

Third Sunday after the Epiphany
(Sunday between January 21 and 27 inclusive)

Jonah 3:1–5, 10   Yahweh People in a Jonah World

"Go to Nineveh . . . and proclaim to it the message that I tell you."
(Jonah 3:1–2)

Jonah is a personal Hebrew name meaning "dove." The book of Jonah, unique among the Minor Prophets, preserves the story of this prophet's ministry. The book of Jonah narrates a major short story about a minor prophet. Jonah's message rings out clearly in one single sentence: "Forty days more, and Nineveh shall be overthrown!" (Jonah 3:4). However reluctantly, Jonah became a steward of God's prophetic word. Despite how much he was at odds with those to whom God called him to prophesy, Jonah was at least a faithful enough believer in God to do as God directed. Likewise, our stewardship of God's good gifts allows each of us to make a declaration about whom we serve. The problem is that when we put ourselves in God's place, we may tend to think God pours out grace and mercy on the wrong people.

The prophetic book of Jonah contains a dual focus. One focal point rests on pagans (1:4–16; 3:3–10), while a second center of attention, as we might expect, is on the Israelite prophet, Jonah (1:17–2:10; 4:1–11). The portrayal of pagans in a positive light as sensitive and submissive to God's will recognizes their worth and potential in God's sight. The writer, however, reveals Jonah's abiding inconsistency: after praising God for rescuing him from death (see chapter 2), Jonah growls when God similarly saves pagans.

One way for preachers and teachers to speak to our culture today using the message of Jonah might be to remind ourselves that Christians are "Yahweh people in a Jonah world." In the Jonah world, hate and prejudice rule. But we are Yahweh people. Yahweh was "concerned about Nineveh, that great city, in which there are more than a hundred and twenty thousand persons who do not know their right hand from their left, and also many animals" (Jonah 4:11). Why would we conceive ourselves as Yahweh people in a Jonah world? Because the way we offer our lives, our substance, and our resources to others in Christ's name hints at a unique biblical inclusivity for all people. At God's table we are to exclude no person. Thus, what God offers to us to manage through our gifts and talents we in turn pass along to other persons as signs of God's realm.

When my son was about three and a half years old, he noticed that we kissed and hugged particular people in our family and at our church. He asked me one day, "Dad, how do we know when people are on our side?" His question startled me, but I later realized that many people ponder this question. Who indeed is on "our side"?

Jonah was angry at God—angry enough to die—because of God's compassion poured out on, from Jonah's perspective, the wrong people. Perhaps we would all be more faithful to God if instead of wanting God on our side, we instead tried consistently to be on God's side. When we commit ourselves—our time, talent, treasure—to God's realm, we make a statement that we choose to be on God's side. Indeed, our giving of self and service to God is what makes us Yahweh people in a Jonah world.

Our stewardship of God's good gifts allows each of us to make a declaration about whom we serve. Small acts of faithful stewardship loom large in our helping God to build our little piece of God's great realm.

Fourth Sunday after the Epiphany
(Sunday between January 28 and February 3 inclusive; if it is the Last Sunday after the Epiphany, see Transfiguration)

1 Corinthians 8:1–13　　　　　Stewards Rein in Freedom of Expression

"Knowledge puffs up, but love builds up."
(1 Cor. 8:1)

Some of the moral issues raised in the New Testament seem appallingly irrelevant today. Why deal with petty sin when Rome is burning? Yet an issue such as whether to eat food sacrificed in pagan cultic worship provides stewards an occasion to deal with church controversy. Attitudes of hospitality may guide us when we address honest differences between individual conscience and peace within the community of faith.

The Epistle lesson is Paul's response to an obvious problem in Corinth. In the ancient world citizens regularly slaughtered animals to sacrifice to pagan gods at pagan shrines. After worshipers burned a small portion of the animals in pagan temples, they sold the remainder. Here is where the congregation's appeal to Paul comes into play. Some Christians in Corinth saw no problem with buying and then eating the "tainted" meat. Yet other believers thought that eating food sacrificed to idols was an affront to God. Plainly this issue created a great deal of commotion at Corinth. Thus, the Corinthian Christian community petitioned Paul for a ruling. But Paul's word surprises.

Acts forbids the eating of meat sacrificed to idols (Acts 15:22–29). So too does Revelation (2:14, 20), in which the heavenly Christ rebukes two churches for eating meat sacrificed to idols. Thus, this issue in the early church shows Paul cutting across the grain of New Testament teaching. Paul writes, "Food will not bring us close to God. We are no worse off if we do not eat, and no better off if we do." In other words, for Paul this is a nonissue because idols are nothing. If so, then food sacrificed to idols is pointless. Paul seems to say, "Eat what you want. You do not violate the ordinances of God."

Just as quickly as Paul gives the green light on all food, however, he adds something else: "But take care that this liberty of yours does not somehow become a stumbling block to the weak." Paul cautions against acting in ways that trouble those who are new believers. Paul understands that some things may be legal but may not be helpful.

Why does Paul say this? I suggest three reasons. First, within the Christian community love takes precedence over individual freedoms. Paul understands that Christ frees people from the religious law. Yet the law of Christ is the law of love. Christian stewards forego freedom in order to encourage other believers and do so out of love. Second, a steward's prime motive for action is the wholeness and health of the body of Christ. Third, Paul advises the believers in Corinth that they should take each individual in the community seriously as a person for whom Christ died—even those without "insider knowledge." For stewards this implies that our actions reflect a compassionate and even restraining consideration for fellow members of the body of Christ.

Our task is to spread Christ's love to the world. It is not to impose a second tier of the Mosaic law on unsuspecting believers whom we welcome into the body of Christ. We all have our work to do here. We might ask ourselves, "How can we help other believers mature in the faith that gives us abundant life?" Sometimes, in acting the part of a Christian steward, we relinquish a part of our freedom in order to help a sister or brother.

Fifth Sunday after the Epiphany
(Sunday between February 3 and 10 inclusive;
if it is the Last Sunday after the Epiphany, see Transfiguration)

1 Corinthians 9:16–23   The Gift of Relationship

"I have become all things to all people."
(1 Cor. 9:22)

Unsuccessful people, those who fall short in their chosen profession, commonly fail because they do not get along with other people. Adults and even children struggle with this. On my own grade school report cards, there was a category labeled "getting along with others." Few people can succeed with others if they are hard to get along with. Of all the households God calls stewards to manage, plainly one of the most vital is the household we call "relationships."

Yet if we have problems in getting along with others, this Epistle text gives us reason to consider the contrary problem of getting along with everyone. It seems that some people in Corinth complained because Paul seemed to get along with everyone. This being "all things to all people," they implied, demonstrated that Paul was indecisive and had no scruples. Paul cites his own behavior to illustrate the kind of self-discipline he recommends to other believers. Paul knows that he is free to behave as other Christian teachers do. He also desires a more effective ministry; therefore, he remains celibate, fasts, and refuses rightful compensation. He does this "so that I might win more of them," as he writes.

Paul refuses to flaunt his freedom; instead, he abides by the Jewish law to win Jews to Christ. When Paul is with Gentiles, by contrast, he diminishes conformity to the law. Paul intends, as a result, "to be all things to all people" for one reason: to win some to Christ. Winning people or converting people to Christ is Paul's central objective. By his willingness to accommodate others' needs, Paul does not transgress his own rules but remembers the lives of those to whom God has sent him. Whether Jew or Gentile, Paul continuously reaches out in Jesus Christ and thus offers a stewardship of relationship.

The lesson stewards can take from Paul's letter is that we are free in Christ but that the most authentic freedom we have is when we look to the good of others for their own sake. When we can do this, then we are truly free and are stewards of relationship.

The Great Wall of China stretches eighteen hundred miles over plains and deserts. The Chinese built it to keep out barbarians, but it ended up impeding China's own progress. Thus isolated from other cultures, the Chinese quit advancing as a people for a time.

When the church turns inward and fails to "be all things to all people," then it ceases to share the gospel with the wider culture for which Christ also came. Of course, great things happen inside churches, but if we never see ourselves as missionaries to the wider culture—those sent out in ministry to the world—then we stagnate and eventually die. Faithful stewards are hospitable to persons of other points of view. We come to understand them first, and then we share the gospel in authentic relationship.

Sixth Sunday after the Epiphany
(Sunday between February 11 and 17 inclusive; if it is the Last Sunday after the Epiphany, see Transfiguration)

2 Kings 5:1–14   A Stewardship Chain

> *"If the prophet had commanded you to do something difficult, would you not have done it?"*
> (2 Kgs. 5:13)

Our culture stresses self-sufficiency. Thus the axiom: "Never let anyone do anything for you that you can do for yourself." Perhaps there is wisdom in this thinking. Maturity implies that we stand on our own feet and are independent of others. We want to be those who help, not those whom others help.

Unfortunately, if everyone is helping and no one needs help, then people obviously have a problem. As basic as it is, self-reliance isolates us at times. Thus, today's 2 Kings text wisely guides us in admitting that often we are to receive— and not merely give—help. Stewardship is more than simply helping others. Stewardship also recognizes that our "help comes from the LORD" (Ps. 121:2).

Second Kings 5 provides an example of a powerful person who needs help. Naaman, commander-in-chief of the army of Aram, suffers from leprosy. Biblically speaking, "leprosy" designated a number of skin diseases. Clearly, Naaman's condition did not exclude him from society, but it was still a burden. Naaman needed healing and help.

Naaman's story entertains us with a chain of random people involved in his healing. First, a young Israelite slave girl tells Naaman's wife about a prophet in Israel who could cure him. Second, the king of Aram writes a letter of introduction to the king of Israel on the army commander's behalf. Third, Elisha hears of the request. He then sends a message to the king of Israel to send Naaman. After Naaman arrives in Samaria, Elisha's messenger gives him some straightforward instructions: Naaman is to wash in the Jordan seven times for healing. But Naaman becomes angry because he expected the prophet to do what prophets do, namely, perform some sort of complicated ritual. Naaman suggests that the rivers in his homeland are just as good as the rivers in Israel. Naaman, in his rage, begins to leave Samaria without following the directions of Elisha.

Naaman's servants prevail upon him, however, to do as instructed, because, they argue, "if the prophet had commanded you to do something difficult, would you not have done it?" Thus, Naaman washes in the Jordan seven times, just as Elisha instructed—and the healing occurs.

Many characters participate in the healing: a slave girl, Naaman's wife, the kings of Aram and Israel, several messengers, and the prophet. Perhaps the story ingeniously tells us that Naaman might not have been healed without each link. In any event, the story implies that many stewards of God's grace play a part in the healing.

The person who began the whole sequence of events was a young, foreign slave girl. This is the biblical way of story-telling. Often an individual we least expect is the one who holds a key to the resolution. Like Jesus' parable of the Good Samaritan, it is the one who has compassion who allows the grace of God to manifest itself. This underscores the principle that all have a gift to offer. We may not have great gifts, or gifts that dazzle, but we do all have something to give.

Seventh Sunday after the Epiphany
(Sunday between February 18 and 24 inclusive; if it is the Last Sunday after the Epiphany, see Transfiguration)

Mark 2:1–12   Sharing the Ineffable

"When Jesus saw their faith, he said . . . , 'Son, your sins are forgiven.'"
(Mark 2:5)

In today's lesson Mark tells us that Jesus "returned to Capernaum." Earlier Jesus taught in the synagogue, and from Jesus' Capernaum healings "his fame began to spread throughout the surrounding region" (Mark 1:28). From Capernaum, Jesus "went throughout Galilee, proclaiming the message in their synagogues and casting out demons" (1:39). What does our text teach those who aspire to Christian stewardship? One thing Mark tries to impart in this narrative is the close alliance of disease and sin. Perhaps stewards can also sense the relationship between faithfulness and health. Mark seems to address a question that Jesus' disciples asked in another place: "Rabbi, who sinned, this man or his parents, that he was born blind?" (John 9:2). Why would the disciples ask such a question?

We can derive an answer from Deuteronomic theology. This theological framework holds that sin causes human suffering. Thus, if someone suffers, then this suffering derives from sin. The reverse is also part of this structure: if one functions in an ethically acceptable manner, then one will prosper. Israel developed this theological system to explain why God's chosen people suffered the kinds of trials that history thrust upon them. Deuteronomic theology's answer suggested that Israel had not lived righteously before God. Clearly, this is a rather uncomplicated way to explain human suffering, and too often this kind of thinking simply blames the victim.

Our lesson today emphasizes that Jesus has the power not only to heal but also to forgive sin. The people who witness the healing "were all amazed and glorified God." Yet in Mark's text we also find Jesus' first encounter with scribal opposition. Evidently, the scribes' concern was not with the healing: "It is blasphemy! Who can forgive sins but God alone?"

No doubt the scribes have Deuteronomic theology in the back of their minds. But they also primarily oppose Jesus' forgiveness. No one forgives sin except God. Mark reveals in this story that Jesus is who Mark claimed at the start: "The beginning of the good news of Jesus Christ, the Son of God" (Mark 1:1). According to Mark, this is not just any prophet, healer, or teacher—this is God's son!

The early church had little, if any, sense of modern psychology. Today many mental health professionals tie a person's physical health to a person's feeling of self-worth. Yet Mark does fuse, at least in this lesson, issues of sin and health.

It seems from Mark's telling that the paralyzed man is interested in healing while the scribes seem focused on forgiveness of sins. Yet if we look carefully at Jesus, the self-described Son of Man seems most attentive to the paralyzed man's friends. Mark tells us that when Jesus "saw their faith," it was at that instant that Jesus pronounced the healing word: "Son, your sins are forgiven." It was this pardoning word that precipitated the healing. In the forgiveness of sin, the healing takes place.

For stewards this is an important insight. We cannot heal people the way Jesus did, but we can provide the faith of the paralytic's friends to others. The church's task is to offer faith for those who have not found their faith yet. In doing so we become stewards of God's ineffable gift—the faith that heals and makes whole. We may not be able to explain it, but faith is a vital stewardship household we manage.

Eighth Sunday after the Epiphany
(Sunday between February 25 and 29 inclusive;
if it is the Last Sunday after the Epiphany, see Transfiguration)

Mark 2:13–22   The Mark of a Disciple/Steward

"[Jesus] said to him, 'Follow me.' And he got up and followed him."
(Mark 2:14)

One of the Bible's best examples of faithfulness is Abram/Abraham. The Lord speaks to Abram those astounding words that create a new people: "Go from your country and your kindred and your father's house to the land that I will show you" (Gen. 12:1). The narrative tells us that "Abram went, as the LORD had told him" (12:4). No questions about clarification from Abram. No points of negotiation or questions about details. Abram does not even ask about the attire for the journey. Rather, he submits completely and immediately.

Mark shares something of this attitude from Levi son of Alphaeus in the Gospel text for today. But although the responses from Abram and Levi are similar, there is a vast difference in their character—or at least as their friends or neighbors might have recognized them. In the case of Abram, Paul writes, "Abraham believed God, and it was reckoned to him as righteousness" (Rom. 4:3). Perhaps Paul uses the example of Abraham's faith as a model of righteousness. Yet Levi as a tax collector would not have enjoyed the benefit of the doubt as to his righteousness, at least from the point of view of those who suffered under heavy Roman taxation. Thus, Mark tells his readers something rather remarkable about God's kingdom when he shares the story of Levi's call to become a disciple of Jesus.

A tax collector was an agent for the Roman Empire. As such a tax collector, he was an example of first-century "outsourcing." That is, Rome hired persons to collect taxes owed Caesar. These tax collectors bid on a territory and built into the bargain enough overage to make a handy profit. The Romans only wanted what they deemed was theirs, and often corruption and overcharging resulted in the collectors gouging taxpayers. The Romans even charged farmers tolls as they carried their goods to market. Therefore, in the New Testament world, as well as what we read from early Greek and Roman literature, common people loathed tax collectors. But Jesus calls Levi anyway.

What a righteous person like Abram has in common with a vile character like Levi we see in their response to the call to discipleship. Each responds immediately and without question. Abram responds to the Lord's call to "go from your country . . . to the land that I will show you." Levi's response to Jesus' call to "follow me" is no less instantaneous: "And he got up and followed him." But a question remains. Why would Jesus call such a person as Levi to discipleship in the first place?

We do not hold IRS agents with the same contempt as first-century Jews held tax collectors. In part, our attitudes are softer because our government regulates tax collection much more strictly. But to people in Jesus' day, when Jesus called Levi, one message that might have been received was "If this tax collector can serve in God's realm and obtain God's grace, then surely anyone can serve in God's realm and obtain God's grace."

Sometimes we stewards of God's grace can be hoodwinked by our culture and church tradition into thinking that God's grace can be obtained by a few select individuals who have the right stuff. But Mark, via Levi and his story, reminds us that God's grace is a gift that God offers all—qualified or not!

Transfiguration Sunday
(Last Sunday after the Epiphany)

2 Kings 2:1–12   A Double Share of Your Spirit

"Please let me inherit a double share of your spirit."
(2 Kgs. 2:9)

The season of Epiphany ends on Transfiguration Sunday. For this reason, the Revised Common Lectionary texts transition between the manifestation of Christ in Epiphany and the observance of Christ's passion during the season of Lent. Today's Gospel reading is of Jesus' transfiguration as recounted in Mark's terse but potent description. The lesson from 2 Kings conveys Elijah's ascension into heaven. Elijah also places his prophetic mantle upon his successor, Elisha. One reason this text appears in the lectionary is because Elijah plays a major role in Jesus' transfiguration. In addition, the passing on of leadership within the religious community is an issue that always confronts the church. Thus, stewards who manage the household of leadership will pay particular attention to the transition of leadership within the faith community.

Elijah and Elisha travel from Gilgal, and the text reads that "the LORD was about to take Elijah up to heaven by a whirlwind." On three distinct occasions Elijah commands Elisha, "Stay here; for the LORD has sent me as far as Bethel . . . Jericho . . . the Jordan." Yet Elisha continues to stick near Elijah and pleads his case with words that echo Ruth's words to her mother-in-law: "I will not leave you" (see Ruth 1:16). In Elisha's steadfast refusal to obey Elijah's command, Elisha reveals his faithfulness to his prophetic mentor.

Although traditionally the focus of this story has been on the ascension of Elijah, we would do well to observe the request of Elisha to his mentor: "Please let me inherit a double share of your spirit." What do Christian stewards make of such a request?

First, Elisha has learned much from his prophetic mentor. In the beginning, as the astute reader recalls, Elisha was not as ready for prophetic ministry as he appears in this text. Earlier Elisha had told Elijah, "Let me kiss my father and my mother, and then I will follow you" (1 Kgs. 19:20). Yet the younger prophet yields to Elijah. Elisha sacrifices his oxen, his only means for making a living, and follows Elijah.

Second, the old prophet asks Elisha, "Tell me what I may do for you, before I am taken from you." Plainly, Elisha might have asked for many things, for example, authority, the ability to do great miracles, or other things worthy of a great prophet. Yet when Elisha asks for a double portion of the prophet's spirit, he essentially asks for *ruach*, or the mighty wind of God (see Gen. 1:2). By asking for a double portion, Elisha wants to make sure he has enough of what Elijah has to continue his mentor's work. That work is speaking the mighty word of God.

Stewards may well want to consider Elijah's response to the "double portion" request. "If you see me as I am being taken from you," then presumably, God grants Elisha's request. Elisha has stuck by Elijah thus far. Thus, if he remains to the end, then Elisha may receive his request. A vital stewardship principle is that we handle traditions our forbears have conferred to us. Whether we are entrusted with the worship customs of a local congregation or a vision by which God guided our ancestors, stewards become guardians of a hard-earned tradition. Time and progress march on, and we adjust accordingly. Yet stewardship preserves those unswerving values that guide believers through the ages.

Lent

Ash Wednesday (A, B, and C)

Joel 2:1–2, 12–17, and Matthew 6:1–6, 16–21   Blow—Don't
Blow—the Trumpet

"Blow the trumpet in Zion; sound the alarm on my holy mountain."
(Joel 2:1)

In an oddity of the texts for Ash Wednesday, the lessons from both the Hebrew prophets and the Gospel of Matthew cite the blowing of a trumpet. For Joel the trumpet, most likely the ram's horn called a *shofar*, sounds the alert. It is like a tornado warning siren by which authorities warn people in parts of the Midwest of an impending storm. Joel's prophecy declares the warning to signal "the day of the LORD." In the lesson for today, Joel's alarm paints a desolate picture for the people of Israel. The day of the Lord will be "a day of darkness and gloom, a day of clouds and thick darkness!" This day is what we modern people frequently understand as the Day of Judgment. The trumpet resounds loudly so that no one will miss the occasion.

Perhaps this is Jesus' understanding of the act of blowing the trumpet—so that no one will miss the occasion. However, the occasion for Jesus' warning is the practice of piety. Matthew writes, "Whenever you give alms, do not sound a trumpet before you, as the hypocrites do in the synagogues and in the streets, so that they may be praised by others." In so doing, Jesus suggests, these persons offering alms to the poor "have received their reward." The circumstances from Joel and Matthew are distinct. Because this is so, biblical interpreters have the opportunity to investigate the context in which people might employ the blowing of a trumpet. But what does this teach us about the subject of stewardship?

As part of Jesus' Sermon on the Mount, Jesus instructs his listeners about the nature and responsibilities of those who dwell in God's realm. In Joel's prophecy the trumpet sounds to warn of danger, and for Christian stewards Jesus' teaching against blowing the trumpet does so as well. Jesus' point is that giving alms, or acting the part of a charitable person in any regard, is a reward unto itself. If stewards offer alms out of altruistic motives, then we act not in order to curry favor or gain stature with regard to public opinion.

Around Christmas each year many local newspapers publish a list of names of persons who have contributed to some community fund or another. Universities and organizations also make public donor names, often in "size of gift" gradations. Perhaps this motivates people to give, and give liberally. Unquestionably, many people give because it is simply the right thing to do. Yet there is something slightly disturbing in motivating people in this fashion. Publishing donors' names, along with the amount of the gift, seems a little like blowing the trumpet.

Offering our time, treasure, and talents to the deprived is its own reward, as surely Jesus meant when he said, "Your Father who sees in secret will reward you."

Joel in a sense closes this circle of blowing the trumpet or not blowing the trumpet when he prophesies: "Blow the trumpet in Zion; sanctify a fast; call a solemn assembly; gather the people. . . . Spare your people, O LORD, and do not make your heritage a mockery, a byword among the nations." When we Christian stewards give of our resources in faith, we need not blow any horns. Our blowing the trumpet is unnecessary. God blows a trumpet in heaven on our behalf. God's music is our reward for faithful service to those who need God's help.

First Sunday in Lent

Psalm 25:1–10   Teach Me, Lord

"Make me to know your ways, O LORD; teach me your paths."
(Ps. 25:4)

Although it is true that most churches address stewardship issues primarily in conjunction with developing the budget for the subsequent year, primarily near the end of Pentecost, a theological focus on stewardship is clearly appropriate during the season of Lent. Lent in its origin was a period of time in which the church prepared new believers for the experience of baptism. Later Lent developed into the forty days prior to Easter, a time of intense spiritual preparation. The Lenten time of preparation includes fasting, prayer, and study. No doubt the early church modeled the forty-day period on Jesus' time in the wilderness (Matt. 4:1–11; Mark 1:12–13; and Luke 4:1–13).

In the book of Ezra is a solid description of God: "The hand of our God is gracious to all who seek him" (Ezra 8:22). Our parents taught us as children a table blessing that describes God as "great and good." In many and various ways, human beings grope about to describe the attributes of God as if to define divinity: merciful, mighty, omnipotent, omniscient, holy, and so forth. Yet to characterize the inexpressible is to flounder in folly.

People can never portray God as God is—indeed, this is what makes God, God. Even so, we do have some of God's qualities to guide us in becoming more of what God requires of us. Thus, Psalm 25 intones, "Make me to know your ways, O LORD; teach me your paths." When God answers our prayer, then God enables us to draw near to God in faithfulness.

During the season of Lent it is appropriate for each believer to examine her or his faithfulness to attributes that define God. We say that God offers providence, which verbalizes simply that God takes care of us. Jesus puts this concept in the form of a question: "Look at the birds of the air; they neither sow nor reap nor gather into barns, and yet your heavenly Father feeds them. Are you not of more value than they?" (Matt. 6:26).

Psalm 25 at its heart addresses the one who prays out of a sense of sinfulness and need for forgiveness. The one who prays asks that God steer his or her life: "Lead me in your truth, and teach me." But the petitioner also suggests even more by way of confession: "For you are the God of my salvation; for you I wait all day long." The promise to wait is in itself revealing. The one who prays offers persistence and endurance as a means to obtain what God alone can deliver. Persistence and endurance also reveal earnestness. Jesus' parable of the Unjust Judge (Luke 18:1–5) praises a woman who received justice only because of her dogged resolve. Likewise, the psalmist promises to wait "as long as it takes."

For stewards, Psalm 25 offers several divine attributes that conceivably those who give and serve faithfully might mimic. Among those divine traits offered by the psalm, we read about God's mercy, truthfulness, steadfast love, and faithfulness. When the psalmist prays to God, "Teach me your paths," he asks for a portion of the essence of what makes God what God is for us. Later in the incarnation, Jesus becomes the character of the Godhead—divine traits assuming human flesh. Christ, consequently, answers Psalm 25's prayer. To learn of God means that stewards assume God's traits with the faithful intention to share these Godlike traits with the world.

Second Sunday in Lent

Mark 8:31–38   A Decision for Discipleship

"What will it profit them to gain the whole world and forfeit their life?"
(Mark 8:36)

During Lent the church examines itself, measuring faithfulness against the life and teachings of Jesus. It is often easy enough for aspiring disciples to confess Jesus as Lord and Savior, yet the proof of discipleship is in the follow-up to the confession. For stewards, what we do with what we have after we make our confession of faith is a litmus test of our stewardship—or how we manage the households God calls us to manage.

In the preceding text from Mark's Gospel Jesus asks two questions. The first is generic enough: "Who do people say that I am?" (Mark 8:27). After the disciples send up some "trial balloon" answers, Jesus then asks pointedly, "But who do you say that I am?" To his credit, Peter answers presumably for all when he says, "You are the Messiah" (Mark 8:29). Jesus forbids the disciples, at this juncture, from sharing this revelation. This prohibition is part and parcel of what scholars term the "Messianic secret."

In a sense, Mark suggests at this point that the disciples seem to be on board with who Jesus is, but now Jesus takes a further step and teaches them. When he teaches them about what awaits "the Son of Man," the thought is so horrific to Peter that he boldly rebukes Jesus. Peter's rebuke, in turn, prompts one of the severest moments of censure in all the Gospels as Jesus tells the impetuous Peter, "Get behind me, Satan!" This scene affords the Second Evangelist the opportunity to let Jesus further instruct his disciples.

Gathering a crowd, Jesus begins to define what those who truly follow him will face. Despite the fact that the crowd has not been privy to Jesus' private teaching to the disciples, Mark nonetheless gives Jesus his teaching moment. Mark's Gospel emphasis as a whole is on the cross, and this passage is no exception.

It is obvious on its face that stewards must first make a confession about who Jesus is. Yet stewardship does more than merely manage a confession. Stewardship assumes the responsibility of living the faith by managing the households of gifts and graces God has loaned us. Thus, what we do with what we have is a "second step" toward full discipleship. In Mark's text, Jesus offers the Twelve a glimpse of what is in store for them if they authentically want to take up their crosses and follow him. It takes great human courage of conviction to go where Jesus leads, as Peter's rebuke of Jesus illustrates with clarity.

I once met a person who followed Jesus as far as she could and without complaint. Mabel immersed her life in being a steward of God's gifts. She may have been the world record holder for visiting people in hospitals or nursing homes. She was the kind of church member that pastors dream about, and she never failed to attend worship and Sunday school. I would regularly encounter her in the nursing homes or hospitals visiting the sick and lonely—those persons who often had few other visitors.

The week before Mabel herself moved into a nursing home at age 92, she visited the residents. On Friday she was a visitor, and by the next Wednesday she was a resident. Initially she was hard to find in her new room, because she was so busy visiting other, not-so-mobile residents. She managed the gift of Christian hospitality, and because of that gift many lonely people received the presence of Christ through her. In Mabel's quiet way, she took up her cross as a steward.

Third Sunday in Lent

Exodus 20:1–17   Our "Merry-Go-Round" of Possessions

"You shall not covet."
(Exod. 20:17)

Now and then we hear a quotation that rings so true that we wonder why we didn't coin it ourselves. One of these, an anonymous one, concerns our modern way of life: "We Americans are people who spend money we don't have to buy things we don't need to impress people we don't like." Welcome to the twenty-first-century culture of materialistic consumerism! We have built our whole Western economy upon this and similar principles, and it is out of this culture of conspicuous consumption that Christian stewards must function. We must swim against the stream of every cultural impulse in our society if we are to function as Christian stewards today.

Why do we buy into this philosophy? Does our culture of conspicuous consumption truly offer us meaning? How do we remove ourselves from such deceptive perspectives on life and its ultimate values? From beginning to end the Bible provides believers clear direction as to what is of crucial value and what is of merely qualified value. Today's lesson from the Hebrew Bible offers such guidance.

The Ten Commandments provide a clear and understandable way to define relationships between people and between people and God. Moreover, the first verse places the commandments within the narrative story of Israel and its liberation from oppression. The context speaks of liberation from Egypt, but it gestures toward liberation from other things as well—including our culture of conspicuous consumption.

The first three commandments speak to faithful people's relationship to God. Moses communicates to the Israelites that they are to shun idols, not misuse the Lord's divine name, and make holy the Sabbath. These directives relate to the connection between the people and their God. Yet the balance of the commandments pertains to the sacred association among those in the covenant faith community.

After Moses discloses regulations for relations between parents and children, he then addresses murder, adultery, theft, and false witness. Moses then speaks of coveting. In this concluding commandment, Moses addresses us modern stewards. Walter Harrelson suggests that one impetus behind the tenth commandment was Israel's "desire to be like the peoples of the surrounding cultures [which] was an understandable temptation."* Moses commands Israel not to covet because God alone provides Israel its identity.

To covet simply means to lust after that which belongs to another. Moses is explicit about possessions that tempt: "your neighbor's house . . . ; your neighbor's wife, or male or female slave, or ox, or donkey, or anything that belongs to your neighbor." If God reveals a higher purpose in life than our having more and getting more, then Christian stewards apprehend a revelation of authentic life. Clearly this is no easy task. Yet recognizing that we are not the first believers who have had to fight this good fight will, perhaps, fortify our resolve. A step toward bona fide Christian stewardship concedes that our battle to obtain more and more material possessions is little worth the struggle.

Fourth Sunday in Lent

Psalm 107:1–3, 17–22   Thanksgiving Is the Steward's Response

"Let them offer thanksgiving sacrifices, and tell of his deeds."
(Ps. 107:22)

For this Sunday, the Psalm text best lends itself to the topic of stewardship. The day's other passages evoke God's power. Numbers 21:4–9 recounts yet another instance of Moses' conflict with the Israelites in the wilderness. As the intolerant people mutter against Moses and God, God sends poisonous serpents that strike many of the Israelites, who die accordingly. Quickly the others repent and beg Moses to intercede with God to remove the snakes. Rather than remove the serpents, God instructs Moses to set a poisonous serpent on a pole. "Everyone who is bitten shall look at it and live" (Num. 21:8).

John's text hints at this account from Numbers. Jesus says, "Just as Moses lifted up the serpent in the wilderness, so must the Son of Man be lifted up" (John 3:14). The Ephesian epistle too affirms life: "You were dead through the trespasses and sins. . . . But God, who is rich in mercy . . . raised us up with him and seated us with him in the heavenly places in Christ Jesus" (Eph. 2:1, 4, 6).

Psalm 107 also speaks to the issue of sickness unto death. We see the most explicit sign in the phrase "they drew near to the gates of death." The first three verses serve as a preface to the entire psalm. In essence the psalm calls on people to offer thanksgiving to God for God's redemption of the people in their time of trouble. Several sections of the entire psalm address specific persons in trouble:

*Walter J. Harrelson, *The Ten Commandments and Human Rights,* rev. ed. (Macon, GA: Mercer University Press, 1997), 125.

those wandering in desert wastes, those relegated to prison, and those lost at sea. Verses 17–22 address those who find themselves ill or diseased. Psalm 107's theme is that no matter in what condition the people of Israel find themselves, it is always the Lord who redeems them from trouble.

Generally, the whole of Psalm 107 recounts the diverse conditions from which the Lord saves the people. In verse 21, the psalmist offers believers an apt response. After the sinful ways, after the affliction, after drawing near the gates of death, after trouble and distress, and after near destruction, the redeemed people have one proper response: "Let them thank the LORD for his steadfast love, for his wonderful works to humankind." In this admonition inheres the steward's wisdom—"Let them offer thanksgiving sacrifices, and tell of his deeds with songs of joy."

Obviously God needs nothing from humankind. God plainly reveals this in an odd and bare divine confession from Psalm 50:12: "If I were hungry, I would not tell you, for the world and all that is in it is mine." Yet what God desires from believers is a sense of grateful thanksgiving. We offer thanks and celebrate with songs and praise.

Doug Lawson writes of the therapeutic value and disease-inhibiting phenomenon of philanthropy. Lawson insists that generous people are healthier people. "Scientists are trying to determine which thought processes and actions have a direct impact on the body. Not surprisingly, some consider concern for others the most important positive factor."*

Psalm 107 suggested long ago much of what recent experiential science has tried to prove. People who are generous are happier, healthier, and better adjusted to life than people who are not. When we consider that God loans us all our resources, then stewards appreciate that faithful household management of God's gifts leads to abundant life. God indeed blesses us for generosity, and it is our way of expressing our thanks.

Fifth Sunday in Lent

John 12:20–33   Lifting a Steward's Material Burden

"Unless a grain of wheat falls into the earth and dies . . ."
(John 12:24)

The church celebrates Lent as a time of repentance. In Lent we assess our behaviors that stand in need of forgiveness. When Jesus says in today's Gospel text that "those who love their life lose it," Jesus speaks to human life. Stewards recognize that we, perhaps out of survival and self-preservation, cling to possessions. The gospel addresses this impulse in many ways. When Luke displays the church at its spotless best, he writes, "All who believed were together and

---

*Doug Lawson, *Give to Live* (La Jolla, CA: ALTI Publishing, 1991), 21.

had all things in common" (Acts 2:44). This is Luke's rendering of a new creation—the church.

We see the perfection of the church in its ability to share with one another. It is to this noble path that God calls his church. Yet as the Ananias and Sapphira story shows, harmony can be a fragile thing (Acts 5:1–11). We who say we want to live in peace often shatter harmonious community over questions about possessions.

In John's Gospel, Jesus teaches about the meaning of his death when some Greeks say to Philip, "Sir, we wish to see Jesus." This request signals a time of fulfillment. It is when Jesus' hour has finally arrived (see also John 2:4; 4:21; 7:6, 8, 30; 8:20). Jesus then teaches about the law of nature concerning death and his destiny. In John's Gospel there is little agony reflected as far as Jesus' vocation—Jesus willingly gives his life for the eternal life of those who believe. As John tells the story, Jesus' sacrifice is part of God's plan for humankind's redemption.

Lent is the season of Christian self-denial. For this reason, this text beckons believers to follow Jesus' lead. While Jesus teaches Philip and Andrew who have come to him, he presumably tells all the disciples—and us: "Unless a grain of wheat falls into the earth and dies, it remains just a single grain; but if it dies, it bears much fruit." Thus, as Jesus dies a natural death, his death also plants a seed—just as in agriculture a seed will eventually produce new growth. Perhaps this is Jesus' manner of teaching the deeper meaning of his death to the disciples, who, no doubt, have little idea about what good can come from Jesus' prophecy about his own death.

When stewards practice selfless giving on behalf of others, then they defy their own instinct for self-preservation. Our culture today lives under the myth of scarceness: it is only by hoarding and keeping possessions that we can assure ourselves of continuous survival. Yet Jesus teaches that within life in God there are ways of living that transcend simple survival. Jesus even reminds stewards, "Whoever serves me must follow me, and where I am, there will my servant be also. Whoever serves me, the Father will honor."

During Lent we believers repent of our sin. A sin for which we all need to repent is the sin of coveting what others have. By sharing our time and treasure, we reveal our heart and we follow the path of discipleship.

A Dayak proverb puts the human quandary this way: "Where the heart is willing it will find a thousand ways, but where it is unwilling it will find a thousand excuses." John's Jesus teaches that the manner of his death leads to life. Perhaps in Jesus' encouragement, we too can learn that the death of our materialistic desires leads to life. As Proverbs promises, "Honor the LORD with your substance and with the first fruits of all your produce; then your barns will be filled with plenty, and your vats will be bursting with wine" (Prov. 3:9–10).

Passion/Palm Sunday
(Sixth Sunday in Lent)

Mark 11:1–11 (Liturgy of the Psalms)   Invest in Obedience to Christ

"The Lord needs it and will send it back here immediately."
(Mark 11:3)

Preachers need to decide on which day's text to focus. Do we choose the Liturgy of the Palms or the Liturgy of the Passion? This decision determines the homily's emphasis. Here Mark's Palm Sunday text will guide us. This lesson also offers a window into stewardship. The window reveals what Jesus needs from his disciples and then what he needs from us today.

I suppose it is an odd question to contemplate: What does Jesus need? Mark narrates this spare story of Jesus' triumphal entry into Jerusalem. Jesus asks two of his disciples to go and find a colt for him. Not only this, but he gives explicit directions about how they are to get the colt. Mark tells the story in a noticeably restrained fashion. We anticipate vast throngs of people lining the streets. Yet besides the "many" who spread coats on the road, Mark's only other mention of a crowd comes when he writes that "those who went ahead and those who followed were shouting." Perhaps the throngs we anticipate never materialized.

Mark draws on an Old Testament prophecy that suggests the reason for Jesus' appeal for a colt: "Lo, your king comes to you; triumphant and victorious is he, humble and riding on a donkey, on a colt, the foal of a donkey" (Zech. 9:9). Thus, from Mark's telling, Jesus' request for a colt connects this scene to Israel's messianic expectations. The disciples ask no further details. They simply respond.

We could speculate about the assorted ways that Jesus might have obtained this colt. Yet Jesus simply asks his disciples to go and get it. The "how" of the attainment is perhaps not as important as the "why." Jesus tells his disciples to undertake the task because, possibly, Jesus knows that someday the disciples' act, offered at this critical moment in Jesus' life, will figure in to their faith story. We human beings create ownership in the things in which we play a part.

In other words, the factors and events that summon our resources also invest us in these same experiences. Perhaps this is why Jesus called upon these disciples for this routine task of rounding up a colt. After all, in another Gospel Jesus announces that he can "appeal to my Father, and he will at once send me more than twelve legions of angels" (Matt. 26:53–54). Jesus does not ask the disciples to do something for him that he cannot do for himself. Rather, Jesus asks the disciples to do something that guides them into the Jesus story. This story will abide with them their whole life long.

Pastors often hear people say they have nothing to offer God. Any discerning steward knows this is untrue. The definition of "steward" comes from a Greek word that means "to manage the whole household." Some common church households include teaching, ushering, listening, visiting, praying, giving, cleaning, and cooking. We manage such households—and many more. Pastors will well note that none of these services is any more complicated than obtaining a colt. Sometimes our flimsy excuses for why we don't offer anything to God sound silly if we only stop to actually listen to them. Some folks repeat their excuses so long that they truly believe them. Yet Jesus teaches all believers that we can authentically serve God using both our treasures and our lives.

Holy Thursday
[See Year C]

Good Friday
[See Year A]

Easter

Easter Day

Acts 10:34–43   Stewards as Shareholders Invest Wisely

"He commanded us to . . . testify that he is the one ordained by God."
(Acts 10:42)

No day is more glorious than Easter Day for the Christian church. For preachers, no day is more difficult to preach. The reason Easter Day is awkward to preach is that on this day we surprise no one about the resurrection. Anyone who attends church faithfully—as well as those who make their semiannual pilgrimage—will be little astonished by the exalting voices proclaiming, "He is risen!" As they say, for most people, "This good news is by now old news."

Miss Manners might urge us to conjure every gracious impulse we have not to mention that we will not see nearly half of those in attendance again until Christmas Eve. Yet hope lingers. In people's response to Easter we hope that the day means at least something to those habitually absent. Maybe we can rejoice that they attend at all. In the light of such a situation, perhaps Easter is a good day to address stewardship as discipleship. After all, Easter is the most gathered that the community will ever be.

The lesson from Acts replaces the common reading from the Hebrew Scriptures—a church/lectionary practice that continues through the day of Pentecost. The lesson outlines Peter's sermon in Cornelius's house. The Spirit brings together Cornelius and Peter via visionary experiences. The import of Acts 10 is hard to overestimate. By the story Luke relates, the church puts forward a theological justification for evangelizing Gentiles, who heretofore had been practically shunned from church membership. Acts 10 achieves what Ephesians observes: Jesus "is our peace . . . and has broken down the dividing wall, that is, the hostility between us" (Eph. 2:14). When the Jew Peter enters the house of the Gentile Cornelius, everything changes. Easter Day proclaims that God's resurrection of Jesus fundamentally changes the entire world.

Presumably, we read the Acts text on Easter Day for its explicit reference to the resurrection. Luke writes that while preaching, Peter announced that "God raised him [Jesus] on the third day." As with Paul's speech in Athens, this claim is the zenith of this sermon. Paul, after taking some time to arrive at the Areopagus sermon's "punch line," tells the only wholly pagan audience of any New Testament sermon that God "has given assurance to all by raising him [Jesus] from the dead" (Acts 17:31).

After declaring Jesus of Nazareth's resurrection, Peter speaks of the witnesses for whom God "allowed him to appear." Peter is clear. Jesus did not appear to all persons, but only to "us who were chosen by God as witnesses." These select believers "ate and drank with him after he rose from the dead." The detail about eating and drinking may have been the church's doctrinal attempt to quell opponents' claims that Jesus only appeared to have risen.

To use an investment analogy, the good news that God raised Christ is encouraging news for shareholders. They have not invested unwisely. All people need assurance that what we give our money to or our life for is worth the risk. For Christian stewards God's resurrection of Jesus comforts believers that what they stake their life on by faith is authentic and lasting. When God raised Jesus, God revealed the One who has authority over life and death. For believers, this truth is potent enough to give Christian stewardship ultimate confidence, and so we invest our lives in Christ.

Second Sunday of Easter

Acts 4:32–35   Overcoming Nature and Nurture

"Everything they owned was held in common."
(Acts 4:32)

For centuries, eminent thinkers such as Rousseau, Descartes, Hobbes, and Locke, as well as armchair philosophers, have debated the "nurture versus nature" theories of human psychological development. Luke appears to counter these arguments in a description of the early church and its relationship to material possessions.

One side of the argument negatively pulls against a full-orbed Christian stewardship. This part of the debate concerns the context in which we live. People in our culture think almost exclusively in terms of private ownership of possessions. We assume this is natural. "Some things are mine," we think, "while other things are someone else's." We think this perception appears inherent in nature, that it is the way of the world.

The other side of the nature versus nurture argument recognizes that we teach our children, after our parents have taught us, that each of us earns, and thereby lays claim to, our property. Our society trains us that people own things in life, whether land, money, or other kinds of possessions. This is in part how humans organize civilization. We nurture one another in this manner. Socialization tutors us in the institution of private ownership.

Yet when Acts says of the early church that "no one claimed private ownership of any possessions," our eyebrows arch slightly. We think to ourselves, "Really? What would cause a community to act contrary to nature or nurture?"

Luke has a penchant for writing here and there summaries of the early church. From time to time, he will pause to let the readers catch their breath, and will then offer a glimpse at the whole church. In this specific summary of the church, it is important to note the lesson's context. It comes on the heels of Peter and John's appearance before the "rulers, elders, and scribes assembled in Jerusalem" (Acts 4:5), where these apostles display boldness.

The next part of Acts 4 speaks of how, after giving an account to the church of the religious authorities' examination, Peter and John join their friends in raising "their voices together to God" (4:24). A few verses later Luke writes, "When they had prayed, the place in which they were gathered together was shaken; and they were all filled with the Holy Spirit and spoke the word of God with boldness" (4:31). Now Luke returns to the narrative to relate the church's first major conflict—the sordid business of Ananias and Sapphira (Acts 5:1–11).

Perhaps one reason that this text from Acts was selected for Easter is its reference to the apostles' testimony regarding Jesus' resurrection. This resurrection faith gave impetus to some startling behavior. In addition to the early Christians' witnessing with great power, Luke tells us that "no one claimed private ownership of any possessions." Not only did the resurrection give great courage to these uneducated and ordinary men (Acts 4:13), it also unleashed the Spirit of God upon these common folk. The Spirit evidently inspired them to share everything they had, for "everything they owned was held in common."

When the spirit of the risen Christ comes upon either the faith community or people within it, believers possess courage to overcome both nature and nurture. Rather than clinging to self-preservation, we now offer our possessions for the common good.

Third Sunday of Easter

1 John 3:1–7   The Righteousness of a Steward

"Everyone who does what is right is righteous, just as he [God] is righteous."
(1 John 3:7)

Easter is not simply a day but a liturgical season. In Christian worship during the season of Easter, the church celebrates not only Christ's resurrection but the church's response to it. On this Sunday the reading from Acts offers one of Peter's several sermons. The Psalter lesson presents a plea to God from the faithful for deliverance from enemies. Luke's Gospel lesson recounts one of Jesus' several resurrection appearances to the disciples. We examine the day's Epistle lesson for stewardship guidance.

In this part of 1 John, the epistle addresses both Jesus' righteousness and the righteousness of believers. The lesson begins by continuing a conversation about what leads believers. The author addresses his audience, saying that he writes "these things to you concerning those who would deceive you" (1 John 2:26). Our lesson concerns God's leading of those who are called "children of God."

To be a child of God signifies those persons led by divine love. This distinction of God's love separates believers from other, "worldly" people. The point of distinction is that those who are God's children know God through Jesus. The world does not know God because it does not know Jesus. We see this clearly in the assertion that "the reason the world does not know us is that it did not know him." Therefore, the world can little recognize those who know Jesus as the manifestation of God. To the point, 1 John does not want its readers to be deceived.

This small text makes two giant claims. The first claim is that Jesus' followers should be like Jesus. In many funeral liturgies we read this verse: "When he is revealed, we will be like him, for we will see him as he is." That is, when God finally and ultimately discloses the full revelation of Jesus Christ, then we will see Jesus with clarity. Until then, we can only catch a glimpse of Jesus here and there. The second claim has to do with Christian perfection: "No one who abides in him sins; no one who sins has either seen him or known him."

The righteousness that God calls forth from us the world can witness best through our acts of stewardship. Perhaps a righteous act involves volunteer time or an extended period of listening to the heartache of another person. Maybe it involves generously giving to the ministries of the church. Whatever God calls us to do, when we act out of righteousness, then it will be an act that is the opposite of sin. It will be an act of self-giving, not an act of sinful separation.

If you want to make an impression on your neighbor, then give generously to others. Generosity without apparent motive or reason is akin to Mark Twain's quip about always doing right: "Always do right—this will gratify some and astonish the rest." So it is with being righteous stewards. If our actions cause others to examine their own actions in a positive way, then we help advance, in our small way, God's realm. Those who demonstrate an abiding relationship with God in Jesus reveal themselves in the small and loving acts shown to others.

Fourth Sunday of Easter

Acts 4:5–12   No Good Deed Goes Unpunished

"If we are questioned today because of a good deed . . ."
(Acts 4:9)

"Peter and John Jailed!" the headline reads. One can only imagine what church members today would think! Yet all through Acts the apostles do jail time. Alas, we cannot read in worship the entire story of Acts 3–4, but the lectionary reading does tell part of the story. Acts 3 begins when Peter and John heal a man in front of the temple. Peter then clarifies the healing with a sermon from Solomon's Portico (Acts 3:11–26). For his trouble, the religious authorities have Peter and John arrested. Yet Luke is careful to assess Peter's sermon by noting, "Many of those who heard the word believed; and they numbered about five thousand" (Acts 4:4). Luke wants us to know that this was some sermon.

What was the apostles' crime? Why were Peter and John put in jail? The best answer we can guess from the story's context is simply "good preaching." Perhaps the healing was also part of the cause. For stewards it is a lesson that goodwill and an effective witness will not always produce applause from "the powerful."

In a certain town where I once lived, there was only one place to get an alcoholic beverage—the VFW hall. One afternoon the bartender's wife called and asked me to go to the VFW. She wanted me to tell her husband that his mother had died at a local nursing home. "I just can't bear to go and tell him myself," she explained.

So I went dutifully to the only bar in town. Inside I found the bartender and told him the news. There were about twenty people inside, and when I walked through the door, everything stopped. What in the world was a local preacher doing in a bar? Because I had a relationship with this bartender, I was the sensible choice to break the news to him. Yet the episode caused a stir in my church. Many demanded to know why I was there, that is, until the bartender's wife came to my rescue. She explained the whole story. At times, stewards do good deeds, and others may punish them for it.

What Peter and John did was disturb the status quo. They healed a man and then spelled out their act as an act of faith in Jesus Christ. To change the world and its view of how things ought to function often threatens those who oversee the world. If faithful to its call, the church tends to threaten those who want to see life continue on an even keel and without incident. However, the church's mandate is to fulfill what Jesus suggests in the parable of the Last Judgment. In this parable, Jesus blesses those who take care of those who have no other source of help. He explains, "I was hungry and you gave me food, I was thirsty and you gave me something to drink, I was a stranger and you welcomed me, I was naked and you gave me clothing, I was sick and you took care of me, I was in prison and you visited me" (Matt. 25:35–36).

Christians pay lip service to feeding the hungry and caring for the homeless. Yet when a church begins to accumulate hungry and homeless people, then some of the members will raise issues. Our congregation housed sixty hurricane evacuees for over a month. Many people lauded the action. But a steady stream of those who had "concerns" about the safety of our members and our children arrived at my office. They had "issues" with all these strangers in our building. They worried about our safety and our "church schedule." They were concerned about the inconvenience of the enterprise. They had a thousand reasons. I empathized, but I said, "We are a church. These people are in great need. After all, what we are doing is what churches do." Stewards do what God calls us to do.

Fifth Sunday of Easter

John 15:1–8   The Vine and the Branches

"Apart from me you can do nothing."
(John 15:5)

Christian stewards in today's world have no easy task. It is akin to swimming upstream. An old axiom puts our stewardship mission in perspective: "Only dead fish swim with the current." We live in a materialistic world. Of this there is little doubt. Yet as Luke quotes Paul, who quotes Jesus, "It is more blessed to give than to receive" (Acts 20:35). But as we face our culture as Christians, how do we give without ceasing?

Today's Gospel text supplies much to ponder and to embrace. Jesus offers in this lesson the final of John's Gospel's seven "I am" sayings. The other six consist of "I am the bread of life" (6:35), "I am the light of the world" (8:12; 9:5), "I am the gate" (10:7, 9), "I am the good shepherd" (10:11, 14), "I am the resurrection and the life" (11:25), and "I am the way, and the truth, and the life" (14:6). With each image John reveals at richer theological planes who Jesus is. If believers understand who Jesus is, then in God's realm we possess a healthier grasp of who we are.

John recognizes that human beings can do nothing on their own. Unfortunately, in the world—and generally John uses the phrase "the world" in a negative sense—we think that we must "go it on our own." This chimera of self-sufficiency John sees as sin. Being cut off from God's Spirit and grace-giving power not only alienates humanity from God but also estranges us from other people.

When Jesus says, "I am the vine," he implies that our being fed by the only source of life-giving grace can help us overcome "the world." The world is hostile to the holy world that God offers in Christ. Consequently, for believers to tap into the divine resource offered by "the vine" simply means that human beings tap into the sole power that truly gives life and gives it abundantly.

John's Gospel repeatedly poses its theology to the church in either/or decisions. That is, one is either a child of the light or not; or one is either for Jesus or against Jesus. One example of John's strategic method occurs when Jesus heals a man blind from birth and John tells us that the religious authorities "were divided" (John 9:16). Or, again, when Jesus says, "I am the good Shepherd," John relates, "Again the Jews [read: "the religious authorities"] were divided because of these words" (10:19). John regularly puts his theology of Jesus in terms that require people to decide for or against Jesus.

The point of Christian stewardship is not to repay God what we owe God. The point of Christian stewardship is to share what God has given us with those with whom God wants us to share. When we share God's bounty, we live up to the promise of Scripture. A grand promise from the Johannine school suggests that "we love because he first loved us" (1 John 4:19). It is the grafting into this love that allows us to give.

We Christians dupe ourselves when we think that we self-generate any of our "good deeds." Indeed, one of the finest marks of genuine Christian stewardship is an acknowledgment that we do not operate out of our own power or goodness. Rather, we tap into the source of all goodness and authentic benevolence when we allow God to graft us into the vine that is Jesus. This is a worthy decision from John's perspective. John also reveals the negative side: "Whoever does not abide in me is thrown away like a branch and withers; such branches are gathered, thrown into the fire, and burned." John leaves the decision to believers. And John trusts that stewards know the life-giving choice.

Sixth Sunday of Easter

Acts 10:44–48   Converting Stewards

"The gift of the Holy Spirit had been poured out even on the Gentiles."
(Acts 10:45).

Jesus had a way of getting right to the heart of matters. When preaching to a great crowd, Jesus once said, "How can you say to your neighbor, 'Friend, let me take out the speck in your eye,' when you yourself do not see the log in your own eye?" (Luke 6:41–42). Part of authentic stewardship is recognizing, then claiming, our own limitations. Most believers understand that finding fault with a neighbor's shortcomings is child's play compared with taking a long hard look at our own inadequacies. Today's lesson helps stewards see that God's grace and mercy extends even to those outside our own zones of comfort. Jew or Gentile—God makes no distinction. We are all God's people.

Today's lesson from Acts connects the so-called conversion of Cornelius to the aftershock in the Jewish-Christian faith community. Perhaps Acts 10 is not so much about Cornelius's conversion as it is about Peter's conversion. It describes the work of the Holy Spirit in getting Peter and Cornelius together. Today's reading completes this part of the story. The "Holy Spirit miracle" is that God brings together two people, representing two cultures, who lived worlds apart. For stewards who manage God's resources, parallel scenarios often function in our faith lives. God calls on us to act on behalf of others—of those we often might not choose to help.

When Luke explains that Cornelius invites Peter to "stay for several days," he means that Peter ate with Gentiles. This table fellowship began Peter's difficulties. The Jewish Christians question Peter's violation of the strict Jewish ritual law prohibiting eating with Gentiles.

Ironically, the quarrel is not over baptism, as we might expect today. Rather, Peter's social relationship with Gentiles is at the heart of the Judaizers' clash with Peter. Peter tells those in Jerusalem that God spoke to him and said, "What God has made clean, you must not call profane" (Acts 11:9). Gerhard Krodel writes of this: "Luke interpreted Peter's vision to mean we 'should not call any *person* common or unclean.' God himself had declared pagans clean and had broken down the barrier between them. No one has the right to preach the gospel to anyone with whom he or she is not willing to associate."*

This is a lesson many believers need to learn over and over. Concerning the lesson of Peter and Cornelius, might we ask, "Do we interpret the Bible, or does the Bible interpret us?" In this lesson Peter has an epiphany. And so might we, for most of us consider that some people in our lives seem beyond the reach of God's good grace. Peter's vision and his encounter with Cornelius unlocked a new possibility.

Our prejudices may include persons of contrary political views. Maybe we shun those whose values clash dramatically with ours. For some Americans, provincial differences or accents elicit negative stereotypes. God converts Peter to a vision in Acts 10 that reveals that God's realm is large enough to include all people. When God calls us to discipleship, God calls us to become stewards. We do not choose those who need our help. Rather, God offers us opportunities in the people that God brings us. As those opportunities to serve God arrive, stewardship connects those in need with those who gratefully offer our divinely given resources.

*Gerhard Krodel, *Acts,* Proclamation Commentaries (Philadelphia: Fortress Press, 1981), 44–45.

Ascension of the Lord (A, B, and C)

Acts 1:1–11   Whiling Away the Time

"Lord, is this the time when you will restore the kingdom to Israel?"
(Acts 1:6)

The concept of time has always fascinated the human mind. Yet the notion of time also overshadows human life, as suggested by the phrase "the tyranny of time." Time regularly oppresses us. It prompts meditation on mortality. As Psalm 90:10 puts it, "The days of our life are seventy years, or perhaps eighty, if we are strong; even then their span is only toil and trouble; they are soon gone, and we fly away." Consequently, along with our aging bodies, time becomes a perpetual signal that "our days are numbered," as Lamentations 4:18 intimates.

Perhaps the "days and years" anxiety lurks behind the disciples' question to Jesus: "Lord, is this the time when you will restore the kingdom to Israel?" They had traveled with Jesus for three years. Although from a distance, they saw Jesus' final hours. The hope of Israel and the disciples' anticipation of Jesus' fulfillment as Messiah was no doubt on their minds. No wonder they want to know whether or not their wait is over. So prior to Jesus' ascension, they figure this is a good time to get Jesus' word about whether or not the time of waiting is drawing to a close.

Near the end of some great task, all of a person's work seems worth the effort. People who run marathons say that once the finish line is in sight, they disregard all pain and shortness of breath. Students at semester's end, or builders at the closing stages of a large construction project, regularly put all the pain of their efforts behind them as they press toward their assignment's completion. This question of time is an important one for Christian stewardship: Are we near the end?

Jesus' answer helps those of us who think this way. Jesus answers his disciples' question by reminding them, "It is not for you to know the times or periods that the Father has set by his own authority." Instead, Jesus gives them two words of assurance. First, he tells them that they will receive "Holy Spirit power." Second, he gives them a task: they are to bear witness from Jerusalem "to the ends of the earth." Accordingly, until further notice they will have the power to provide testimony to Jesus' life, death, and resurrection. Until further notice they witness to what they have seen: God's working through Jesus. God offers in Jesus all the grace the human family needs.

Through his use of the word "witness," Jesus suggests testimony in the legal sense of giving evidence to the truth as one might do in a court of law. Today, when a legal representative calls witnesses before the court, they swear to tell the whole truth. This testimony is the disciples' task. They bear witness to the truth.

For stewards this is an important function. Our term of service as Jesus' stewards has no exact timeline, at least from the human side. Rather, God calls us to make our witness day by day until our testimony is no longer required.

We manage the gifts God has loaned us until God informs us that the time of our stewardship is complete.

Near the end of his life, a young man asked St. Francis of Assisi, as Francis was hoeing his garden, what he would do if he found out that he was soon to die. His answer is instructive for all stewards: "I would continue to cultivate my garden." This is a good word for Christian stewards; we continue to do what God has called us to do until God says, "Stop."

Seventh Sunday of Easter

Psalm 1   What Offers Stewards Happiness

"They are like trees planted by streams of water."
(Ps. 1:3)

When I read Psalm 1, it brings to mind my twelfth-grade English teacher. Her favorite student assignment was for us to read a passage from an essay, novel, or poem. Our task was then to "compare and contrast" the elements of the assignment. Today's psalm contrasts the life of those who follow God's law with those who do not. It prompts a question with respect to stewardship: What nourishes the life of disciples as stewards?

Walter Brueggemann provides a helpful taxonomy of the Psalter. He suggests that all psalms fall into three distinct categories: psalms of orientation, psalms of disorientation, and psalms of a new orientation (or reorientation). Using Brueggemann's categories enables those who preach to better interpret the psalms for modern believers.

About Psalm 1, Brueggemann writes: "In terms of our theme of orientation, this psalm, didactic in character, affirms that the well-oriented life fixed on torah expectations is one of happiness and well-being. The violation of that orientation is a sure way to diminishment and disintegration."* It seems as if Brueggemann, too, detects a "comparing and contrasting" theme in Psalm 1.

We sometimes hear people speak about "donor fatigue." This notion suggests that the needs of the world have overwhelmed many otherwise willing donors. Thus, these donors feel drained by endless appeals on behalf of some group or cause. The world tells people that human beings find ultimate happiness in obtaining and protecting the things they accumulate. Yet the Christian faith offers the opposite kind of logic. Jesus tells those who aspire to live under divine authority to "give to everyone who begs from you, and do not refuse anyone who wants to borrow from you" (Matt. 5:42). This kind of thinking the world sees as hopelessly naive.

Yet Psalm 1 offers a perspective on human happiness that is in accord with

---

*Walter Brueggemann, *The Message of the Psalms: A Theological Commentary* (Minneapolis: Augsburg Publishing House, 1984), 39.

Jesus' instruction: "Happy are those who do not follow the advice of the wicked. . . . Their delight is in the law of the LORD." Happy people follow the dictates of God's holy laws. We might cite numerous examples, but one will suffice. When Leviticus lays down the law of the harvest, for example, it says to Israel, "You shall not reap to the very edges of your field, or gather the gleanings of your harvest; you shall leave them for the poor and for the alien: I am the LORD your God" (Lev. 23:22). God builds provisions for the poor and hungry into the fabric of Hebrew social relations. An adequately fed society tends to be a happy society.

On this last Sunday of Eastertide we observe a power enabling believers to delight in God's law. Certainly the world's needs wear us down. Plainly the best stewards cannot provide for all needs that arise. Yet by God's power that resurrected Jesus from the dead, we too can cling to God and God's abundance. That abundance we can share with those through our management of the grand and ample gifts God offers to us.

Because our resources are in most cases not unlimited, we must discern how to exercise stewardship to maximize their effectiveness. The cure for donor fatigue is to use resources judiciously. By resurrection grace, we can apply God's gift of wisdom—a wisdom that offers authentic happiness and well-being.

Pentecost

Day of Pentecost

Psalm 104:24–34, 35b   Singing Stewards

"I will sing to the LORD as long as I live."
(Ps. 104:33)

Pentecost is the birthday of the church. Because all three cycles of the lectionary suggest Acts 2:1–21 as a reading, I have chosen for Year B the lesson from the Psalter. This is a lesson for the day, no doubt, because it speaks to the wonder of creation, which comes about as a result of God's creative spirit: "When you send forth your spirit, they [created beings] are created." The overall theme of Pentecost captures the wonders of the Holy Spirit, and Psalm 104 clearly addresses this theme.

A group of laypersons from my congregation gathered one Saturday morning to discuss the lectionary texts for the next day. In that discussion they focused on this psalm, which because of its content drew their interest. In the course of the conversation, these folks decided that God was a good steward because of "God's care for God's creation." Some suggested that God was a steward of creation; others said God could not be a steward because as Creator, God was also the "owner" of creation.

One of the bedrock principles of Christian stewardship is that everything belongs to God. A corollary is that one cannot be a steward over that which one owns. Thus, by definition, God is not a steward over God's creation. That stewardship God gives over to those who profess God—that is, we manage that which God creates and owns.

Psalm 104 offers a suggestive, although not exhaustive, list of those things that God created. Not only does the psalm delineate the living things created, but it also addresses the relationship between the creatures and the creation. The creatures look to God for food: "When you give to them, they gather it up; when you open your hand, they are filled with good things." In a vital sense, these creatures manage the gifts that God puts before them.

Psalm 8 helps us see the responsibility that human creatures have to God's creation—a responsibility that no other creature possesses. Rhetorically, the psalm puts the question like this: "What are human beings that you are mindful of them, mortals that you care for them?" The answer comes in that God has created us "a little lower than God" and has "given [us] dominion over the works of your hands" (Ps. 8:4–6). Human beings have much over which to exercise stewardship—the whole of creation!

In the case of stewardship of creation, a question arises. Are we stewards as a world community, or as individuals? On the one hand, we as creatures have our individual responsibilities as stewards, but we also live communally. What happens to one part of creation affects all other parts. As the saying goes, "None of us can say to another that your end of the lifeboat is sinking." We are all in the same boat.

The spirit by which God created the world is the same spirit that God sends at Pentecost to create a new community—the church. As a created people even today God charges us, like the aboriginal man and woman, to "till and keep the garden" (Gen. 2:15). If we can lend a hand in preserving God's creation as God's created community of stewards, then we will also sing with the psalmist, "I will sing to the LORD as long as I live; I will sing praise to my God while I have being."

Trinity Sunday
(First Sunday after Pentecost)

John 3:1–17   A Stewardship of Influence

"How can you believe if I tell you about heavenly things?"
(John 3:12)

Since the Middle Ages the church has celebrated Trinity Sunday the first Sunday after Pentecost. The celebration explores the triune God as revealed in traditional language as Father, Son, and Holy Spirit. The broad doctrine of the Trinity is more implicit in Scripture than it is explicit. Yet Trinitarian theology sets our inexpressible faith in God's three persons into human language—inexact and provisional as it may be.

In the 1970s and 1980s an individual known publicly as "Rainbow Man" held up signs reading simply "John 3:16" during many televised events. In the church's tradition, however, this verse has been a staple of memorization for countless Sunday school pupils. Those inclined to explore the larger text for stewardship purposes might ask, "Why does Nicodemus come to Jesus by night?"

One of stewardship's notable "households" is that of influence. Nicodemus was not just any first-century rank-and-file Jewish person. Rather, he was "a leader of the Jews." Leaders have responsibilities. Leaders have followers. Thus, Nicodemus as a prominent leader cares about how people see his actions. When Nicodemus approaches Jesus, he does so recognizing the controversy that Jesus creates. By associating with Jesus in any way, Nicodemus takes a calculated risk.

Jesus created divisions between people wherever he went and whenever he taught. Both Luke and John play on Jesus' divisiveness with regard to the status quo. For example, John comments, "There was a division in the crowd because of him" (John 7:43; see also 9:16; 10:19). Luke too accentuates the deep divisiveness that Jesus calls forth. Jesus says, "Do you think that I have come to bring peace to the earth? No, I tell you, but rather division!" (Luke 12:51). Nicodemus, as a Jewish leader, must be wary that his meeting with Jesus does not create leadership difficulties. For Nicodemus, dealing with Jesus is tantamount to handling poisonous snakes. Jesus openly teaches that "from now on five in one household will be divided, three against two and two against three; they will be divided: father against son and son against father, mother against daughter and daughter against mother" (Luke 12:52–53). Nicodemus knows that Jesus is a perilous fellow for a Jewish leader to be seen with.

Perhaps unfairly over time, some in the church have branded Nicodemus a coward. However, Nicodemus dutifully understands his stewardship of leadership and influence. There is a vast difference between being reckless and being brave. In the first, we disregard our actions and the effect they may have on others. In the second, we recognize our obligation to those whom we influence. True leadership takes these matters to heart before acting; it counts the cost, as Jesus said (Luke 14:28).

John completes his story about the relationship between Jesus and Nicodemus by recounting that, after Jesus' death, "Nicodemus, who had at first come to Jesus by night, also came [with Joseph of Arimathea], bringing a mixture of myrrh and aloes, weighing about a hundred pounds" (John 19:39). After weighing his allegiance and stewardship, Nicodemus acts by faith. He brings his final offering for Jesus. It may have taken Nicodemus longer than others about whom John writes, but in the end he exercises his stewardship of influence in a most genuine way.

Sunday between May 29 and June 4 inclusive
(if after Trinity Sunday)

Psalm 139:1–6, 13–18   Inside-Out Stewardship

"How weighty to me are your thoughts, O God!"
(Ps. 139:17)

The psalm's exact versification also appears in the lectionary for two other Sundays—the Sunday between September 4 and 10 (C) and the Second Sunday after the Epiphany (B). A slightly different set of verses occurs on the Sunday between July 17 and 23 (A). Perhaps the beauty and truth of this psalm prompted its inclusion in the lectionary in so many places.

In verses 13–18 the psalmist treats the reader to an intimate and engaging picture of the God who created us. He writes that God "knit me together in my mother's womb" and that he has been "fearfully and wonderfully made." The psalm praises God's care in creating this particular human being, perhaps as a shorthand way of suggesting God has done this work with every part of creation. The psalmist tells nothing particularly new or even newsworthy; yet in an elegant way the writer pays homage to the care that God exhibits in forming God's creation.

What strikes the careful reader with respect to stewardship is the psalmist's phrase in verse 17: "How weighty to me are your thoughts, O God! How vast is the sum of them!" An interesting dichotomy presents itself here—and a question: "Do we think the thoughts of God?" Isaiah prophesies, "My thoughts are not your thoughts, nor are your ways my ways, says the LORD" (Isa. 55:8). Yet we faithful human believers want to cling to the promise of creation that "God created humankind in his image, in the image of God he created them; male and female he created them" (Gen. 1:27). Thus, are faithful people of the mind of God, or not?

It is possible that in inviting people into a fulsome life in God, the phrases Isaiah uses highlight God's greatness. God is the unspeakable, and has mercy and desire for God's people. The human mind cannot grasp this truth. Therefore, the people must receive the divine invitation on terms they cannot understand or explain. Paul does speak of having "the mind of Christ" (1 Cor. 2:16; Phil. 2:5), so it is possible for those who are truly faithful to think, in some manner, as God thinks.

God forms faithful stewards in heart and mind. It is what God forms deep within us that produces the volition by which we act. If we have hearts and minds full of grace and mercy, then we act accordingly. Jesus said much the same thing when he argued to the crowd against the Pharisees that "what comes out of the mouth proceeds from the heart, and this is what defiles" (Matt. 15:18).

A truth this psalm suggests is that our thinking sets our course of action. If we have a true heart, then right action follows. Ironically, life's greatest battles are frequently those we wage within ourselves. When warships used heavy cannons, sometimes these massive guns would escape from the chains that held them in place. In such instances, the peril of a cannon piercing a ship's hull was much greater than any enemy fire. We could say much the same of Christian stewards and believers. Our matchless and routinely faced hazards are not from external threats, but rather from an enemy that lurks within. To get our minds right with God and Jesus offers us the possibility of faithful actions and authentic stewardship.

Sunday between June 5 and 11 inclusive
(if after Trinity Sunday)

1 Samuel 8:4–20 (11:14–15)   Stewardship of Following

"They have not rejected you, but they have rejected me."
(1 Sam. 8:7)

Today's lesson from the Hebrew Bible presents us with a negative stewardship example. Odd as it may seem, "all the elders of Israel" display what we might call poor stewardship in terms of their "household" of following. If following does not seem to be part of vital stewardship for believers, then consider Jesus' words as he called his community together: "Follow me." Each of the four evangelists underscores the importance of following Jesus. In fact, the command "follow me" occurs in the NRSV translation of the Gospels in twenty-one verses.

Our lesson from 1 Samuel relates the story of how Israel came to the decision to install the monarchy. Earlier in the narrative the daughter-in-law of Eli gives birth after finding out that her husband has been killed in battle. The name she chooses for the child, "Ichabod," not only bespeaks her mood but also reminds readers that "the glory has departed from Israel" (1 Sam. 4:21). Given the persistence of Israel's enemies, the besieged nation appeals to Samuel for a king. Part of their rationale is so that Israel might be "like other nations."

The irony is that the people want to surrender the one thing that makes them unique among the nations. They are a people governed by God. Samuel, displeased, turns to God in prayer and receives a surprising answer. The Lord tells Samuel to grant their request and, in so many words, not to take it personally. God says, "They have not rejected you, but they have rejected me from being king over them."

When our leaders do not perform up to our expectations, or when life throws difficulties our way, it is a natural human instinct to look for another leader. In this case, Israel craves another system of leadership by which to function. When we read about a failing Fortune 500 company or an athletic team that has a woeful won-loss record, many of us reason that a change in leadership will occasion a change in status. Perhaps this kind of thinking operated among Israel's leaders.

Another reason is more factual. The first verses of chapter 8 explain, "When Samuel became old, he made his sons judges over Israel. . . . Yet his sons did not follow in his ways, but turned aside after gain; they took bribes and perverted justice" (8:1–3). As subsequent biblical history exposes, this decision proved a disaster. Israel exchanged generations of effective leadership for a new system that would spell its ruin.

In the stewardship household of following, God trusts believers with discernment about whom or what to follow. The decisions that followers make is part of our management of following. Sometimes people choose leaders who offer what looks like the easy way out of one problem or another. Too often, the court of popular opinion selects the path of least resistance. Often this trail reveals itself as a thornier path. As stewards, we must follow wisely.

Sunday between June 12 and 18 inclusive
(if after Trinity Sunday)

1 Samuel 15:34–16:13   Each Believer Has a Task

"Are all your sons here?"
(1 Sam. 16:11)

Today's lesson from 1 Samuel narrates a momentous change in Israel. After God directed Samuel to anoint Saul as king, things went fine for a time. Yet eventually God called for a new king. This story is one of the Hebrew Bible's most exquisite, one with which most readers are familiar. After Jesse parades his seven sons before Samuel—each of whom is rejected in turn—the prophet asks, "Are all your sons here?" Jesse replies, "There remains yet the youngest, but he is keeping the sheep." Samuel informs the assembly that "we will not sit down until he comes here." Perhaps Jesse either has forgotten David or considers him too young. Yet upon David's arrival the Lord commands, "Rise and anoint him; for this is the one." As it is often true, the surprising choice is the Lord's choice.

We can all recall unlikely circumstances that we could never have imagined. Some suggest these circumstances imply God's hand. I remember my father laughing about his friend, Harry S Truman, whose own mother-in-law didn't think he had a chance to win the 1948 presidential election against that "nice Mr. Dewey."

The process of choosing teams for a playground game was a painful experience for many people. Alternating, two captains chose everyone—from best to worst. For many people, life is like this. We sometimes feel as if we are not tall enough, fast enough, pretty enough, big enough, smart enough, popular enough, or good enough. Yet as stewards in God's realm, each of us has a task that God has gifted us to do. God can and will choose according to God's purposes. Each of us has the abilities and gifts to contribute something to God and God's people.

This story about Jesse and Samuel nearly neglecting David reminds us that in God's sphere it is not what others think of us that matters. Rather, it is what God thinks. David is no human accident but a divine intention. Unlikely and heroic people dot Scripture: Abraham, Sarah, Moses, Hannah, Joshua, Rahab, Hosea, and Jeremiah, to name but a few. Paul was the least likely candidate to plant churches and to make faith in Jesus Christ a worldwide phenomenon. Yet God's choices always win the day.

"Each believer has a task" is a basic stewardship principle. Christians are commonly guilty of doing either too much or not enough as their response to the grace and talents that God freely gives them. Ephesians cites a suggestive list of gifts: apostles, prophets, evangelists, pastors, and teachers (Eph. 4:11). Yet there are many households, perhaps too many to name. We all have specific talents that we can use to build up God's realm.

Taken together, all of our unique talents build up the church. Every baptized person receives a call to ministry. All of us can engage in some form of ministry or another. Yet not every appearance of ministry is high profile, nor does the church celebrate well enough what we might call "behind the scenes ministries." Still, God endows with significance each manner of ministry. In the church, all tasks are important to us and to Christ. We diminish Christ's work among us when we forget that each believer has a task for which God gifts him or her.

Sunday between June 19 and 25 inclusive
(if after Trinity Sunday)

2 Corinthians 6:1–13   Working Together

"We urge you also not to accept the grace of God in vain."
(2 Cor. 6:1)

In this part of 2 Corinthians, Paul addresses faithful living and his ministry of reconciliation. Indeed, Paul has spoken to the work of Christ and God's work in creation. Today's lesson continues with Paul's addressing the work of ministry. In the NRSV the text begins, "As we work together with him." But this may also be translated more simply as, "As we work together." This alternative reading can be found in the textual notes in most Bibles. In terms of stewardship, however, whether we work with God or with one another, the point is plainly that we work together.

One of the primary standards of Christian stewardship is that God includes people as partners in creation. But even more than that, believers labor together in the Lord's vineyard. Because the work is great, kingdom work needs all available hands. As an old proverb puts it, "Many hands lighten the load." By sharing work we can accomplish much more as we till and keep God's garden.

Yet this is often a bone of contention in local communities of faith. Too many believers either feel left out of the work, or worse, that they are the only ones who can do the work. How often have we heard someone complain, "I have to do everything around here," then, after someone volunteers to offer a hand, say, "No, that's all right. I will just do it myself"?

Whether Paul is suggesting here that he works with God or that he works with other believers, what is important is the stewardship attitude that people are partners with God and with others in the work of God's creation and its redemption.

Paul quotes a text from Isaiah to urge cooperation: "Now is the acceptable time; see, now is the day of salvation." We sense Paul's urgency in these words. He does not want the Corinthians to perceive him as setting up obstacles for their ministry. He even trots out a laundry list of his enduring afflictions: "hardships, calamities, beatings, imprisonments, riots, labors, sleepless nights, [and] hunger." Paul wants the Corinthian church to feel his sincerity. He and his ministry companions want this church to know, "Our heart is wide open to you." This "open heart" suggests Paul's willingness to work with others for Christ's claim on the world.

Have you ever wondered that perhaps God created people not because God *needed* people to work but because God *wanted* us "to till and keep the garden"? There is a world of difference between God needing and God wanting. Can you imagine playing tug-of-war alone? In the Christian life, stewardship is a task we share with others and with God. We do our part, others do their part, God does God's part. God created people for the sole enterprise of making the divine creation what God first imagined it.

God incorporates us as partners in creation. This is a vital stewardship tenet. God does not need us in any ultimate sense but wants us in every ultimate sense. It is on the basis of alliance that God builds stewards. For this reason Paul and his companions enter into congregational ministry. By doing so, they minister to the world for which Jesus died. As partners in Christ's ministry, we become partners with Christ.

Sunday between June 26 and July 2 inclusive

2 Corinthians 8:7–15   Remember Your Promise

"The gift is acceptable according to what one has."
(2 Cor. 8:12)

Although many people fail to give liberally, perhaps nothing tugs at our sentiment quite like the spontaneous outpouring of generous giving. Several events in recent history give evidence of the human impulse toward substantial giving to people in need. We only need to remember the relief effort surrounding 9/11, the Asian tsunami, or Hurricanes Rita and Katrina to be encouraged by the generosity of Americans. Only God can be the source of such gracious giving. Of course for stewards, generous giving is not a now-and-then activity. Christian stewardship is a daily choice and a way of life.

In today's Epistle lesson, we note how diplomatic Paul can be when the situation warrants gentle persuasion. Paul and his ministry partner, Titus, have a mission. They are receiving offerings from their Gentile churches for the poor in the Jerusalem church. Paul believed this would not only create goodwill but affirm the Jerusalem Council's decision for Paul to evangelize Gentiles (Acts 15).

Paul cites the example of the churches in Macedonia, which are much poorer than the church in Corinth. They have "overflowed in a wealth of generosity. . . .

They voluntarily gave according to their means, and even beyond their means, begging us earnestly for the privilege of sharing in this ministry." Paul attempts to persuade the Corinthians by showing them that the poor, in the case of the Macedonians, are helping the poor.

To further bolster his case, Paul writes of Jesus Christ, who "though he was rich, yet for your sakes he became poor, so that by his poverty you might become rich." And then Paul adds to these first two arguments the Corinthians' own record as a generous church.

Paul stresses their initial enthusiasm for the collection. They had been the first among the churches to approve of the Jerusalem collection. He urges them to "now finish doing it, so your eagerness may be matched by your completing it according to your means." Paul does not command but does suggest that the collection is a matter of balanced stewardship.

Finally, Paul prompts the Corinthians to remember that life has an odd way of evening things up. The Bible and experience teach us that the measuring vessel we use to give to others is ultimately the same vessel given to us. Whatsoever we sow, that shall we also reap.

Paul urges the Corinthian church to match with commitment their earlier eagerness to help others—in this case the Jerusalem church. This church is in every sense the "mother church" for all of Paul's missions.

I knew a man once who gave lavish gifts to his son, who lived with his mother. The couple had divorced, and there was still much bitter feeling between the child's parents. This father who appeared so generous to the child failed to pay his child support. He was willing to give "big ticket" items like bicycles and video game systems, yet he failed to offer support for the more mundane features of life—like food, clothing, and shelter. For this behavior he was taken to court and severely chastised by the judge, who commented that his "self-gratifying gifts to the boy did not feed or care for him in important and fundamental ways." Perhaps Paul makes much the same point.

Christian stewards recognize that special appeal offerings in emergency situations never replace steady, week-in, week-out charity. We often offer our money to the church's ministry in understated ways—the steward's response to life's many needs.

Sunday between July 3 and 9 inclusive

2 Corinthians 12:2–10   Power to Give Comes from God

"I will not boast, except of my weaknesses."
(2 Cor. 12:5)

Today's reading is the third consecutive passage in this section of the commentary from 2 Corinthians. The lectionary enables preachers to construct a three-part stewardship sermon series from these texts. For preachers who find it helpful to string consecutive lectionary texts together around one coherent theme, then this is a happy circumstance.

Paul begins this text by telling the story of a person who "was caught up to the third heaven." No doubt, Paul is speaking of himself here. Evidently some of Paul's opponents have undermined Paul's authority in order to enhance their own claims for influence. One piece of evidence for Paul's argumentative tone occurs when he writes the church concerning those who have obviously evaluated his ministry: "For they say, 'His letters are weighty and strong, but his bodily presence is weak, and his speech contemptible'" (2 Cor. 10:10).

Usually Paul avoids matching his revelatory encounters against those of his opponents. He sees this as "foolishness" (1 Cor. 2:14). Yet in our lesson Paul chooses to play his authority card. Paul's foes roll out one vision experience after another. They allude to divine wonders and signs to validate their ministry. By tooting their own authority horn they also diminish Paul's authority in the process. Paul writes explicitly about these persons: "Such boasters are false apostles, deceitful workers, disguising themselves as apostles of Christ. . . . Their end will match their deeds" (2 Cor. 11:13, 15).

As the passage unfolds, Paul moves from the third person to more self-revelatory language. He says he refrains from boasting in contrast to his antagonists. But if Paul did boast, he would be speaking truth. To keep him from boasting about the quality of his revelations, Paul goes so far as to mention the thorn given him from a messenger of Satan. Thus, it is not from on high but from his grounding in the human condition that Paul receives his authority. He tells the church at Corinth that he appealed to the Lord three times about his affliction. The answer he receives from the Lord discloses a key stewardship theme. According to Paul's own words, the Lord tells him, "My grace is sufficient for you, for power is made perfect in weakness."

Where does the power come from for our ability to become Christian stewards? In a world where we are encouraged to grab all we can get and then hold on to it for dear life, the idea of giving liberally to others seems naive. Paul's own life is evidence of the source of such power. He writes, paradoxically to human reason, "For whenever I am weak, then I am strong." Why is this so for Paul, and by extension, for us?

The reason we as Christians derive power through our weakness is twofold. First, when we recognize that in our own aptitude we have little power, then we look elsewhere for it. Our pride melts before the power of God's grace. We know that we are nothing in ourselves, but we can say, with Paul, that "I can do all things through him who strengthens me" (Phil. 4:13). Paul understands that his power comes from divine grace and that this is sufficient—for Paul and for believers as stewards.

Second, from the gospel, we see that bona fide power takes a crucified form. On the cross, Jesus demonstrates the power of humility, surrender, and yielding to God's will. In Jesus' act on the cross, Jesus' power extends over death itself.

Sunday between July 10 and 16 inclusive

Ephesians 1:3–14   Owners, Not Renters

"In Christ we have also obtained an inheritance."
(Eph. 1:11)

On this Sunday the lectionary begins a series of seven consecutive Epistle lessons from Ephesians. Whether or not one believes that Ephesians is a genuine letter from Paul's hand, few can argue that most of the epistle's ideas are Pauline. In fact, one of the unusual features of today's lesson is that in the original Greek the whole text is one sentence. Translators have broken the English text into five distinct sentences, but the idea is compact. The concept of inheritance is one that speaks to stewardship.

After Paul puts forward praise to God, he turns to the idea of the people of God being chosen "to be holy and blameless" before God in love. God has destined God's people "for adoption as his children through Jesus Christ." The reason for our adoption is as simple as it is unexplainable: it is God's pleasure and goodwill. The densely packed text goes on to delineate benefits to those adopted. We are redeemed, offered forgiveness, and have had the mystery of God's will revealed to us. In addition, we have obtained an inheritance that "according to his counsel and will" will offer hope to those who trust God. Therefore, we "might live for the praise of his glory." All this—"the word of truth" and "the gospel of our salvation"—is sealed by God's Holy Spirit. This "thickly packed" theology that begins the epistle will be unpacked throughout; it is something of an abstract of the whole letter.

For our purpose of stewardship, we will do well to note the distinction between being simple believers and being those who are adopted as daughters and sons. Family relationships tend to be closer and more dependable than other kinds of human associations. When a person has been adopted, that person has all the rights and privileges of a person born biologically into a family. This is God's pledge to faithful disciples.

Recently I talked with the president and CEO of my city's chamber of commerce. One of the most striking things he said in the course of our conversation was that the most effective way to help lower-income people move toward middle-class status is to facilitate home ownership. He said, "When people become homeowners, rather than renters, they immediately become stakeholders in their communities." When people become vested in their community as owners rather than renters, the entire community benefits.

As offspring of the living God, stewards are stakeholders in God's realm. We are more than beneficiaries of God's forgiveness and mercy. We are those who now pass these benefits along to others. At each point, God initiates our good fortune. We do not beg or pray for these benefits. Rather, God gives them to us by God's "good pleasure" and "according to the purpose of him who accomplishes all things." We did not ask for our good standing before God, but we rest in God's good graces nevertheless.

As stewards, we are not casual passersby. Rather, we are those who have been commissioned to manage the households God has deposited with us. How we share God's mercy and forgiveness is the way in which we honor the immensity of the gift. This gift is of such magnitude that we could have never earned it— but we can share it. Stewards handle the things of God not as renters but as if they were owners.

Sunday between July 17 and 23 inclusive

Mark 6:30–34, 53–56   Rest Is Essential

"Come away to a deserted place all by yourselves and rest a while."
(Mark 6:31)

"Overscheduled and overworked" describes modern life. Yet do we really expend more energy now than our ancestors did? Survival conditions likely compelled our ancestors—until recently—to endure daily toil. Today we choose to be busy. If stewardship is managing the gifts and graces that God loans us, then how do we value rest and contemplation as part of that management?

Mark's lesson relates that the apostles have been hard at work. We infer this from their telling Jesus "all that they had done and taught." Clearly Jesus senses their fatigue. He says, "Come away to a deserted place . . . and rest a while." All the activity that swirled around Jesus, no doubt, had worn on the Twelve. Their activity had so absorbed them that "they had no leisure even to eat." Jesus' suggestion about rest for the disciples is not unique. God long before wove respite into the fabric of Hebrew life.

We find in Exodus the first mention of Sabbath in the Hebrew Scriptures. Moses tells the people what God has related to him: "Tomorrow is a day of solemn rest, a holy sabbath to the LORD" (16:23). Solemn rest appears to be the primary purpose for Sabbath. Of course, later in Israel's life Sabbath also functioned as a day of worship (Exod. 20:8, 11) and a day of remembrance for what God had done for God's people (Deut. 5:15). Indeed, Sabbath observance reminded the people of God's covenant (Lev. 24:8). In a nutshell, Sabbath keeping occasioned rest, remembrance, worship, and covenant renewal for Israel. Jesus knew this commandment well.

According to worship statistics, modern people observe Sabbath less and less. Yet we seem to need rest and renewal more than ever. What separates us from the ancients is not decreased faith; rather, our life's outlook is more utilitarian. Modern people often ask, "Is this worth my valuable time?" Today we rarely value rest's restoring capacity.

Into this perspective of modern life Jesus' wisdom guides believers as stewards. The gospel's labor of love in teaching, feeding, and caring for people's minds, bodies, and souls is demanding work. From time to time those who offer themselves to God's world must retreat from the fray. Jesus assumes that the rest Sabbath offers for Israel will likely benefit the apostles. By extension, Jesus' counsel of rest makes good sense to our culture of utility. More and more activity does not bring success or effectiveness. This life of hectic activity looks astonishingly like hamsters running on a wheel. The Bible is clear about Sabbath keeping. Jesus extols rest to his disciples and therefore to modern stewards.

Perhaps we today think we are too sophisticated to accept ancient wisdom's directives regarding rest. However, something interesting is happening in secular thinking. Stephen Covey uses an analogy of taking a break while sawing wood in order to sharpen the saw. This seemingly minor interruption makes the worker more fruitful. This is what rest, and especially Sabbath rest, does for those engaged in the challenging work of discipleship as stewards. Covey urges modern folks to "cultivate the habit of sharpening the saw physically, mentally, and spiritually every day."* This is what the Bible has told us all along and what Jesus advises, too.

Sunday between July 24 and 30 inclusive

Ephesians 3:14–21   From Nature and the Ocean

"I pray that you may . . . know the love of Christ."
(Eph. 3:18–19)

What fetters Christian stewardship to the overall mission of the church? What is it that unites believers to a far greater degree than all the small issues that seem to divide us? How can the church offer a comprehensive delivery system of God's grace and mercy to a hurting world? The writer of Ephesians addresses the theological groundwork of these kinds of questions. Ephesians 3:14–21 is the foundation upon which God builds the church.

Sometimes when people look at the church, it may appear as a collection of individuals who function independently. The church often seems to move in a myriad of directions. One of the greatest challenges in leading a congregation toward fulfillment of biblical mandates for ministry is to help believers all get on the same page. How can congregations focus their power and influence on the task of converting the world? As stewards of leadership, one household we manage is that of lucid vision.

These days many secular businesses try to focus their organizations with documents they label "mission statements" or "vision statements." These statements allow everyone in an organization to understand what it aims to accomplish. In a sense, a vision or mission statement is to a business what a job description is to an individual employee. The mission or vision statement offers something of a map by which businesses can move into unknown territory.

Today's Epistle lesson informs the church of its mission purpose. The text

*Stephen R. Covey, *Principle-Centered Leadership* (New York: Simon & Schuster, 1992), 140.

explores theologically God's relationship to believers. Paul (perhaps the author) first offers thanksgiving, proclaiming the God "from whom every family in heaven and on earth takes its name." Second, Paul offers petitions. He prays that God strengthen readers through the Spirit but also that "Christ may dwell in your hearts through faith." Paul assumes that God will root and ground them in love. This "love of Christ" surpasses all human knowledge. If so grasped, then the Ephesian church will "be filled with all the fullness of God." This text has no story line. Rather, it is pure theology. Yet this passage plainly offers the source for the church's divine vision and intention for mission.

Years ago I sat next to an oceanographer on an airplane trip across the Atlantic. As we looked out the aircraft's window, we observed floating specks below. She tutored me about the phenomenon of icebergs. She remarked that small icebergs flow in one direction but more substantial icebergs move in another direction. She explained that surface winds propel the smaller pieces of ice. However, the deeper ocean currents control the flow of the large icebergs. Stewards can learn a lesson from nature and the ocean.

We may liken people to icebergs in this respect: life conditions move some people by elements as elusive as surface winds. Even Jesus said that "the wind blows where it chooses" (John 3:8). Yet when stewards ground their Christian vision and mission in what Ephesians describes as "the love of Christ that surpasses knowledge," then the foundational currents of God's love lead us. It is the deep channel of God's love that inspires us to work in God's vineyard. Stewards follow the deep current of God's love, and in so doing God empowers us to manage God's gifts for mission and ministry.

Sunday between July 31 and August 6 inclusive

Ephesians 4:1–16   Teaching a New Dog Some Old Tricks

"The gifts he gave were . . . for building up the body of Christ."
(Eph. 4:11–12)

We often hear people speak about "God-given talent." Typically, the phrase is simply a cliché employed by a sports or an entertainment celebrity. Perhaps they use the phrase because they cannot explain their ability. "God-given talent" covers a mass of mysteries, just as the phrase "act of God" works for the insurance industry to define occurrences that are beyond human control or explanation.

Ephesians, however, brooks no mystery concerning what "each of us was given." The writer is clear. God gives believers gifts to "build up the body of Christ." The early Christians believed they had all the essential gifts and talents to accomplish the ministry God gave them. Today, however, in the age of specialists we aren't too sure. The "spectator mentality" has sapped the stewardship potential of many rank and file believers. In fact, the spectator mentality has two chief and unfortunate outcomes.

The first is that for the handful of folks truly involved in the hands-on ministry of the church, an undermining sense can develop leading to protestations that "I have to do everything around here." Of course, resentment has no place in the church. Yet sinful antipathy creeps into Christ's church when only a few individuals offer their gifts.

A second unfortunate outcome of poor participation in the church is when spectators feel the brief thrill in another's success. This vicarious participation is fleeting. As experience teaches, success doubles in enjoyment when we have a hand in it. The idea of participation—every believer in ministry—was one of the early church's most brilliant strategies. All took part, and no one watched while others lived out their faith. During the Middle Ages when priests assumed the faith tasks for the laity, the church's strength waned. When Reformation Protestants read the Scriptures in their native tongue and prayed for themselves without a priestly intercessor, the church regained its vitality.

Too often modern believers see the church as existing for its members. Such people belong to churches so that someone can minister to their needs. However, Jesus taught that the function of disciples is always "inside out." Jesus' disciples existed to share the gospel with a world captured by a narrow view of life's purpose. The disciples' wishes were not nearly as important to Jesus as what God wanted.

What does this look like for today's church? Modern Christian people too often ask questions like, "What is in this for me or my family?" or "How does this protect what I think is important?" Perhaps today's good stewards might ask, "What is the good of this ministry for God and God's people?" or "How can God best use my gifts?"

A healthy church fills itself with servant leaders. A servant church appreciates that each person in a congregation is a gifted steward. As Ephesians plainly states, there are a host of necessary gifts: "some would be apostles, some prophets, some evangelists, some pastors and teachers." We will have to adjust our thinking and serving in order to adopt this two-thousand-year-old model. Perhaps we can adjust by learning how to trust each other, how to cooperate—not compete—and how to cultivate a common image of what it means to be God's stewards with many gifts. Ephesians offers us today a picture of the early church and its management of gifts. From "one body and one Spirit" we can learn anew.

Sunday between August 7 and 13 inclusive

Ephesians 4:25–5:2   Stewards Behaving Well

"Therefore be imitators of God, as beloved children."
(Eph. 5:1)

We might say that the sum of stewardship is sharing what we have with others. While this may be true, it is also true of stewardship that the *way* we share with others may be just as important as *what* we share. In today's Epistle lesson Paul offers tangible instruction. Some think that it is nothing more than a behavioral laundry list of things your mother might warn you to avoid. Yet Paul knows that when people live together, as God calls the church to do, then friction will result. Believers' conduct, however, has a practical end in harmony in God's household. We can describe Paul's exhortation as a template for the stewardship of relationships.

Essentially Paul's pragmatic directions begin at chapter 4 (see last week's commentary). Paul writes of God's multiplicity of gifts to build the household of faith. In the verses between last week's text and today's, Paul contrasts the believers' old life with their new life in Christ. Today's lesson offers a catalog of things for the faithful both to shun and to embrace. This inventory of "don'ts" includes telling falsehoods, letting anger fester, making room for the devil, stealing, engaging in evil talk, and grieving the Holy Spirit. In the place of such negative behavior, Paul urges telling the truth, laboring honestly, speaking words that build up, employing kindness, being tenderhearted, and displaying forgiveness. Paul teaches believers, then and now, that we forgive "as God in Christ has forgiven [us]." Summarizing the inventory, we read Paul's weighty words: "Therefore be imitators of God, as beloved children."

One day a pharmacist friend of mine, a solid church member, shared a concern he had. The substance of his problem was that he did not feel like the Christian people he saw on television. He said, "There seem to be two kinds of Christians. The first are those people that the TV preachers tell are horrible sinners—drug abusers, child molesters, drunks—and unless they confess how bad they are, then Jesus can't (or won't) help them. The other kind of Christian is like Mother Teresa or Billy Graham. I feel left out because I am not like either kind."

My friend is a decent person and a good steward. Yet the way the media portrays the Christian life, he feels left out. Perhaps his problem is similar to where a good many mainline believers are today. We are not so good or bad to bring notice. Rather, we spend our time in seemingly unheroic ways—coaching Little League baseball, cooking for the Sunday night youth group, or singing in the church choir.

It may be that our Ephesian lesson addresses people like this—people like us. The text is straightforward, almost commonsensical. None of Paul's suggestions seem unusual in degree or kind. We hear them, even offer them, every day. Truthfully, the best-led Christian lives rarely make headlines. Like good umpires, these faithful stewards do their best work unseen. In quiet, unassuming ways, they carry out Paul's mandate to "be imitators of God." These kinds of people regularly and systematically do the right things for the right reasons and do them for a very long time.

One should never be ashamed to do what God calls us to do as stewards. We may not make a splash in newspaper headlines. Yet it is in the fidelity of day-to-day life with other people that Christian stewards like my friend make a difference in our world.

Sunday between August 14 and 20 inclusive

1 Kings 2:10–12; 3:3–14   Wise Stewards Ask for What They Need

"Ask what I should give you."
(1 Kgs. 3:5)

Today's lesson puts the finishing touches on the story of David's successor to Israel's throne. The monarchy that Samuel so resisted has had its predictable problems. Saul's reign was short-lived, and while David's time in power was long, it also revealed ethical missteps along the way. As we turn to Solomon's reign, we see the ominous clue dropped by the text: Solomon "sacrificed and offered incense at the high places." No doubt the writer believed that the true place for sacrifice was Jerusalem. First Kings 3:2 explains this situation by telling readers that "the people were sacrificing at the high places, however, because no house had yet been built for the name of the LORD." Depending on the sermon's slant, the preacher may want to address this issue.

For stewardship, a fruitful place to explore is the dream scene in the middle section of the text. While at Gibeon, Solomon dreams about an encounter with the Lord. The dream is important, because Solomon is at the beginning of his reign. In the dream God tells Solomon, "Ask what I should give you." The Lord points out to Solomon that he does not ask for "long life or riches, or for the life of your enemies." Rather, the new king asks for "an understanding mind to govern your people, able to discern between good and evil." Commenting positively on this request, the writer of 1 Kings records approvingly, "It pleased the Lord that Solomon had asked this."

God has given Solomon the responsibility of ruling over God's people. God has also offered to grant Solomon what he desires. Contrary to a foolish or selfish request, Solomon asks for the one thing that those who manage the household of leadership most need—wisdom. In this request is revealed the good judgment of Solomon.

Solomon clearly understands the role of servant-leader. He has the insight to ask for that which would help him become an effective leader. We often look for tasks to do rather than asking, "What task needs to be done?" It is a wise steward who makes this distinction.

A Girl Scout leader came to me near Christmas one year and said, "My troop wants to help some poor children, and I thought a pastor might help give us some guidance." I told her that one of the pressing needs for some of the community's children was school supplies. In addition, I told her that many children also needed coats and shoes. She replied, "Well, we are not interested in those kinds of things. We really want to give them toys and candy. It is Christmas, after all."

I am not opposed to toys or candy, yet when people give to others, they err if they give out of their need rather than responding to others' needs. This Girl Scout leader wanted to please those who gave more than help those who received.

Solomon proved to be a good steward of his leadership household. He recognized that the wisdom he desired would help the people he was to lead. We can learn from his request and pray for the gifts that will help us become more faithful stewards.

Sunday between August 21 and 27 inclusive

1 Kings 8:(1, 6, 10–11) 22–30, 41–43   Stewards of the Incarnation

"But will God indeed dwell on the earth?"
(1 Kgs. 8:27)

The Christian faith is incarnational if nothing else. We Christians believe that the final, decisive, and most ample revelation of God that humans will ever see came in Jesus of Nazareth. This Jesus, who was divinity in human form, departed earth as the resurrected Christ. Incarnational theology has important implications for Christian stewardship. In fact, one of the most egregious misunderstandings of Christian stewardship resides in our common attitudes toward "bricks and mortar," or as some have called it, the Christian "edifice complex."

Today's lesson is the story of the dedication of Israel's temple. This was the temple David never built (see 1 Chr. 17). Our text relates the prayer of Solomon. After assembling Israel's elders in Jerusalem and after the ark of the covenant arrives, Solomon begins this extended liturgical prayer.

In the prayer Solomon praises God, speaks of his father David's faithfulness, and asks God's fulfillment of the promise to David. Then Solomon asks a rhetorical but pertinent question: "But will God indeed dwell on the earth?" In Solomon's answer is evident the king's proverbial wisdom. Solomon prays, "Even heaven and the highest heaven cannot contain you, much less this house that I have built!" This statement may be more true than the king realizes. And it is a truth with which each new generation of Christian stewards must contend.

In our modern world, we get caught up in the spirit of efficacy. We are ever planning, implementing, and evaluating our transactions. In this often laudable exercise, however, we at times lose the deeper purposes of God. We habitually suppose that our building plans and the like are ends in themselves. Periodically we forget that our churches and places of worship serve a greater purpose.

Near the end of the prayer, Solomon gestures at what stewards of the gospel try to practice. Solomon prays, "When a foreigner, who is not of your people Israel . . . [sees the temple, then] they may know that your name has been invoked." Solomon here speaks of Gentiles who may hear the word of the Lord and thereby come to faith. Is this not what we Christians do when we preach the gospel? Too often when a church completes a building project, those involved consider that this is the end. However, as Solomon's prayer implies, completion of a building may only be the beginning of ministry.

Evangelical theology at its best understands that God's ultimate connection with human beings is in the space between people. In the area of relationship between persons who trust one another, people can broach the subject of fidelity to God, worship, discipleship, and stewardship. When we sing that we "serve a risen savior," we do so because we have met a savior who became one of us. And in that meeting we now can become more like the one who sent Jesus. On occasion God is incarnate in our witness.

Good stewards know that all the other things we do with regard to the church—caring for buildings, worshiping, educating children and youth, and so forth—we do for one purpose. That purpose is to lift up the name of Jesus. We exist to introduce people to the risen Christ. In other words, we believers as stewards do what Psalm 116:13 suggests: We "lift up the cup of salvation and call on the name of the LORD."

Sunday between August 28 and September 3 inclusive

James 1:17–27   Practicing What We Preach

"[God] gave . . . so that we would become a kind of first fruits."
(Jas. 1:18)

Of all the books of the Bible, James may be the most practical. When I read James, it brings to mind the word "praxis," which comes from the Greek word for "action" or "practice," and so sensibly the word emphasizes useful concerns. Praxis signifies that we can only learn spiritual truth through experience. Thus, praxis engages the totality of our being—body, soul, mind, and spirit. Praxis, to say it another way, is where theory and practice meet. Stewardship reveals praxis at its most elemental embodiment.

Today's lesson reminds stewards that "every perfect gift is from above." God gives to believers in order that they may "become a kind of first fruits of his creatures." In this story of creation, God elects humankind as the crown of creation—a sort of icing on creation's cake. In making humankind creation's culmination, God also has given us great responsibility.

After offering a theological rationale for human accountability, James then offers some practical advice for believers: "Be quick to listen, slow to speak, slow to anger. . . . Rid yourselves of all sordidness and rank growth of wickedness." James also advocates the positive attribute of hospitality. The urging of believers to "be doers of the word, and not merely hearers" is as applicable to the Christian life today as it was in the first century. James also admonishes his readers to curb the tongue, care for the weak, and "keep oneself unstained by the world."

From a Christian perspective, praxis is where our profession of faith and our serving in God's realm meet. Of course, we have another and more familiar word for this phenomenon—we call it discipleship. We might even say it is good stewardship. People from West Texas might say that praxis is "where the rubber meets the road."

From time to time we hear people say, "Practice what you preach" or "I'd rather see a sermon than hear one any day." These statements imply that our actions are ways to measure Christian sincerity. The most cutting description of a Christian is "hypocrite." That dreaded word "hypocrisy" simply means to "play a part" or pretend to be something that one is not. Hypocrites are those persons who say one thing and then do another. They are people who playact for gain. Jesus was so insistent about faithfully following the way of God that he addressed hypocrisy this way: "Whenever you give alms, do not sound a trumpet before you, as the hypocrites do in the synagogues" (Matt. 6:2).

Stewardship puts our lives where our profession is. Praxis is a way to say our stewardship is active and based on solid biblical principles. Praxis means we do not divide our faith into the spiritual part and the service part; instead, we blend them into a life pleasing to God. Although James is exceptionally practical, he is, of course, also right!

Sunday between September 4 and 10 inclusive

Proverbs 22:1–2, 8–9, 22–23   Sharing Creates Relationship

"Those who are generous are blessed, for they share their bread with the poor."
                                                    (Prov. 22:9)

As many preachers know all too well, a gap exists between what preachers want to say from the pulpit and what people want to hear from the pulpit. Although not all lay folks crave practicality, many others want to hear something "down to earth." Such persons want something useful to help them live the Christian life. Their comments after sermons often go like this: "Well, preacher, what you said may be true enough, but what am I going to do with that sermon this week?" Perhaps this is a perennial problem. Proverbs is one of several biblical books that focus on the truth that is embodied in the "nickels and dimes" of life. That is, Proverbs speaks directly to the issues that people encounter daily.

Our lesson today from Proverbs is tailor-made for stewardship. It tells us not only that "a good name is to be chosen rather than great riches," but that a person who "sows injustice will reap calamity." These statements are true enough on their face that one might have heard them from grandparents. Yet the lectionary only uses four readings from Proverbs in its three-year cycle. Is it because these verses seem to be platitudes? Maybe the writer knows that human beings need reminding again and again of life's most basic truths.

This proverbial wisdom is not the "give-to-get" gospel that we all too frequently hear on TV and radio. Rather, it is a sound truth that God blesses generous people. Most people gravitate to persons who are generous in spirit. Generous people are winsome people. We like to converse with people who are generous in listening and with their time. We like to work in the company of those who are generous with their labor. We like people who are generous in spirit, who give others the benefit of the doubt and do not rush to judgment. Thus, when Proverbs

22:1 says that "a good name is to be chosen," it means that a reputation for integrity and honor is a most valuable possession. In cultures that function in an honor and shame mode, generosity puts one in an honorable category.

This is good news for Christian stewards. We hold fast to Jesus' words, quoted by Paul as he says goodbye to the Ephesian elders at Miletus: "It is more blessed to give than to receive" (Acts 20:35). The words seem counterintuitive in our avaricious culture, where we latch on to everything we can get our hands on. Yet Jesus tells us, via Paul, that the one who gives is more blessed than the one who receives.

This part of Proverbs teaches that those who cling to God are the faithful stewards who take on the persona of generosity. God blesses such persons because "they share their bread with the poor." Underlying this practical piece of folk wisdom is the fact that those who share also create a relationship between giver and receiver. In God's world, imagined at creation, relationship is everything. It is prized above all else. It is in relationship that a good name becomes more priceless than silver or gold.

Faithful stewards create relationship in giving. They create relationship between themselves and God. They create relationship in the community of faith. Nothing closes the space between one and another sooner or more wholly than sharing.

Sunday between September 11 and 17 inclusive

James 3:1–12   Stewardship of the Tongue

"From the same mouth come blessing and cursing."
(Jas. 3:10)

One of the households that stewards manage is the household of our words. In a practical way, James guides those who want better to manage "the tongue." James uses "the tongue" as a metaphor for verbal communication. He writes of the tongue's power, "With it we bless . . . and . . . curse." From the biblical standpoint this little organ possesses a great deal of power. To manage the tongue's power habitually takes all the control and grace we can muster.

This pericope begins with a warning that not all should aspire to teach. For Christian education leaders who are in constant need of Sunday school teachers, this advice seems almost painful. From this point on James makes his case for control, which to his way of thinking leads toward perfection.

In addressing control, James uses two analogies. The first is that a trainer controls a large horse by a small bit placed in the horse's mouth. A skilled horse person can effectively restrain a 1,200-pound horse this way. Second, James turns naturally to ships, suggesting that those who steer large ships maneuver them by a small rudder. James's images demonstrate that people can control something large by something comparatively small.

James then completes his circle of logic, which he began in writing about "making mistakes in speaking," by reminding readers that although the tongue is small in contrast to the whole body, it does have great power. James uses a case from nature to remind readers that "every species of beast and bird, of reptile and sea creature, can be tamed and has been tamed by the human species." Yet the human tongue remains untamed! To James's thinking the tongue is plainly "a restless evil, full of deadly poison."

To manage a household as a steward is to recognize that the gifts we possess are ours only as God's loan. Therefore, the ways we use God's gifts either honor or shame God. When James states that "from the same mouth come blessing and cursing," we discern both good and bad news. The bad news reveals that we may use the tongue for cursing our fellow creatures, but the good news follows. From this same mouth or tongue we may also bless God, and presumably other people. The faithful steward is one who knows how to use the gift as divinely intended. The steward manages the tongue.

Isaiah declares optimistically that "the Lord GOD has given me the tongue of a teacher, that I may know how to sustain the weary with a word" (Isa. 50:4). We can hearten others. As James and Isaiah remind us, teaching is a gift or household that some stewards manage. James beckons believers to perfect their speech in order to perfect their lives. It seems simple enough but so difficult to accomplish.

For rank and file believers, this modest guidance on proper speech comes as a welcome rain in a parched desert. We all know of circumstances in our own lives when we wish we could take back words spoken in haste or in the heat of passion. For people like us, stewardship of our words is counsel we might all heed.

Sunday between September 18 and 24 inclusive

Mark 9:30–37   Servant Leadership

"Whoever wants to be first must be last of all and servant of all."
(Mark 9:35)

In Christian stewardship Jesus asks believers to step into a world where everything seems upside-down. In the natural world where survival is not only a priority but *the* priority, an animal either eats lunch or is lunch. Biologists write of the food chain, and we humans sit at its summit. Yet even within the human family there appears to be an unquenchable need for competition. We thrive on beating others in everything from jump rope to securing the best marriage partner. We compare ourselves with others incessantly. As social creatures we measure, grade, score, and evaluate every endeavor we can think of.

The world into which Jesus invites disciples is an alternative to the world of nature and society in which we live. In this alternative world Jesus teaches that "if anyone strikes you on the right cheek, turn the other also" (Matt. 5:39) and commands, "Love your enemies, [and] do good to those who hate you" (Luke

6:27). For those who aspire to be faithful Christian stewards, Jesus' word is "Give to everyone who begs from you; and if anyone takes away your goods, do not ask for them again" (Luke 6:30). In our world this is utter nonsense.

Mark's lesson today concerns the stewardship of leadership. Jesus has just healed a boy with an unclean spirit and Jesus has made his second passion prediction (the first in Mark comes at 8:31–33). After this Jesus and his band of disciples move on, but on the way an argument crops up among the disciples. Arriving at Capernaum, Jesus asks, "What were you arguing about on the way?" Jesus' question meets with silence. The disciples feel shame because after Jesus had spoken of his death, they had argued about who was the greatest.

As sometimes happens in the Gospels, Jesus perceives the conversation without the words being spoken out loud (Mark 2:8; Luke 5:22). We readers expect a rebuke. Instead Jesus offers a life lesson to the gathered disciples. First Jesus tells them, "Whoever wants to be first must be last of all and servant of all." Second, he takes a child and suggests that hospitality to one of these little ones is hospitality extended to him. Moreover, one who welcomes a child welcomes the one who sent Jesus in the first place. This is a similar lesson to the one Jesus teaches in the parable of the sheep and goats (Matt. 25). In the first century, children dwelt at the bottom of the social order, and children remain the most vulnerable humans in nature's food chain. How disciples or stewards treat the lowly and helpless is a measure of obedience.

In the upside-down Gospel world, in order to be great one must serve others—whether great or small. This is difficult, because we are not built that way. We strive to succeed, and we struggle to survive and triumph. Yet in God's created world, we who believe are "to be in love and charity with our neighbors." And as Jesus teaches, the neighbor is the one who is in need, and we are neighbors—and great in the realm of God—when we show mercy (see Luke 10:37). Good stewards of leadership are ones who have the heart of a servant.

Sunday between September 25 and October 1 inclusive

Mark 9:38–50   Sometimes We Just Get Out of the Way

"Whoever is not against us is for us."
(Mark 9:40)

Today's text may offer us an opportunity to think about the negative actions we attempt on God's behalf. Sometimes we get so engrossed in what others are doing that we forget to "set our own house in order."

The verses preceding the Gospel lesson for the day have Jesus not only foretelling his death but also blessing a child. This blessing comes as a response to the disciples' arguing among themselves about who is the greatest. Jesus takes the child in his arms and teaches the disciples, "Whoever welcomes one such child in my name welcomes me, and whoever welcomes me welcomes not me but the one who sent me" (Mark 9:37). The point Jesus makes gently here with a child is a point he will make more unambiguously in the next chapter. There Jesus says, "For the Son of Man came not to be served but to serve" (Mark 10:45). The disciples are concerned about honor and status; Jesus teaches them about humble usefulness in God's realm.

Today's text takes another of the disciples' blunders and allows Jesus to teach from it. John, no doubt speaking for the Twelve, complains to Jesus, "Teacher, we saw someone casting out demons in your name, and we tried to stop him, because he was not following us." Evidently, "the insiders" thought Jesus would congratulate them on their discernment. However, he rebukes them by telling them, "Whoever is not against us is for us." From the perspective of the disciples, it may seem that Jesus is confused as to who is an "insider" and who is an "outsider." Perhaps, again, Jesus' point is that in God's realm we do not divide into insiders and outsiders.

As odd as it may sound, we church folks spend a good deal of time determining who can and cannot do certain things in the name of the church. Many a church governing body spends energy laying down church rules and procedures. (Several people in my own congregation yearn for me to try to stop our bishops from speaking out on a number of issues, such as war or capitalistic materialism.) It may be necessary for the church on occasion to lay out guidelines for ministry. Rarely, however, should this activity be the order of the day. Jesus implies that the disciples should not be so concerned about those who can cast out demons. Maybe, Jesus seems to suggest, the disciples should be concerned with why they could not (see Mark 9:14–19).

The role of stewards is not so much to prevent others from using their perceived spiritual gifts as it is to employ their own gifts to the glory of God. Perhaps Acts has a good word for us here. In Acts the council is trying to decide what do with Peter and the apostles who have been doing great signs and wonders. Gamaliel, a respected teacher of the law, says to the assembly, "I tell you, keep away from these men and let them alone; because if this plan or this undertaking is of human origin, it will fail; but if it is of God, you will not be able to overthrow them—in that case you may even be found fighting against God" (Acts 5:38–39).

Faithful stewards recognize that all those who are in Christ have gifts to give. Occasionally our best course of action with regard to others' gifts is to simply get out of the way and allow God to work.

Sunday between October 2 and 8 inclusive

Psalm 25   What the Humble Have to Learn

"He leads the humble in what is right, and teaches the humble his way."
(Ps. 25:9)

One of the principles by which faithful stewards live is that God loans us our gifts and talents. Consequently, what we stewards possess is not really ours.

According to Proverbs, "Wisdom is with the humble" (11:2). The humble possess nothing of which to boast. This makes them wise. To be a humble person means that before God one not only is meek but also has no foundation for pride.

The lesson from Psalm 25 (Psalm 26 is also an option for the day) reflects the psalmist's appeal for forgiveness as one who is estranged from God and others. For this reason, the heartfelt prayer, "Do not remember the sins of my youth or my transgressions; according to your steadfast love remember me, for your goodness' sake, O LORD" reflects earnest humility. This prayer is used in the lectionary on four occasions (Pentecost, Year A and B; and the First Sunday of Advent and Lent, Years C and B, respectively). Psalm 25 understands humbleness before God!

A friend once told me a story that relates the wisdom of those who are of "humble means." Several years ago an earthquake in Pakistan damaged the country's sewage treatment plants. Pakistan engaged several international companies to repair the damage and hired a respected project supervisor to work with local people. Mammoth trucks transported the new equipment, some of which contained components larger than an average-sized home. Oversized sheets of cardboard and wood protected the components during shipping.

The project supervisor hired local laborers to uncrate the massive equipment as it arrived on the job site. The supervisor, via an interpreter, struck a deal with the laborers. He allowed the workers to sell the leftover crate material to local people for temporary housing. The project supervisor had done this previously in other countries where he had done similar work. Someone estimated that in about three years he earned roughly the equivalent of one year's salary by selling the cardboard and crate waste.

In retrospect, the project supervisor became a good steward of material that might have otherwise been thrown away or burned. But because he was a good steward, he provided for people who had nothing and made a profit by helping others. As Jesus himself said of the slave who invested wisely, Jesus might have said to this project supervisor as well, "Well done, good and trustworthy slave; you have been trustworthy in a few things, I will put you in charge of many things" (Matt. 25:21).

When we read in Psalm 25, "He leads the humble in what is right, and teaches the humble his way," we assume that what the Lord will teach, the humble will learn. Good stewards not only recognize the gifts of God, but they also discern the possibility of using God's gifts in ways that build up the realm of God. Providing housing, however temporary it may be, is a sign of good stewardship and shrewd judgment. Indeed, from time to time we may even encounter persons who know how to stretch a little into a lot. These kinds of stewards are both humble and wise. They are stewards who have learned the humility of letting the Lord teach them.

Sunday between October 9 and 15 inclusive

Mark 10:17–31   Turning Loose

"Go, sell what you own, and give the money to the poor."
(Mark 10:21)

Possibly we never say it out loud; after all, we are modern and urbane people. Yet in the back of every person's mind who desperately wants to trust the goodness and providence of God lurks the question "What must I do to inherit eternal life?" We may pose the same question in different ways: "Karl Barth said that people come to church on the Sabbath with only one question in their minds: Is it true? The providence of God, the saving power of Jesus Christ, the comforting presence of the Holy Spirit, the resurrection from the dead, the forgiveness of sin: Is it true?"* Barth's question replicates our text's inquiry: "What must I do to inherit eternal life?"

Before we can develop a theology of stewardship, we must develop a theology. Developing a theology presupposes God as the provident owner of all. We yearn for eternal life, at times referred to in the Gospels as the kingdom of God or the kingdom of heaven. From his affirmative answer to Jesus' assertion about God's commandments, the man appears to have met his obligations. He, by his own confession, has kept all these commandments since his youth. Jesus then drops the hammer: "You lack one thing; go, sell what you own, and give the money to the poor, and you will have treasure in heaven; then come, follow me." The man leaves without another word.

Some may smugly think, "He was possessed by his possessions." Yet who of us is not? In our world of investements, mortgages, car payments, school bills, compensation packages, pensions, and insurance, we are all frauds if we think our possessions do not possess us. How could it be otherwise? We have to put food on the table, after all.

Jesus spells out for the disciples exactly what his teaching entails. He speaks of wealth and of camels. This leaves the disciples with one question: "Then who can be saved?" After professing to having left everything for Jesus, they seem hopelessly troubled. The shocked man who asked Jesus about eternal life departs grieving. The disciples remain, although no less troubled. However we ask the question about "eternal life" or "who can be saved" or "is it true," it hangs over us like Damocles' sword.

When Jesus tells the disciples that "for God all things are possible," he offers a way out of the dilemma. When the man poses his question, the operative word is "I," as in "What can *I* do?" Yet Jesus reveals his divine wisdom by indirectly teaching these disciples that all is absolutely dependent on God—even human striving. An authentic and faithful theological understanding of stewardship

*Joanna Adams, "The Only Question," in Thomas G. Long and Cornelius Plantinga Jr., eds., *A Chorus of Witnesses: Model Sermons for Today's Preacher* (Grand Rapids: Eerdmans, 1994), 268.

apprehends this: God is the owner of all, and we merely borrow for a time the gifts God offers.

Stewards gain confidence by knowing that whatever gifts we bring to God's realm, whether great or small, God multiplies our offering as Jesus multiplies the fish and loaves (see Mark 6:33–44 and parallels). So whatever we offer, God increases. When God provides, even by use of our hands, then there will always be enough. Eternal life is God's gift to us. Our lone task is to receive God's bounty and pass along the gift.

Sunday between October 16 and 22 inclusive

Job 38:1–7 (34–41)   God Provides

> *"Who provides for the raven its prey, when its young ones cry to God?"*
> (Job 38:41)

Lincoln and Douglas had their debates as did Socrates and his opponents. In world literature, however, it may be difficult to locate a superior, more passionate argument than the one that comprises the book of Job. What makes this protracted discussion so germane is its topic—human suffering. Of all the deliberated and perplexing subjects that have occupied people's minds throughout history, human suffering must be at the very top of the list.

In essence, the Lord's reply to Job from the whirlwind simply puts the debate into a grander perspective. It consists of four chapters of rhetorical questions (Job 38–41). For stewardship these divine questions remind us that God provides.

Thus far in the book of Job, Job obstinately disputes his suffering. As well, Job's so-called friends weigh in with assorted theological resolutions to Job's bewildered queries. None seem satisfactory, at least from Job's viewpoint. Finally, the Lord speaks from the whirlwind. The whirlwind assumes the status of a theophany. From the whirlwind the Lord inaugurates the blistering sequence of questions. The Lord's questions are addressed to Job, but they may as well be addressed to Job's friends—and by extension to all of us who ponder the theological topic of theodicy, the justice of God.

The final verse of today's lesson will capture the attention of those chiefly interested in stewardship themes. The Lord asks, "Who provides for the raven its prey, when its young ones cry to God, and wander about for lack of food?" This question is a question of providence. Who provides what and to whom? The writer grants no space for the human debaters to answer. The context, however, robustly implies that the provider is the Lord God.

Jesus, when addressing human anxiety about what to eat and what to wear, reminds his listeners: "Look at the birds of the air; they neither sow nor reap nor gather into barns, and yet your heavenly Father feeds them. Are you not of more value than they?" (Matt. 6:26). Jesus alludes to the all-caring and all-compassionate nature of God to provide for God's children. We worry and we fret, but to what end? God will provide.

God's providence is the bedrock of Christian conviction. If there is anything that convinces people of God's authentic existence, it is this: God gives us what we need and when we need it. In Exodus God demonstrates this divine attribute plainly in the giving of manna (Exod. 16).

The lesson from Job reminds all of us of a constructive truth in our habitually troubled world: despite our questions concerning God's ways in the world, and despite our despair at what little we have to offer, God will provide. When we take the gifts God has put at our disposal and use the discerning spirit with which God endows us, then what we offer as stewards will be sufficient. If God provides for unclean birds of the air, then think what God can do for us—and through us.

Sunday between October 23 and 29 inclusive

Job 42:1–6, 10–17   When Friends Fail

"The LORD *restored the fortunes of Job when he had prayed for his friends."*
(Job 42:10)

When Jesus said, "Love your enemies and pray for those who persecute you" (Matt. 5:44) or "Bless those who curse you, pray for those who abuse you" (Luke 6:28), we may doubt that he had Job's friends in mind. But he could have.

Job's friends do indeed play the part of "enemy" if we read the whole text with care. At one point Job cries out, "My friends scorn me" (Job 16:20). If prayer is one of God's households we stewards manage, then our prayer life entails the spiritual management of God's sacred gifts. God entrusts us to oversee our prayer life. To pray for and with the downtrodden, the sick, the grieving, and the helpless is no stretch for most believers. Yet we recoil at the suggestion of praying for our enemies.

In today's text Job answers the Lord with all the humility that he can muster. He confesses, "I have uttered what I did not understand, things too wonderful for me, which I did not know." He "repent[s] in dust and ashes." This repentance is all the more remarkable when we recall that the Lord said to Eliphaz, "My wrath is kindled against you and against your two friends; for you have not spoken of me what is right, as my servant Job has" (42:7). By this time in the "great debate," the Lord is advocating on Job's behalf.

The final verses (10–17) have troubled biblical exegetes. The horrible story of Job's suffering now seems to have a fairy tale ending. Many scholars presume that a later editor came back and "fixed the text" because the original ending was simply too raw. This kind of thinking is not unusual; Mark 16 has similar editorial issues. Bible readers may find texts with several alternative endings of Mark, much as a movie on DVD may have multiple endings.

Yet we have a text and must make the best of it. What could the faith community have been trying to teach when it included in the canonical record that "the LORD restored the fortunes of Job when he had prayed for his friends"?

Satan's question, regardless of who asked it, is certainly worthy of theological consideration: "Does Job fear God for nothing?" (1:9). The restoration of Job's fortune indicates the fitting acuity of such a question. It is crucial to note the sequence, however. The Lord restores the fortunes of Job only after he has prayed for his friends. In the text there is no intimation that restoration is likely. Job may not have considered it. He simply prayed for his friends after the divine rebuke. Make no mistake, this prayer would have been challenging.

When we remember Job's litany of woe—"I am a laughingstock to my friends" (12:4); "My relatives and my close friends have failed me" (19:14); and "All my intimate friends abhor me" (19:19)—we can be sure that Job's prayers did not trip off his tongue. Yet in the end Job is what he was in the beginning, which is "blameless and upright" (Job 1:1). Job's prayer reflects not only who Job is but also what he understands the Lord to be, namely, one who offers forgiveness.

Genuine stewards know that we manage our prayer life. God asks us to pray for others, but God never draws up short. God knows that we cannot simultaneously have hate in our heart and prayers on our lips for people that the world calls "enemy." To put a human face on the enemy is to hope for reconciliation. God's will is that as stewards of prayer, we can learn to love our enemies—even when they are disguised as friends.

Sunday between October 30 and November 5 inclusive

Mark 12:28–34   The Good Scribe?

"One of the scribes came near and heard them disputing."
(Mark 12:28)

Good stewards are judicious disciples who evaluate God's gifts and deploy them in ways that build up God's realm. Today's text highlights a scribe with whom Jesus resonates.

Usually the appearance of a scribe in the New Testament signals a confrontation between Jesus and one arm of the Jewish religious establishment. Up to this point in Gospel, there have been an assortment of occasions pertaining to the scribes' importance in Mark's story of Jesus. For example, Mark suggests that the scribes do not have authority (Mark 1:22), that they question Jesus "in their hearts" (2:6), that they ask questions or make remarks that throw a negative light on Jesus' ministry (2:16; 3:22; 7:5), and that they will reject Jesus in company with the elders and chief priests (8:31). The scribes are among the Jewish authorities who consistently argue with Jesus (9:14). Because of Jesus' spellbinding effect on the crowds whom he teaches, the scribes look for a way to stop him (11:18).

Thus, when Jesus says to the scribe, "You are not far from the kingdom of God," Jesus' affirmation offers us a circumstance for consideration. Jesus' offering praise to one of the religious authorities is worth documenting—and Mark has done this. The astute Bible reader and steward of the "mysteries of God" promptly detects that Jesus resonates with this individual, unnamed scribe. Mark tells us that "Jesus saw that he answered wisely." The scribe's wise answer elicits Jesus' response that he is not far from the kingdom of God.

The scribe responds to Jesus' assertion, which boils down the whole law to the essentials of loving God and neighbor. The scribe pronounces that Jesus' teaching "is much more important than all the whole burnt offerings and sacrifices," which is to say, "Although ritual may be essential, what is most indispensable is the loving of both God and neighbor." Maybe we could say that loving neighbor is loving God and vice versa.

In the realm of stewardship, we church folk at times put too much emphasis on pledge cards or annual estimates of giving. Jesus' encounter with the "good scribe" reminds us of a vital truth of proper relationship to God. Perhaps our pledge cards or estimates of giving—in other words, our equivalent of "burnt offerings and sacrifices"—can too habitually become substitutes for something deeper and more consequential than our outward devotion. Loving God and neighbor in heartfelt ways continually motivates whatever other outward manifestations our fidelity may reveal. As one of my old preacher-mentors repeats as a mantra, "People can give without loving, but no one can love without giving."

We suffer the same temptations first-century people did. We like control. We control our lives and even our relationship with God. But when we see Jesus and a scribe in accord, then we fittingly pay rapt attention. Possibly the scribe and Jesus agree with Isaiah's question: "What to me is the multitude of your sacrifices? says the LORD." Isaiah provides a steward's answer: "Wash yourselves; make yourselves clean; remove the evil of your doings from before my eyes; cease to do evil, learn to do good; seek justice, rescue the oppressed, defend the orphan, plead for the widow" (Isa. 1:11, 16–17).

All Saints'
(November 1, or may be used on the first Sunday in November)

Isaiah 25:6–9   God Stewards God's People

"Then the Lord GOD will wipe away the tears."
(Isa. 25:8)

All Saints' Day may be one of the most important Sabbaths that we celebrate as God's people. Stewardship and what saints (or believers) have done for God's people fit like a bowstring in a nock. Sometimes the day overwhelms our ability to articulate its meaning. Emotion renders our tongues practically inarticulate today. Nonetheless, we offer our beloved sisters and brothers back to God in death as we honor their sacred memory.

Beside a six-foot open grave we celebrated the life of a saint from our little church. People were grief stricken. They genuinely loved this man. He had been kind to all and unfailingly helpful to those he encountered. I too was anguished when I intoned the words of a thousand years: "And I heard a voice from heaven saying, 'Write this: Blessed are the dead who from now on die in the Lord.' 'Yes,' says the Spirit, 'they will rest from their labors, for their deeds follow them'" (Rev. 14:13). Later as I reflected on the day, I remembered our friend as a blessed fellow who could legitimately rejoice that his deeds followed him, for his deeds were pure, righteous, and full of Christian virtue. We did not need to say much about our departed friend because his life had written a whole new Gospel.

In the Isaiah text for All Saints' Day, the Lord of hosts throws a great banquet for the faithful—a feast, as they say, "fit for kings." Accompanying this good news, Isaiah reminds readers of the earlier desolation of an unnamed city. The Lord left this city as "a fortified city [in] a ruin" (Isa. 25:2). In addressing human pride, Herbert N. Schneidau writes: "A most revealing demonstration of this devaluation of cultural attainments is the Bible's treatment of cities, which after all give their name to 'civilization' . . . Cities are only a symbol of what arouses Yahweh's wrath."* Haughty pride in people's cultural achievements sows seeds of ingratitude to God.

By definition, stewardship denotes the management of another's property or resources. No one can steward that which that person owns. Therefore, faithful stewards plainly appreciate that their Christian stewardship derives from managing God's resources, given to believers to administer for the benefit of God's people.

At death we Christians believe that God will take care of us. God indeed "will wipe away the tears from all faces," both the quick and the dead. In the meantime, that is, before we die, our stewardship necessitates our managing on earth what God provides from heaven's storehouse. When a church opens a soup kitchen for the hungry, it merely prepares food resources already provided by God. When we bless our food during table grace, we simply bless a second time that which God first blessed at its creation. When we lodge evacuees of a natural disaster, we put into play the resources that God has previously provided for such compassionate purposes.

The psalmist sings, "This is the LORD for whom we have waited; let us be glad and rejoice in his salvation." As we wait for the Lord, we use the means that God has provided us to care for God's people and God's world. Faithful stewards simply redirect God's resources, by way of our meager talents, toward persons in need. In other words, God's distribution of blessings often comes indirectly through human discipleship. Might we say that discipleship is synonymous with stewardship? To follow Jesus as learners is to become those who offer their best stewardship households to the master.

---

*Herbert N. Schneidau, *Sacred Discontent: The Bible and Western Tradition* (Berkeley: University of California Press, 1976), 5–6.

Sunday between November 6 and 12 inclusive

Mark 12:38–44   A Mentor for Good Giving

"She out of her poverty has put in everything she had."
(Mark 12:44)

"You've come a long way, baby," the old commercial suggests to a new age of women whom a particular cigarette company hopes will become a new generation of smokers. This signals but one of thousands of changes in the status and role of women from days gone by. Women not only vote today but hold significant political offices. Women are leaders in many Christian denominations, and they hold many professional positions: doctors, lawyers, judges, and such. The economy of women has undergone a seismic shift from the day when Jesus told this story, traditionally known as the "Widow's Mite."

Women in general, and widows in particular, control a vast amount of wealth in the United States. Often this wealth comes from inheritance at the time of a spouse's death; however, hard-working women accumulate riches through professional compensation and also by being shrewd investors. Thus, in some ways the social circumstance that Jesus established his parable upon is no longer in force. Yet women and children are most vulnerable to poverty, a fact that should never escape people with a conscience.

Nonetheless, the Widow's Mite is a dearly beloved story. As originally told by Jesus, it embodies the stewardship law that all persons have some gift to give, no matter how large or how small. Thus, the story is more about the willingness to give rather than the ability to give.

Recently a friend shared a letter with me from an inmate in a Texas prison. The inmate had addressed his letter, "Dear believers in Christ." Through participants in our church's prison ministry, this man had learned that our congregation was helping relocate fifty families from Hurricane Katrina. Writing out of his profound thanksgiving for the grace of God, he told us, "I am indigent at this particular time, but I'm still very eager to help with the little that I have."

He enclosed in his letter, as far as we could determine, pretty much everything he had that inmates can mail out of prison—twenty stamps, which we used to send thank-you letters to all who contributed from outside our church. "Hopefully you would please be kind enough to sow these twenty stamps toward the fifty families of the disaster," he wrote. He closed his letter by announcing, "During my troublesome time, God has taught me that when I have little, I have just enough to help someone else, and when I have plenty, I have nothing because it all belongs to God!"

This inmate caught the widow's spirit of faith. As Jesus said of the widow, Jesus says of all who offer themselves completely to God: "Truly I tell you, this poor widow has put in more than all those who are contributing to the treasury. For all of them have contributed out of their abundance; but she out of her poverty has put in everything she had." Our incarcerated friend, despite his outward circumstances, contributed what he could. Jesus' widow and our friend are mentors to those who want to learn about Christian stewardship.

Sunday between November 13 and 19 inclusive

1 Samuel 1:4–20   Parenting as Total Dedication

"[Hannah] prayed to the LORD, and wept bitterly."
(1 Sam. 1:10)

Good stewards know how to "count the cost," to use a phrase from Luke's Gospel. Jesus speaks about what it means to be a disciple and asks, "For which of you, intending to build a tower, does not first sit down and estimate the cost, to see whether he has enough to complete it?" (Luke 14:28). Good stewards understand the terms of discipleship. The lesson from 1 Samuel illustrates a mother's dedication to answered prayer. In getting what her heart desired Hannah must also give that desire back to God.

The story that begins 1 Samuel is the account of answered prayer—but prayer that occasions a condition. Hannah, a barren woman, prays fervently for a child. Hebrew culture commonly stigmatized childless women, and Hannah's husband's other wife, Peninnah, taunts Hannah without mercy. Hannah even bargains to dedicate her child to the Lord's service should one be born to her. In time she conceives and bears a son whom she names Samuel.

Eager parents want to see their child's first step, but not Hannah. She knows that each day brings her closer to satisfying her vow to God. Even Samuel's first word reminds Hannah that she will soon surrender him. Finally, after weaning the boy, Hannah offers Samuel to Eli, Shiloh's priest. In offering Samuel, Hannah tells Eli, " 'Therefore I have lent him to the LORD; as long as he lives, he is given to the LORD.' " (1 Sam. 1:28).

My wife once noticed that my sermon title had to do with parenting. She asked, "Are we having a pulpit guest Sunday?" Honestly, who among us can set ourselves up as experts on parenting? When it comes to parenting, even the most capable folks become dizzy and unsure of their footing. Trying to raise children reminds me of the old Peace Corps slogan, slightly altered: "Parenting is the hardest job you will ever love."

No matter how our children turn out, we love them. I have seen dozens of mothers whose children are scheduled for execution interviewed on television or in newspapers, and not one mother has ever said, "My child deserves what he is getting." Rather, they invariably say, "He is a good boy." This sentiment makes Hannah's willingness to offer Samuel to the Lord all the more remarkable. When she uttered her prayer, she was earnest. When she negotiated with God in prayer, Hannah lived up to her end of her bargain. Hannah counted the cost and completed what she had vowed to do—she offered her only son to the God who had given him to her in the first place.

Perhaps we parents all sacrifice our children to some god or another. Would that we faithful stewards offered our children to the God who provides a basis for human wholeness. Would it not be better to surrender our children to a life of full-time Christian service than to nurture them within a materialistic world of buying and selling?

Hannah recognized, as emotional as that recognition no doubt was, the psalmist's truth: "For a day in your courts is better than a thousand elsewhere. I would rather be a doorkeeper in the house of my God than live in the tents of wickedness" (Ps. 84:10).

Good stewards measure the gift of God and respond in faith. Faithful parents grasp that what they do with and for their children is part of their stewardship of God's gift. God offers us children with the knowledge that we will give them back to God.

Christ the King/Reign of Christ
(Sunday between November 20 and 26 inclusive)

Psalm 132:1–12   Do We Look Out for God?

"I will not give sleep to my eyes . . . until I find a place for the LORD"
(Ps. 132:4–5)

One of the key declarations a steward makes is that everything belongs to God. Because God creates everything, God owns everything. The Nicene Creed, in affirming our belief in the one God, announces God's sovereignty. It reminds believers that God is "maker of heaven and earth, of all that is, seen and unseen." Sovereignty is the order of the day as we celebrate Christ the King/Reign of Christ Sunday. Worship acknowledges today that Jesus Christ is God's crown prince, our Messiah. The final Sabbath of the Christian year offers a piece of the good news we need not overlook or take for granted: Jesus, our Sovereign, is God incarnate among us.

A friend once told me of visiting Scotland and seeing two things that elated him. The first site he visited was the Old Course at St. Andrews, where golf purportedly originated. He also visited St. Giles, the Edinburgh cathedral where John Knox was a pastor and writer and played his role in the Protestant Reformation. St. Giles's tower depicts a crown. As people pass by and see the crown, it reminds them that Jesus is the "King of kings" (see 1 Tim. 6:15; Rev. 17:14; 19:16).

It is fitting that Psalm 132 is in the lectionary on this Christ the King/Reign of Christ Sunday, for this is a day in which believers measure the past year against Christ's reign in all its purity. Psalm 132 is a "psalm of ascent," or a "royal psalm." Some scholars suggest that Israel used this psalm when the community moved the ark of the covenant to Jerusalem. The ark for Israel, of course, signified God's presence among them. It may have represented a "stool" upon which God sat.

The psalm's opening prayer implores God not to forget David and all he has undergone to "find a place for the LORD, a dwelling place for the Mighty One of Jacob." For Israel, David was plainly the prototypical monarch. David was brave in battle, shrewd in politics, and an individual that "the LORD has sought out . . . after his own heart" (1 Sam. 13:14). Yet from hindsight a reflective person might ask, "Should not David have been a little more concerned about looking after himself and his behavior than worried about a dwelling place for the Lord?" Perhaps.

Yet Psalm 132 provides readers a double-barreled promise. The first pledge comes from David, via the psalmist's lips, that "I will not give sleep to my eyes . . . until I find a place for the LORD." However, a second promise also emerges from verses 11–12. This promise states, "The LORD swore to David a sure oath from which he will not turn back: 'One of the sons of your body I will set on your throne.'" Further, the Lord will do this if the sons of David keep covenant with him. Kings promise to serve the people, and likewise the people promise to serve the king. It may not always come to pass, but that is part of the covenant between the ruler and the ruled.

Believers make promises to God, and God makes promises to us. This is the nature of covenant faith. Yet faithful stewards also know that while our human promises may be well intentioned, they remain less than reliable. However, the covenantal promises God makes to God's people are always unswerving. In Psalm 132, among other things, we recognize the earnestness of human promise making to God. At the same time, we also read about the steady and consistent promise that God makes on our behalf. To become a faithful steward is to rest in the assurance that God's promise to God's people is a promise that not only is reliable but also eternal. We serve Christ the king.

Thanksgiving Day

Matthew 6:25–33   Therefore Do Not Worry

"Is not life more than food, and the body more than clothing?"
(Matt. 6:25)

I have occasionally pondered Alfred E. Neuman's question from *Mad* magazine: "What? Me worry?" If Mr. Neuman indeed does not worry, then he is surely unique among the human beings God created—and for this reason he may be, in fact, mad. Theologians spanning Christian tradition from Augustine to Luther to Reinhold Niebuhr and Karl Barth have written about the aspect of the human condition that we know as anxiety. This tradition extends, in fact, back at least as far as Jesus, who speaks of worry in the Gospel passage for today.

If the Christian calendar presents a liturgical day tailored for stewardship at its most weighty, then that day would be Thanksgiving. Naturally, many worship purists hold that Thanksgiving is more national holiday than Christian holy day, the argument being that every day is a day of thanksgiving for the faithful. Yet Thanksgiving offers us an appropriate time to pay homage to the human impulse for thankfulness.

Thanksgiving is difficult to preach. Why? Because almost everyone believes that "we all ought to be more thankful." What does a preacher say after "We should be more thankful"? It is at this point that Jesus' teaching from the Sermon on the Mount becomes constructive. Nothing comes as a bigger shock than when Jesus begins this sermon with the Beatitudes: "Blessed are those who mourn, for they will be comforted. . . . Blessed are those who are persecuted for righteousness' sake, for theirs is the kingdom of heaven. Blessed are you when people revile you and persecute you and utter all kinds of evil against you falsely on my account"—when Jesus says this, is it not enough to make us scratch our heads and wonder? Worldly people simply cannot comprehend this thinking—either in Jesus' day or in our day.

This may be the point. The world that Jesus creates in the faithful human imagination is not a world created by human effort or ingenuity. Rather, it is a world created in the image, or better, the imagination of God. The world Jesus offers us is what Jesus calls the "kingdom of God," which is a sort of shorthand rendering of the world God envisioned at creation.

Thus, for Christian stewards thanksgiving is not so much directed at "the many blessings God has already bestowed upon us." Rather, faithful stewards direct their thanksgiving to an unknown future where we experience life—God's greatest gift, a gift that we will live into and out of as we stewards function as God's people.

In today's Gospel lesson Jesus implies that all people are anxious about the necessities of life: food, clothing, and shelter. He in no way discounts the importance of these life requirements. Neither, conversely, does Jesus grant material things the pride of place that they routinely demand. God provides these essentials, yet Jesus knows that there is something more important to life. This is a human-divine relationship based on being nonanxious about material well-being. The basis of relationship with the divine is the knowledge that God sustains by something else—that something is the assurance that only God provides. Faith and trust replace our slavery to anxious feelings. This faith is indeed something over which to give thanks. It is the very essence of the good news.

YEAR C

Advent and Christmas

First Sunday of Advent

Luke 21:25–36   The Confidence of a Steward

"When these things begin to take place, stand up and raise your heads."
(Luke 21:28)

God promises abundance to God's people. Abundance is having enough—more than enough—to survive and even to thrive. Americans live amid plenty. The world's majority envy such prosperity. These people who suffer want are victims of unjust economic systems, war, famine, or disease. Oddly, we Americans exist as if we lived in a circumstance of scarceness. I recently heard a radio personality describe a scene where team officials at the door of a bus passed out "per diems" for meals and incidental expenses to multimillion-dollar athletes. The commentator described these athletes receiving their "lunch money" as "waifs and strays opening presents on Christmas Day at an orphanage." Millionaires with few fears about material security live as if they

165

occupied a world of scarceness. However, stewards live with poise in God's abundance.

Our lesson today comes from Luke's Gospel. The text relates Jesus' response to a disciple's question: "Teacher, when will this be, and what will be the sign that this is about to take place?" (Luke 21:7). Jesus speaks not only of signs and persecution but also of Jerusalem's destruction. Next Jesus turns to today's theme: the coming of the Son of Man and the lesson from the fig tree.

Typically, fear compels preachers to offer these texts as warnings of "the wrath to come." Yet notice what Jesus tells the disciples to do when they see these apocalyptic signs. Contrary to Revelation's account (6:15–16), where "kings . . . and the generals and the rich and the powerful . . . hid in the caves . . . calling to the mountains and rocks, 'Fall on us,'" Jesus instructs the disciples to "stand up and raise your heads, because your redemption is drawing near." In this counterintuitive teaching, Jesus reminds the disciples of God's absolute power and providence. If and when the wrath of God comes, we can do nothing to save ourselves. Instead, faithful people remember that all human hope is pinned on God. Only God can save. This is the reliable essence of the gospel.

This is a counterintuitive teaching because from our human experience we know that when startled, most people duck or hide. When frightened, we tend to hunker down and seek cover. But here, in the midst of "distress among nations" and "the powers of the heavens [that] will be shaken," Jesus directs believers to look up. Jesus suggests this because our help will come from on high in the figure of the Son of Man.

The kind of confidence that God offers us in Jesus is simply divine. Despite all evidence to the contrary, faithful people remember that God alone is our only salvation. When handling the gifts and households God gives us to manage as stewards, it is vital that we remember this promise. While we may hoard our possessions and time, God does provide. Faithful stewards function out of this dependable confidence.

A foster parent once told me about two little girls who had been starved and had a difficult time trusting adults. The older child had lived with the family for about six months. She tried to persuade the youngest child that she would always have enough food to eat. The foster parents had hid food all over the house so that the first child could tell the new arrival, "Come and see—there is food everywhere!" As confident stewards we know that God provides. Our task is to look up and notice the abundance all around us—and share that abundance with others.

Second Sunday of Advent

Luke 3:1–6   Stewards Formed in the Wilderness

"The word of God came to John son of Zechariah in the wilderness."
                                                         (Luke 3:2)

One of Christian stewardship's most pernicious myths is that one must possess a lot of money to be a good steward. Yet stewardship concerns not how much but how well we manage what God has given us. Even in the wilderness of poverty or of pain, God summons believers to be faithful stewards regardless of circumstance.

The lectionary attends to the ministry of John the Baptizer on the second Sunday in Advent in all three years of the lectionary cycle. Today Luke describes John's opening prophetic salvo. As he often does, Luke couches his narrative in the historical details of people and places of his time. Some biblical scholars dispute the precise historical detail that Luke offers. However, Luke is more interested in theology than the dates and places of events. Bible readers catch a historic sense from this story—Emperor Tiberius, Pontius Pilate, and Herod offer an authentic feel. Luke also mentions genuine places too: Ituraea and Trachonitis. This story has a historic texture.

After setting the context, Luke relates John's preaching. John goes for the emancipation jugular in "proclaiming a baptism of repentance for the forgiveness of sins." Thus, he ties together Isaiah's prophecy of the voice in the wilderness to the coming of the Messiah who reveals "the salvation of God." For John, the wilderness is a place of forming the spiritual life for believers. This wilderness image suggests that God often shapes our spiritual life in desert moments. Regularly, the wilderness becomes the crucible in which our most cherished values develop. At times, modern people stumble into a wilderness not so much in arid regions but in places such as prison.

For some, prison incubates hate. For others, prison becomes a site to find the divine will that hammers out a vision of what pleases God. For example, some of the seeds of Egypt and Israel's 1978 Camp David Peace Accord were sown in Anwar Sadat while in prison. Eldridge Cleaver recreated his life and vision in prison. Many biblical personalities found themselves tested in prison. The Bible's inmates include Joseph, Jeremiah, Samson, Peter, Paul, Jesus, and John the Baptizer. A good steward recognizes that even in the bleakest experiences God fashions our spirits. The wilderness both tests and shapes stewards.

When God finds us, it may not be at the optimum moment of our spiritual seeking. Yet out of our depths and even in "our dark night of the soul," God can and does transform us. In dire circumstances, those whom God shapes most fundamentally God also makes into good and faithful stewards. God fashioned a people, Israel, while they were in Egyptian bondage and then called them into the wilderness. In Acts, God constructed the church with apostles who kept finding themselves in Roman jails.

During the season of Advent we focus on gifts for others. Too often many things essentially tangential to the deepest meaning of Christ's coming overwhelm us. We rarely, if ever, hear the word stewardship uttered. Yet genuine disciples are faithful stewards. Therefore, if for some reason this season we think, "It sure doesn't seem like Christmas," then do not worry. The great gift of Advent/Christmas is God's gift of Christ—the Word made flesh. We remember these words to encourage us when we feel un-Christmassy: "The word of God came to John son of Zechariah in the wilderness." In John's proclamation we remember that stewardship is not forged in ease, but rather in the wilderness where God is. Good stewards are tested and found faithful.

Third Sunday of Advent

Luke 3:7–18   The Stewardship of Good Questions

"What then should we do?"
(Luke 3:10)

Via Luke's Gospel, we continue today to explore John the Baptizer's ministry. Two questions arrest the attention of attentive readers. The first is the challenge John throws down to those who come for baptism: "Who warned you to flee from the wrath to come?" Clearly this is a rhetorical question, for plainly John expects no answer but asks it to capture the listener's attention. The text's second question is one stewards may want to consider. After John's scorching harangue, the people ask: "What then should we do?" It is a good question. It is an earnest question that seeks direction. The people want to know how to respond to John's prophetic word.

There are many kinds of questions. There are statements that pose as questions. There are questions for information and clarification. There are questions that wax hypothetically as well as kindhearted questions that ask how someone feels. The people's question to John asks what action they might take to avoid being those who do "not bear good fruit." To be a steward of questions is to be a faithful disciple. Those who steward questions recognize that our minds are a stewardship household we manage. These conscientious stewards recall Jesus' words, broadening Deuteronomy 6:4–5, about loving God "with our mind" (Mark 12:30).

Nobel Prize winner Isidor Isaac Rabi is an example of the consequence of good questions. Rabi said that when his mother inquired about his school day she never asked what he had learned, but rather, "Did you ask a good question today?" This, Rabi said, made him a scientist.

Luke portrays Jesus as full of wisdom. In a remarkable passage about Jesus' own youthful precociousness, he writes, "After three days they found him in the temple, sitting among the teachers, listening to them and asking them questions" (Luke 2:46). Our text today highlights good questions. The right question at the right time creates new visions and new means by which faithful stewards can become better disciples.

In the church we too often deflect questions. This inclination stifles mature faith. In truth, God expects seeking people to ask of faith strong questions. In good conscience we ask, for although God's ways are not our ways, we never get closer to God's mind than when we ask candid questions.

The stewardship of the doctrine of God and the insights garnered for daily life reside in our questions about how faith and life intersect. To steward such questions reveals a willingness not to settle for simple answers. It also spurs us on to better and more compassionate discipleship. We embrace our questions as stewards of the mind.

Rainer Maria Rilke, more than many literary figures, could describe the torment of the human heart without giving way to a cynical mind. Rilke's words are similar to Scripture; we may not understand them, but somehow we trust that we will someday live into them. He wrote:

> Have patience with everything unresolved in your heart and . . . try to love the questions themselves as if they were locked rooms or books written in a very foreign language. Don't search for the answers, which could not be given to you now, because you would not be able to live them. And the point is to live everything. Live the questions now. Perhaps then, someday far in the future, you will gradually, without even noticing it, live your way into the answer.*

Rilke understood the value of questions.

Fourth Sunday of Advent

Hebrews 10:5–10   A Steward's Christmas Gift to God

"See, I have come to do your will."
(Heb. 10:9)

If the homiletic tendency of late is "narrative preaching," then preaching this Hebrews text poses a clear-cut challenge to preachers. The text is linear and pursues an understanding of the incarnation. For this doctrinal reason, the creators of the Revised Common Lectionary selected this Epistle passage for the last Sunday in Advent. There is no narrative to work with, for example, such as a miracle story or parable. Add to this the challenge that this is the last Sunday prior to Christmas and our focus is on stewardship. Thus, the preacher has her work cut out for her. Yet despite these hurdles, this Hebrews text does offer a portal through which we can see God's intention for sending Jesus into the world—a distinctive Advent theme.

*Rainer Maria Rilke, *Letters to a Young Poet,* trans. Stephen Mitchell (New York: Modern Library, 2001), 34.

Most parishioners are in the throes of last-minute gift shopping. Many gifts are heartfelt, although some we give out of obligation. This is the common perspective for the Sunday before Christmas. For stewards, gifts signify something important. What Hebrews ponders in this passage emerges out of a meticulous discussion of high priests, sacrifices, and salvation. When the author writes "consequently," the inference is that worshipers offer sacrifices year after year. Yet because the sacrifices are repeated, the implication is that the worshipers have not been "cleansed once for all" (Heb. 10:2). The writer urges readers to recognize that the annual sacrifices simply underscore that "there is a reminder of sin year after year."

Thus, "consequently" denotes how God healed the human state of sin for a people who could not remedy their sin for themselves. Crediting a quotation from Psalm 40:6–8 to Jesus, the epistle proposes God's desire is more than sacrifice. God wants obedience.

When we read, "I have come to do your will" (vv. 7 and 9), we see adherence to God's will. The next sentence in verse 9 then reveals the purpose for Christ's coming: "He abolishes the first in order to establish the second." Thus begins a "new earth."

One of the chief reasons to preach this text is to remind believers that from cradle to grave, Jesus is God's incarnation. The church usually divides Jesus' passion from Jesus' birth. Yet to understand the full salvific role of Jesus, at times we need to remember that in Jesus' birth we also see the shadow of the cross. From this reality we recall Simeon's blessing to Mary: "This child is destined for the falling and the rising of many in Israel, and to be a sign that will be opposed so that the inner thoughts of many will be revealed—and a sword will pierce your own soul too" (Luke 2:34–35).

What does this Hebrews lesson tell stewards about the gospel of Jesus Christ? Hebrews reminds us that we are like our spiritual ancestors. They too offered sacrifices to God but failed to "do God's will." Today we live in a world in which critical judgment has more to do with the whims of popular opinion than it does with the experience, expertise, or judicious reasoning of people who actually possess knowledge. We have built our culture on the likes or dislikes of the masses. However this eliminates society's pretensions, we are now at the mercy of marketers and packagers of culture who, as a rule, appeal to our culture's lowest common denominator.

An enduring gift of Advent/Christmas is to appreciate that God has a precious gift for us. This gift is the gift of holiness and perfection. It comes wrapped in swaddling clothes. We find it not under the Christmas tree but in a Bethlehem manger. For stewards this is a Christmas gift from God. Our thank you to the divine is simply the life we give back to God. Stewardship begins when we say, "I have come to do your will."

Christmas Eve
[See Year A]

Christmas Day
[See Year B]

First Sunday after Christmas Day

1 Samuel 2:18–20, 26   Stewards of the Promise

> *"May the LORD repay you with children by this woman*
> *for the gift that she made to the LORD."*
>
> (1 Sam. 2:20)

One of the blessings of God is that through faith we can strive to be more godly people. For stewardship this means that what God does for us, God then enables us to do for others. For example, the little yet powerful phrase "We love because he first loved us" (1 John 4:19) can illumine a host of divine characteristics within us. Playing with the wording we might say, "We promise because he first promised us." God in Christ has offered humankind a splendid promise, which we in turn can offer others. In so doing, believers become stewards of a household we call "promise."

Today's lesson is a condensed part of an ample story. First Samuel begins by addressing the power of a promise. Hannah is a barren woman who prays fervently to God for a child. The story also relates that Hannah's husband, Elkanah, has another wife, Peninnah. She has children, but Hannah has none. Peninnah taunts Hannah incessantly. For years Hannah has bargained with God to dedicate any child to God's service if God will give her a child. This was Hannah's promise to God. The biblical text tells us, "In due time Hannah conceived and bore a son. She named him Samuel, for she said, 'I have asked him of the LORD'" (1:20).

Today is the calendar's final Sunday of the year. It is a time when many make New Year's resolutions. We resolve to make promises to ourselves, others, or God, but breaking promises commonly seems easier than keeping them. We have become so familiar with other people's broken promises that we see promise breaking as a likely human penchant. Advertising promises, political promises, economic promises, and the broken promises of those who love us make us a bit pessimistic when someone offers us yet another promise.

However, the promises we make before God and one another help us recall that a promise is a pledge or a covenant. Thus, reliable stewards manage the household of promise. We promise our children at baptism that we will raise them in a Christian home and place them in the worshiping community. The church promises to help raise them and teach them the faith. We promise to "love, cherish, and honor" one another in the church's marriage ritual. We build strong families on such promises. When we promise to be faithful to our church community by "being loyal to it with our prayers, presence, gifts, and service," we build a strong church by way of that promise. Genuine church growth is not numerical. It is rather a result of people keeping their vows to God.

Israel's history changed because Hannah made a promise to God and kept it. As we approach a new year, may we never miscalculate the importance and freeing exercise of making promises. A promise is what makes us who we are and what we are to become with God's help. Perhaps our promise to God comes in the form of a pledge to the new budget. Perhaps it is a commitment to teach the seventh-grade Sunday school class. Whatever your promise is, remember that you are a steward of the sacred promise, like Hannah.

January 1–New Year (A, B, and C)

Ecclesiastes 3:1–13   On Being and Time

"For everything there is a season, and a time for every matter."
(Eccl. 3:1)

When the Preacher begins musing on life, these meditations seem peculiar when set against the background of the biblical witness. Some Bible scholars see this writer of Ecclesiastes as an accomplished cynic, while other scholars point out bursts of joy within the text. It is difficult to discern an obvious literary structure to the work. Each of these issues, no doubt, contributed to the decision by the Revised Common Lectionary's creators to use only one text from Ecclesiastes during the full three-year lectionary cycle. New Year's Day is the day for Ecclesiastes.

For most people, New Year's Day is a day to take stock of one's life. In the secular world there is much focus on parades and college football. But in the church's life believers examine where they have been and where they are going. The calendar encourages this kind of contemplative attitude—and the calendar is a tool of stewardship. A used and somewhat soiled calendar from last year reminds us of commitments made and commitments kept. A fresh calendar is a map of where we may want to go in the year to come. The calendar reminds us of what Ecclesiastes suggests when it tells us, "For everything there is a season, and a time for every matter under heaven." A spotless new date book suggests that we can now schedule "every matter under heaven."

There are logically many stewardship households. Some easily named are money, volunteerism, listening, leadership, prayer, voting, and influence. Yet the way we spend our time is one of the elemental gauges of what we value. Ecclesiastes understands the significance of time—the word "time" appears thirty times in the NRSV translation.

The problem with the Preacher's meditation on time is that it seems so relative. How much help to the steward can the statement that there is "a time to kill, and a time to heal" be? I appreciate Will Willimon's remark in his sermon "Untimely Word": "There is a time for everything and only God knows what that time is! There's a time to speak and a time to keep silent, but you'll never know what time it is! I despise Ecclesiastes."* Yet it does appear in the midst of all this relativity with respect to time that God has placed us as stewards over time. We may use it wisely or not. When we use time recklessly, then Will Rogers's retort has a ring of familiarity: "Half our life is spent trying to find something to do with the time we have rushed through life trying to save." Good stewards not only remember to smell the roses, so to speak, but they also know the fitting time to do so. One of the gifts of the discernment God gives believers is knowing how to use time appropriately.

No doubt the Preacher's perception is a grim reminder that we can experience life as a dismal affair indeed. Nonetheless, there is a dependable word for Christian stewardship. Although life often seems fleeting and our experiences of it vain, yet time is a gift that God has given us. Every person has the same number of hours and minutes each week. Our gratitude for God's gift of time is shown in how we employ it as we do our part to be in harmony with God's realm.

As we wade into the new year, we might want to make a covenant with ourselves. In this covenant, although it might not be that we always use our time wisely, we attempt to recognize "a sense of past and future" that God offers us as stewards of time.

*William Willimon, *Conversations with Barth on Preaching* (Nashville: Abingdon Press, 2006), 40.

Epiphany

Epiphany of the Lord
[See Year A]

Baptism of the Lord
(First Sunday after the Epiphany; Sunday between January 7 and 13)

Acts 8:14–17 (18–24)   Money Cannot Do Everything

"Peter said to him, 'May your silver perish with you.'"
(Acts 8:20)

Today's Acts lesson offers a great insight about the power of the gospel and the occasional impotence of money in the light of the good news. Although the lesson ends at verse 17, I wish to extend the text to include the "rest of the story." Peter confronts Simon and teaches us about stewardship.

At times the church has referred to Acts as the "Acts of the Holy Spirit," because the Holy Spirit is evident throughout Acts. For example, the NRSV refers to the Holy Spirit in forty verses, while the KJV uses the equivalent term "Holy Ghost" in forty-one verses. In Acts 8 Simon desires the power of the Spirit, but not for faith. Rather, Simon seeks the power of the Spirit for personal gain.

Luke addresses the conflict with Simon, a reputed magician, by writing that he "amazed the people of Samaria. . . . All of them, from the least to the greatest, listened to him eagerly, saying, 'This man is the power of God that is called Great.' And they listened eagerly to him because for a long time he had amazed them with his magic" (Acts 8:9–11). Yet Philip's eloquence persuades many people of Samaria to believe in God's kingdom and they are baptized—including Simon.

The Jerusalem church soon receives word of the miraculous circumstance in Samaria and quickly dispatches Peter and John to assess this extraordinary situation. After Peter and John pray that the Holy Spirit will come upon the people, Simon observes that "the Spirit was given through the laying on of the apostles' hands." Simon then offers to pay for the ability to control the Spirit as Peter and John have apparently done. Peter, displaying his celebrated righteous indignation, snarls, "May your silver perish with you!" Peter's wrath burns hot because Simon thinks he can buy God's gift of the Spirit. Peter leaves no doubt as to the odious nature of Simon's request.

While almost all people of faith would decry someone using gifts to their congregation in exchange for influence, some modern church people "vote with their checkbooks." This behavior is little different from the sin for which Peter censures Simon. Indeed, later the church names the buying of ecclesiastical offices as the sin of "simony." No one can influence the grace or Spirit of God with human purchasing power. A gift is a gift. We give to God through the church not to get, but as a faithful response to what God has already given us free and clear.

We may use money for good or ill, but God pours grace freely on all who would receive it. Our money, offered to the ministries of God and administered through the agencies of the church, is our gift to the church. Our money is not a weapon we use as a means to influence or establish our wants. Nor are our gifts given to leverage others or impose our will. Using our monetary gifts to God in this way does not demonstrate faith, but rather it smacks of intimidation and coercion.

Simon's sin was to offer his money to obtain a gift of God that is freely given. Simon wanted to use the gift of the Holy Spirit for his personal financial gain and for the economic exploitation of others. This imprudent behavior is not in the Spirit of the Christ who gave all so that we might respond to God in faith, discipleship, and stewardship. We give because the Spirit prompts us; we do not give to prompt the Spirit.

Second Sunday after the Epiphany
(Sunday between January 14 and 20 inclusive)

1 Corinthians 12:1–11   Each Gift Is a Blessing

"Now there are varieties of gifts, but the same Spirit."
(1 Cor. 12:4)

In today's lesson, Paul embarks on a new section of his Corinthian correspondence. He has concluded a long discussion relating to the Lord's Supper. He now turns to the topic of spiritual gifts. Paul's task with this congregation is to bring them together as a church. Getting any group on the same page is an arduous task. Getting the church together—to work, live, and be the church together—takes as much effort as the saying goes, as "sorting out salt from pepper with boxing gloves on."

Most believers have preferences and self-perceived talents to offer. Yet it is at the point of spiritual gifts that Paul reminds these Corinthians of an essential truth—that is, as Christian believers God alone supplies all our gifts and talents. We do not generate these gifts. Rather, God gives them as spiritual gifts of the Holy Spirit. Paul even begins his deliberation by telling the church that he does not "want you to be uninformed." The KJV reads here "ignorant." Either way, Paul wants them to understand.

When Paul writes that "there are varieties of gifts, but the same Spirit," he hits on an important principle of Christian stewardship. This principle states that we all have gifts to offer Christ's ministry. Paul then offers a "laundry list" of gifts: wisdom, knowledge, faith, gifts of healing, the working of miracles, prophecy, and so on. He is convinced that all believers have something to offer God.

Sometimes people say, "I have no gift to offer." Yet John's story of the feeding of five thousand people (John 6:1–14) recounts that "Andrew, Simon Peter's brother, said to [Jesus], 'There is a boy here who has five barley loaves and two fish. But what are they among so many people?'" Jesus takes this meager gift and feeds the people. He then instructs his disciples to gather up the leftovers. The disciples proceed to fill twelve baskets. The faith assurance that Jesus conveys to the disciples that day is that God can do a lot with a little. This is a message for modern stewards too.

Each of us has special contributions we can offer by way of gifts and talents to God's realm. We also recognize that not all gifts are identical. As Paul reminds the Corinthian church, so too Paul reminds us: "Now there are varieties of gifts, but the same Spirit; and there are varieties of services, but the same Lord; and there are varieties of activities, but it is the same God who activates all of them in everyone."

We all have gifts to give. As my friend Ellsworth Kalas reminded me, the word "retirement" is not in the Bible, nor is it an emblem for those who seek the high calling of God's sovereignty. I once almost burned down a parsonage in my first year in ministry. Yet eighty-year-old Pete Ruth rescued me by repairing the fire damage before the women's group found out. They had been concerned that I was too young to live in the parsonage by myself anyway. Pete had told me that he never wanted to pray in public or teach Sunday school. But finally, with my help, we found a gift for him to give. Clearly, his wonderful remodeling job did not bring in the kingdom, but then none of our gifts do.

We only offer our spiritual gifts in a response of gratitude to the God who does indeed bring his kingdom near to those who love him and serve him in gladness of heart. Good stewards recognize that we all have a gift to give. These gifts plainly differ, but they are each important nonetheless.

Third Sunday after the Epiphany
(Sunday between January 21 and 27 inclusive)

1 Corinthians 12:12–31a   Sacraments Connect Stewards

"In the one Spirit we were all baptized into one body."
(1 Cor. 12:13)

From the beginning God wanted people as partners. In Genesis we read, "The LORD God took the man and put him in the garden of Eden to till it and keep it" (2:15). God certainly did not *need* people to work, but God *wanted* us to till and keep creation's garden. God created partners to make creation what God designed it to be. Can you imagine playing tennis by yourself, or singing a duet alone? Sharing with others and with God is a fundamental element of the Christian life. We do our part, others do their part, and God does God's part. Partnership in God's creation is a solid stewardship touchstone. And although God does not need us in any ultimate sense, God wants us in every ultimate sense. God builds stewardship on partnership.

Occasionally, however, believers get the idea that if God has blessed them, then it makes them better or more holy than others. Overly "spiritual believers" were a prevailing problem in Corinth. Some church members exalted themselves over others because they believed God had blessed them with unique spiritual gifts and graces. In today's passage Paul argues against the abuse of spiritual gifts, "gifts given by God through the agency of the Holy Spirit."

The topic of spiritual gifts is so critical to Paul that he spills more ink on spiritual gifts than any single topic in Corinthians. Paul ties this reflection back to what he earlier wrote: "Whether you eat or drink, or whatever you do, do everything for the glory of God" (1 Cor. 10:31). Paul also reminds the congregation of unity in Christ: "In the same way he took the cup also, after supper, saying, 'This cup is the new covenant in my blood. Do this, as often as you drink it, in remembrance of me.' For as often as you eat this bread and drink the cup, you proclaim the Lord's death until he comes" (11:25–26). Thus, Paul uses both sacraments to illustrate spiritual union.

Paul realizes that either people have forgotten the principle of unity of the body of Christ, or they have never grasped it. Someone in Corinth wrote to Paul, evidently trying to comprehend the church's common life together. Thus, Paul begins the segment on spiritual gifts: "Now concerning spiritual gifts, brothers and sisters, I do not want you to be uninformed [or "ignorant" KJV]" (12:1).

Today we occasionally forget that in the life of the church each believer is crucial. Certainly we each have different abilities and graces to offer the community of faith, but every gift is important. Some people spend too much time and energy in the church trying to jockey for the best positions and places of honor. However, Paul is clear—all gifts are important to the work of God in Christ's church.

God's will for the church is for the Holy Spirit to edify the church through the gifts offered by that same Spirit. When we place our gifts at Christ's feet and offer ourselves to Christ's ministry, then we satisfy Christ and we respond to God's call. As Jesus admonishes us, "Strive first for the kingdom of God and . . . all these things will be given to you as well" (Matt. 6:33). Of all possibilities open to him, it is remarkable that Paul selects the image of baptism (and earlier, the Lord's Supper) as a uniting feature for the faith community. It is also ironic that today's church divides itself over these specific issues. But Paul thinks otherwise. The sacraments unite believers. Paul suggests that God unites stewards into one body. We stewards each have a gift to offer.

Fourth Sunday after the Epiphany
(Sunday between January 28 and February 3 inclusive; if it is the Last Sunday after the Epiphany, see Transfiguration)

Luke 4:21–30   Grace: The Foundation of Stewardship

"Elijah was sent to none of them except to a widow . . . in Sidon."
(Luke 4:26)

When many pastors preach from this text, their focus is upon the messenger Jesus, rather than on the message. This is Jesus' triumphal return home after teaching in the synagogues and being praised by everyone (Luke 4:15). We can almost see the newspaper headline: "Local Boy Does Good!" Curiosity strikes us Bible readers. How will the home synagogue folks receive Jesus?

From the angle of stewardship, what Jesus preaches in his hometown sermon sets the tone for his ministry. What will Jesus tell those who watched him mature? No doubt, not a few ponder the question "Is not this Joseph's son?" (see also Mark 6:3). Thus, for purposes of stewardship, Jesus' message captures our attention. What will he say?

First, Jesus tells them, "Today this scripture has been fulfilled in your hearing." In Jesus, the messenger becomes the message. Because the lectionary divides Luke 4 into two readings, the fulfillment of which Jesus speaks concerns Isaiah's prophecy. The Lord has put "the Spirit of the Lord" upon Jesus as Messiah and anointed Jesus "to bring good news to the poor . . . [and] to proclaim the year of the Lord's favor" (Luke 4:18–19). In other words, Jesus announces that in him the Lord's favor is manifest.

Second, after the crowd speaks well of Jesus, he then issues a prophetic warning: "No prophet is accepted in the prophet's hometown." Then to prove the point, Jesus tells two stories that reveal God's grace falling upon those who would have been outside the circle of Judaism. The stories are about the widow at Zarephath (1 Kgs. 17) and Naaman the Syrian (2 Kgs. 5). Each speaks of God's favor falling on those whom the people in the synagogue would not have considered as part of the chosen people. Jesus is talking about the favor of God falling upon adversaries of Israel—Gentiles!

Jesus' stories, from his audience's own Scriptures, infuriate the people, and they try to throw Jesus off a cliff. What causes such an emotional about-face? Perhaps this story reveals something about our relationship to the grace of God. Grace always looks and feels good when we receive it. However, when God lavishes grace on others, especially those whom we do not consider worthy, then grace does not look so noble. Jesus, as both message and messenger, reminds these synagogue worshipers that God offers grace to whom God wills. This divine expression of grace is part of God's essential nature. We too might react as those in the synagogue that day.

Years ago I saw a former mentor-pastor at a church conference. We agreed to have lunch together. I was excited to have him all to myself for a meal because I wanted him to know how well I was doing. He had taught me a lot, and I rarely had a chance to see him. I looked forward to our private lunch all morning. Leaving the meeting and on our way to the car, an annoying, boorish colleague saw us and shouted, "Hey, wait! Can I come, too?" I cringed because I knew that my mentor friend would say what he did: "Sure, come on. We always have room for one more." My countenance fell, but my friend's invitation was fitting.

Our source of graciousness as stewards stands on God's previous grace to us. But make no mistake—God is gracious far beyond our grasp and our kindred circles. God loves all people because God created all people. As stewards it is good for us to remember that God's grace is always good—no matter how we happen to feel about it.

Fifth Sunday after the Epiphany
(Sunday between February 4 and 10 inclusive; if it is the Last Sunday after the Epiphany, see Transfiguration)

Isaiah 6:1–8 (9–13)   The Stewardship of God's Call

"Whom shall I send, and who will go for us?"
(Isa. 6:8)

Baptism is one of the many ways that God calls believers into ministry. As one ordination liturgy puts it, "All Christians are called through baptism to share in

Christ's ministry of love and service."* How God reveals divinity in the world is a focus of Epiphany. One way we experience God is by God's call to labor in God's vineyard.

Whether or not we respond to God's call as an ordained clergyperson, our response to God's call is a stewardship household we manage. God calls people in many ways, but if one believes, then one responds to God's call. Sometimes the call summons us to teach or to pray. Sometimes the call beckons us to feed the poor or clothe the naked. Occasionally the call entails surrendering to the ministry. But one way or another God calls all of us. How we steward God's call measures our faithfulness and discipleship.

Today's text from the Hebrew Bible is a classic "call story." Of course, we remember the calls of Moses and Abraham. Samuel's call occurs while he is quite young. Jeremiah prophesies that God called him even earlier: "Before I formed you in the womb I knew you, and before you were born I consecrated you; I appointed you a prophet to the nations" (Jer. 1:5). Yet the singularity of Isaiah's call makes it most memorable.

First, the time is fixed—"in the year that King Uzziah died." In addition, the scene is rich in detail: the Lord, the throne, the temple, the seraphs, the singing, the wings. Moreover, Isaiah discloses that "the pivots on the thresholds shook at the voices of those who called, and the house filled with smoke." A memorable call, indeed!

To this summons of God, Isaiah responds appropriately. The prophet makes a confession of sin as well as a confession of faith: "Woe is me! I am lost, for I am a man of unclean lips, and I live among a people of unclean lips; yet my eyes have seen the King, the LORD of hosts!" On the heels of Isaiah's confession is his absolution. This divine pardon takes place in a visible act. One of the seraphs takes a live coal from the altar and touches it to the prophet's lips. From now on Isaiah speaks through singed and blistered lips. Is this bodily emblem similar to the dislocated hip of Jacob (Gen. 32:25, 32)?

We hear in the last verse of the primary text (verses 9–13 are optional) the Lord's summons: "Whom shall I send, and who will go for us?" As painful as articulating the answer no doubt was, Isaiah responds to God's call. The prophet says through his tender lips, "Here am I; send me!" Isaiah becomes a steward of the word of the Lord.

In Deuteronomy 12:5–6, Moses tells the people that God said, "You shall seek the place [and bring] your burnt offerings and your sacrifices, your tithes and your donations." We are modern people. We do not bring burnt offerings, but we might consider that our "modern" offerings include many things. From the beginning God understood the human tendency for fear, insecurity, and the grasping of material possessions. Most Christians understand about giving of our time and treasure. We recognize that we offer the things we earn and the things we create as signs of our connection with God.

*The United Methodist Book of Worship (Nashville: United Methodist Publishing House, 1992), 688.

Yet the most crucial gift we ever "give back" to God is the gift of our lives to God in ministry and relationship. It is upon yielding to God's upward call in Jesus Christ that we genuinely become stewards of all that passes through our hands.

Sixth Sunday after the Epiphany
(Sunday between February 11 and 17 inclusive; if it is the Last Sunday after the Epiphany, see Transfiguration)

Luke 6:17–26   The Stewardship of Eschatological Promises

"Blessed are you . . . but woe to you . . ."
(Luke 6:20, 24)

The first part of today's Gospel lesson gratifies Christians who care about people in difficulty. Yet this is also a troubling passage because of the "woe section." Stewards understand shoring up poor and despairing folk, but Jesus frightens us when he says, "But woe to you who are rich." Why? Because most of us readers are comparatively rich by any worldly yardstick. How can stewards get a handle on these words of Jesus?

Earlier in the chapter Jesus ascends a mountain to pray (6:12–16). For Luke, mountains are always fitting sites for prayer. Jesus chooses twelve apostles and then descends to a "level place" where he finds people from Israel, Tyre, and Sidon. He heals their diseases and removes their unclean spirits. These miseries had rendered the people ritually "unclean," excluding them from corporate worship. Luke relates Jesus' four beatitudes and the corresponding woes for the age to come. But the story's rub comes at this point. Some are "blessed" by inclusion in Jesus' realm; to others, Jesus offers "woes." Jesus' woes are prophetic warnings, but to the rich they seem biased.

It may seem that if one is poor, hungry, weeping, or persecuted, then Jesus' message is good news. However, if one is prosperous, eats well, laughs, or is admired, then Jesus' message seems like bad news. If Jesus came to save all people, then this seems neither right nor fair. What is going on here?

Perhaps a key to unlocking this text comes from Jesus' audience. Who was Jesus speaking to then, and to whom does Jesus speak now? Of course, the poor came to hear Jesus' promises and be healed of their diseases. These were not wealthy or healthy people. They were needy people who longed to hear a word of hope in the midst of their despair. The gospel's good news plays well to this crowd.

Many stewards in modern American churches are folks who have worked hard and achieved a degree of success. When Jesus says, "Blessed are you who are poor, for yours is the kingdom of God," we moderns are not sure what to make of this. Yet this is part of God's eschatological promise that assures believers that despite current circumstances, God remains faithful to God's providential promises. It is on par with the promise in Revelation that "God himself will . . . wipe every tear from their eyes. Death will be no more; mourning and crying and pain will be no more" (21:3–4). The promise is that God will reverse the order of this age in the age to come.

The Christian life is not just about the result of what we do, but it is also about the way we do what we do. For although the Christian life concerns "the ends," it also concerns "the means." God could have zapped us into salvation, but God used the means of Jesus' self-sacrifice for divine purposes. Consequently, the Christian life often makes little sense to our managed, linear, logical way of doing business with the world. The gospel way is not always the way of efficiency—and efficiency is our motto.

The "poor" of whom Jesus speaks are those who concede their dependence on God, while the "rich" in this text reluctantly commit themselves to God's realm. The rich appear at ease with their self-created existence. The word translated "consolation" in verse 24 is a financial term. Perhaps the rich do not grasp what they owe Jesus. The "hungry" hunger for the word of God, while the "full" are satisfied.

An authentic steward recognizes that the basis for all our benevolence is God's benevolence toward us. Good stewards confess their dependence on God.

Seventh Sunday after the Epiphany
(Sunday between February 18 and 24 inclusive;
if it is the Last Sunday after the Epiphany, see Transfiguration)

Psalm 37:1–11, 39–40   Stewards Eschew Envy

"Refrain from anger, and forsake wrath. Do not fret—it leads only to evil."
(Ps. 37:8)

"Do not fret" sounds like something a wise grandmother might say. This wisdom in fact echoes Jesus' teaching of long ago: "Do not worry about your life" (Matt. 6:25). Although we rarely consider managing our attitudes or anxieties as "stewardship households," nonetheless our self-control—or better, letting God control our thoughts and feelings—is part of stewarding the life God has given us.

Psalm 37 has the psalmist pondering how well the wicked appear to fare in this life. This person of prayer finds this circumstance not only unjust but also distasteful. The response Psalm 37 offers serves well those of any age who ponder this situation. Today, as in every generation, people long to compare their condition to others who seem to thrive thanks to "ill-gotten gains." We work and play by the rules, yet we do not seem to be able to get ahead. Yet this psalm is clear: "Do not fret because of the wicked; do not be envious of wrongdoers." Envy ends up on the list of what folk theology calls the Seven Deadly Sins. The Bible deems envy sinful, for it isolates believers from others and God.

There has always existed in church circles one form or another of what we euphemistically call "the gospel of prosperity." In this theological perversion, churches or individual preachers urge believers to give to God so that God will give back to them. Ben Franklin wrote that God helps those who help themselves. Often the prosperity gospel devotees use this slogan as if it were scriptural. The sin of envy worms into this manner of thinking, since people naturally see the good fortune of others and want to grasp it as well. For all our preachments about living lavishly, Jesus taught that the human heart was something of an incubator for evil intentions. Jesus, we also note, includes envy as defiling believers, along-side adultery and murder (see Mark 7:21–23).

However, Psalm 37 offers steady wisdom for modern stewards. It advises believers to "trust in the LORD, and do good." This sage counsel reverses the transactional, tit-for-tat character of the prosperity gospel. God is not good to us because we first give to God. Rather, God frees us from our insecurity about earthly things and liberates us to give to and for others. We do this by merely offering to God our gifts and talents. In turn God assures us "the desires of [our] heart." With our modern sense of time, waiting for God to give us our desire is grueling. We want what we want—now. The true hearers of Psalm 37 cultivate patient waiting for God. As Paul paraphrases Isaiah for the Corinthians, so Paul reminds us: God indeed "works for those who wait for God" (1 Cor. 2:9; Isa. 64:4). It is God who prepares life for us. We do not grab it by the horns.

God offers us prosperity as a gracious gift—no strings attached. For believers who practice faithful stewardship in the midst of other people's plenty Augustine's words ring true: "God's work done in God's way will never lack for God's supply." We do not "give to get," but we give because God fosters generosity in our hearts.

Eighth Sunday after the Epiphany
(Sunday between February 25 and 29 inclusive; if it is the Last Sunday after the Epiphany, see Transfiguration)

Luke 6:39–49   The Identifying Mark of a Steward

"No good tree bears bad fruit. . . . Each tree is known by its own fruit."
(Luke 6:43–44)

Because of the way Easter typically falls within the liturgical calendar, preachers seldom preach the texts for this Sunday. The church rarely celebrates the Eighth Sunday after the Epiphany. Yet on that rare worship occasion, the day's Gospel lesson from Luke concludes Jesus' Sermon on the Plain. The text seems like a bundle of sayings of Jesus gathered here by Luke to conclude Jesus' sermon. Similar teachings are scattered in several places in Matthew's Gospel. In fact, on the surface there seems little reason for Luke to have collected these teachings here. At the same time, we can understand something about stewardship from Jesus' image of trees bearing fruit. Psalm 92 also uses this arboreal image.

The lesson of the day begins with Jesus teaching about disciples and about

learning from a teacher. In Jesus' mind there were good teachers and those needing improvement. A shrewd disciple will follow the good teacher. Then Jesus uses
the images of the speck and the log in a person's eye. He then moves to the statement that "figs are not gathered from thorns, nor are grapes picked from a bram-
ble bush." The lesson for discipleship is that "each tree is known by its own fruit."

Jesus does not suggest here any kind of "works righteousness." He does not
mean that if we do enough good deeds then we will somehow sway God's judgment of us. Rather, he says that those who follow the master and those who offer
compassion to others reflect the spirit of Jesus.

Pastors encounter many grieving people; it comes with the territory. Regularly
I hear people say to those grieving, "If you need anything, please do not hesitate to
call me." Yet it is unlikely that those who are grieving will call for help. They may
welcome and accept other people's assistance, but in the midst of grief they are
unlikely to call on others—regardless of how well they know them or how much
they need another person's aid. Sometimes the pain is too raw to call for help.

Faithful stewards do not wait for others to ask for assistance. Rather, they discern what is necessary and lend a hand. Small acts of kindness—providing a meal,
mowing the family's lawn, taking care of small children—each of these is a concrete demonstration of care for those in grief. As Jesus said, a "tree is known by
its own fruit." A person who possesses a steward's heart will know what to do and
the right time to do it. Our text implies that the disciple acts the part of a steward: "It is out of the abundance of the heart that the mouth speaks."

Once while reading a church newsletter, a wonderful quotation by T. S. Eliot
caught my attention: "Most of the trouble in the world is caused by people who
want to be important." In our lesson today Jesus shares something of great value
to stewards. He seems to be saying that bearing good fruit is what makes people
important or of value to God's realm. Too often too many of us are held captive
by those who merely want to be important.

In the realm of God those who serve others in tangible and helpful ways are
those who are stewards of God's mysterious love, which God offers us in Jesus
Christ. Anyone can talk about the value of discipleship; stewards know how to
put value into practice.

Transfiguration Sunday
(Last Sunday after the Epiphany)

Luke 9:28–36 (37–43)   Stewards Astounded by God's Greatness

"All were astounded at the greatness of God."
(Luke 9:43)

Perhaps I read too much Karl Barth to fit into the modern theological landscape.
Near the end of today's Gospel lesson (the extended text option), after Jesus
rebukes the unclean spirit, heals the boy, and gives him back to his father, Luke

comments, almost nonchalantly, "And all were astounded at the greatness of God." Luke often recounts simply the reaction of those who witness Jesus or the apostles at work (see, for example, Luke 5:26; 7:16; Acts 2:43; 5:5, 11). The Barth part of me suggests that Luke's objective is to engender a faith in God's greatness that astounds us. Luke accomplishes this as he shares God's mysterious grandeur via Jesus' life. Luke's transfiguration story certainly astounded three disciples.

Perhaps the foundation of stewardship begins in utter awe. The life that manages God's stewardship households originates in pure wonder. Moses comes to mind as a faithful steward of the multiple talents that God saw in him. Yet Moses evidently failed to discern these talents and thus denied them (see Exod. 3:11 for one of many of Moses' arguments against being sent). Conceivably, our modern neglect of standing before God's grandeur makes it difficult to identify the magnificent gifts God offers to us to manage. In many churches there is a lot of "me and Jesus" and too little heeding of the God who spoke to Moses, "Come no closer! Remove the sandals from your feet, for the place on which you are standing is holy ground" (Exod. 3:5). Authentic stewardship recognizes the immensity of the steward's task. Our task is not to revel in ministry's success, but to rejoin the fray. We know that God's greatness offers stewards new challenges.

In a way, transfiguration is a prelude to resurrection—God's greatest miracle. When Jesus went to the mountain to pray, Luke recalls, "the appearance of his face changed, and his clothes became dazzling white." Not only this, but Moses and Elijah appear and talk to Jesus in front of Peter, John, and James. Naturally, the transfiguration changes Jesus, but are not the three disciples also transfigured in some way? Whatever we make of the disciples' experience, Peter speaks for all when he blurts out the first thing that comes to mind: "Master, it is good for us to be here; let us make three dwellings, one for you, one for Moses, and one for Elijah." Luke's next phrase is the evangelist's comment on Peter's suggestion: Peter did not know "what he said."

In the extended text option, we read of Jesus' healing of the child that suffered seizures. What is remarkable about this healing story is that it comes on the heels of Jesus' talking with Moses and Elijah, two of Israel's greatest faith heroes. Despite the heady experience, Jesus subsequently returns to the seemingly ordinary and mundane business of healing bona fide human beings. There is little time for Jesus to absorb the transfiguration moment. It is back to common life and the problems life presents. Luke's Jesus offers God's stewards a sterling stewardship example.

A great temptation for stewards is to revel in whatever small successes we enjoy. Many of our tasks, however, are routine, even mundane. We offer our best effort preaching or teaching Sunday school and someone kindly says, "Thank you. I'm sure next week will be just as good." While we want to soak in such compliments, the world's needs beckon. What fires the steward's passion in God's realm is what Luke noted long ago: "All were astounded at the greatness of God." In this amazement resides our call to stewardship. As we leave a peak worship event, we at that moment search for ways to use God's gifts. Astonishing!

Lent

Ash Wednesday
[See Year B]

First Sunday in Lent

Deuteronomy 26:1–11   Offering First Fruits: A Teaching Ritual

"I bring the first of the fruit of the ground that you, O LORD, have given me."
(Deut. 26:10)

When the Hebrew Bible speaks of "the first of the fruit of the ground," it signifies for ancient people an acknowledgment that God holds the means to agricultural success. The Hebrews were among many ancient peoples to recognize the tie between agriculture and providence, although naturally Israel celebrated God as the sole source.

The text from Deuteronomy is an ancient thanksgiving liturgy and tells the story of faith. As the people enter the land of promise, they are to take some of "the first of the fruit of the ground" and offer it as a sacrifice of thanksgiving. As the people perform this tangible act of sacrifice, they repeat what is a more or less creedal statement: "A wandering Aramean was my ancestor. . . ." This article of faith recounts the story of Israel from the Exodus to God's leading the people into "a land flowing with milk and honey." Then the Hebrews are to "celebrate with all the bounty that the LORD your God has given to you and to your house." What can stewards learn from this act of thanksgiving and praise?

This ritual of thanksgiving reminds us that people are not born generous. Rather, we learn altruism from those who model this trait. In fact, ritual has a deep teaching function. Ritual helps us pass along significant things of meaning that are larger than our words can explain. This is why ritual is so vital in the life of stewardship. Stewardship is a habit of thanksgiving.

Ritual helps people act out faith. Ritual tells others about the things we hold dear, although many people cannot articulate why these matters are so essential. Ritual is important in the church's stewardship realm, although many modern people forsake it. Many modern people neglect the church's ritual of thanksgiving because they fail to understand that for the past two thousand years the church has tried to help people value life and faith in ways too deep to express.

Deuteronomy reminds us that previous to the church's life, Israel too celebrated faith's ritual of thanksgiving. As they offered back to God from God's bounty, the Israelites recollected other ways that God had acted on the community's behalf—the exodus being the immediate case in point. Faithful stewards connect the story of faith to "the first of the fruit of the ground" as well as other tangible ways God provides for God's people.

When we celebrate our "ritual offering," we model for children and others new to faith that Jesus' story results in a concrete response to this story. Today many people offer their gifts to God via electronic fund transfers or by credit cards. Yet the ritual of "passing the plates" is a tangible gesture by which we respond in physical and concrete ways to God's prior gifts to us. If we did not take up an offering each Sabbath, then how would our children understand that giving to the church is our response to the story of God revealed in Jesus?

For Israel, a ritual of firstfruits and the story of God's work on their behalf celebrates the people's faith. Ritual teaches about valued community matters. Ritual helps groove people into good habits. Thanksgiving rituals become faith habits—living responses to God's gift of bounty to God's people.

Second Sunday in Lent

Psalm 27:1–14   The Lord Gives Stewards Confidence

"The LORD is the stronghold of my life; of whom shall I be afraid?"
(Ps. 27:1)

In some American churches a great impediment to funding church ministries is the lack of confidence a congregation has in its leaders. Although many churches struggle because of poor stewardship development, another factor is the lack of trust a congregation has about what it gives. In terms of stewardship, trust is everything.

Psalm 27 is both a prayer of assurance and a prayer calling for God's assistance. In fact, logically we might more easily understand the psalm if it began with verses 7–14. These verses constitute something of a prayer for divine help. Verses 1–6 are a hymn to the confidence a believer has in God. Some biblical scholars suggest that originally these halves were two distinct psalms. However, as in life, confidence and pleas for assistance often exist side by side. Perhaps this psalm is an example of that circumstance. The psalmist reverses the fear of enemies and of being forsaken by God with a confession of confidence in the Lord at the psalm's beginning. In other words, the fear in the psalm's last half is conquered by a trust in the first half.

As stewards mature, we develop wisdom that what we do for God and others has a deep and abiding purpose. If we did not believe that what we did with our time and treasure was of worth, then we would invest our stewardship in other ways. Yet we stewards have full confidence that what we do with what God has loaned us has some greater significance than what often meets the eye. It is out of this conviction that we willingly offer what we have to the Lord. As verse 1 asks, "Whom shall I fear?"

In the second half of Psalm 27 the psalmist prays that the Lord "not hide your face from me." The one who prays earnestly seeks not to be cast off or given "up to the will of my adversaries." Rather, the psalmist prays that God will "teach me your way" and "lead me on a level path." This last part of Psalm 27 also extols the virtue of patience: "Be strong, and let your heart take courage; wait for the LORD!"

We become stewards not because we live in terror of what God will do to us if we do not give. Instead, we respond as stewards in faith because of the trust and assurance that God has already offered us in Christ. Anthony de Mello relates a wonderful parable about the relationship between our fear and God's assurance:

> A sheep found a hole in the fence and crept through it. He was so glad to get away. He wandered far and lost his way back. And then he realized that a wolf was following him. He ran and ran, but the wolf kept chasing him until the shepherd came and rescued him and carried him lovingly back to the fold. And despite everyone's urgings to the contrary, the shepherd refused to nail up the hole in the fence.*

It is the confidence we have in God's providence and protection that gives stewards the courage to do what many modern people are too fearful to do. With glad and generous hearts, we share out of the bounty that God provides. In our culture the idea of survival reigns paramount. People wonder why a person would give away what he or she has worked so hard to obtain. Perhaps the only answer

*Anthony de Mello, SJ, *The Song of the Bird* (Anand, India: Gujarat Sahitya Prakash, 1982), 200–201.

is that no one can understand giving until they have a faith that moves beyond such questions.

At its end, Psalm 27 asks all-too-human questions regarding being forsaken and about our enemy. Psalm 27's beginning has an answer. We trust the God of providence.

Third Sunday in Lent

Luke 13:1–9   Give Us Another Chance

"If it bears fruit next year, well and good; but if not . . . "
(Luke 13:9)

In the Gospel lesson today, Jesus is at his best. Some of the multitudes bring to his attention the situation of some people who died violently at the hands of sol-diers. They tell Jesus, as Luke puts it, about these "Galileans whose blood Pilate had mingled with their sacrifices." They no doubt broach the subject to see how Jesus will address undeserved human suffering. But Jesus ups the ante by responding with a horror story of his own. He tells them about "eighteen who were killed when the tower of Siloam fell on them." Then Jesus asks, "Do you think that they were worse offenders than all the others living in Jerusalem?" In fact, Jesus warns those who by now wished they hadn't asked, "Unless you repent, you will all perish just as they did." Later we will explore Jesus' teaching for stew-ards. But for now we will ponder Jesus' words.

By these two examples, Jesus pretty well covers the waterfront of human suf-fering. The first example speaks of unfair suffering at the hands of a foreign mil-itary occupying force. The second example illustrates by way of an accident. People ask Jesus about human suffering, and he tells them a parable. The para-ble of the Fig Tree divides neatly into two parts. The first part addresses the ques-tion about what to do with a fig tree that has not produced for three years, even as the owner has habitually come looking for figs. Despite all the vinedresser's care, the fig tree has yielded nothing. Accordingly, for the owner there is only one alternative: "Cut it down." This is a realistic approach. A nonproductive fig tree is as useful as a nonproducing oil rig. Why put time, energy, and resources into something that will never produce? This is good, old-fashioned common sense.

But the second part of the parable surprises. The vinedresser, in a subordinate role, negotiates on behalf of the ill-fated plant. He offers to dig around the roots and apply fertilizer to help the plant reach its potential. The vinedresser goes far beyond what we would expect for his role. He tries to provide a "last chance" for the fig tree. The vinedresser becomes an advocate for the fig tree.

The people want to know about other people's suffering, and Jesus forces them to examine their own lives, asking what they will do with a new chance. Although spared Pilate's soldiers or a tower falling on them, they could have died this way. So now, Jesus' parable implies, what are you going to do with your second chance?

This is where Jesus indirectly teaches us about stewardship, and it is a Lenten type of lesson.

Sometimes people to whom God has given much question what other people's response has been—or should be. We wait and see what others may give to a certain church mission project or what others may pledge to the church for the next year.

But sometimes our questions are not for information or clarification. Our questions instead become ways to dodge our responsibilities before God. Plainly, we can ask why this or that happened. More practically, we might ask, "Since this did not happen to me, then what will I do with my second chance?" As stewards the parable of the Fig Tree reminds us that what we or others have done in the past is not as important as what we, as people of faith, intend to do today and tomorrow with God's gifts to us.

Fourth Sunday in Lent

Luke 15:1–3, 11b–32   Bountiful Love, Plentiful Gifts

"All that is mine is yours."
(Luke 15:31)

One of the best-loved stories of the Bible, Luke's parable of the Prodigal Son, has been replayed many times over by modern novels and films. As a short story, this parable finds its way into many college writing classes as an exemplar of the genre. Despite its familiarity, it never loses its force. For stewards, each son's attitude toward the father's goodwill offers clues about managing God's good gifts.

The younger son demands, "Father, give me the share of the property that will belong to me." The father without delay does so. But with a pocketful of cash and little awareness of how to manage it, the younger son soon finds himself penniless in the far country. We imagine that one swindler after another "shakes down" the boy, cajoling him into picking up checks for ill-spent evenings on the town. After a time of soul-searching, the younger son "comes to himself." Luke uses this phrase again at Acts 12:11 when an angel frees Peter from Herod's prison. During his long journey home, this younger son rehearses a speech. He is surely astonished when his father says, "Let us eat and celebrate; for this son of mine was dead and is alive again."

Despite the boy's audacity, the father welcomes him home as a conquering hero. Such is God's love for God's people. One of the principles of stewardship concedes that God owns all but nonetheless shares with human beings. We manage God's generous gifts while God offers us multiple chances to express our gratitude.

The elder brother more or less demands that the father abandon the feast for the younger son. His rationale is that "this son of yours" does not merit consideration. Out of his anger, and no doubt envy, he accuses the father of a gross injustice: "For all these years I have been working like a slave for you, and I have never disobeyed your command; yet you have never given me even a young goat so that I might celebrate with my friends." Despite the light in which Luke casts this elder brother, he does have a point. Grace and forgiveness always seem right when we are the recipients. Yet when God lavishes grace and forgiveness on the unworthy, it is easy enough to become righteously indignant. Jesus made this point in another context when he said that God "makes his sun rise on the evil and on the good, and sends rain on the righteous and on the unrighteous" (Matt. 5:45).

Two brothers offer us two ways to understand God's good gifts offered to us without price. The younger—the prodigal, or wasteful—brother reveals his inner thoughts by demanding his share of the family inheritance while his father still lives. This request suggests that the father is useless to him while he is alive.

Conversely, the elder—the frugal or envious—brother reveals his raw feelings by leading his father to take into account his industriousness. He has done what his father has expected and his social role has dictated. Now he expects his father to regard him in a special manner.

Neither son proved a sturdy steward. One squandered resources. The other sulked about merely doing his duty. Faithful stewards remember that God loves us for who we are as God's creatures. How stewards respond reveals how stewards love God back.

Fifth Sunday in Lent

Psalm 126:1–6   The Divine Impulse for Giving

"The LORD has done great things for us, and we rejoiced."
(Ps. 126:3)

On this Lenten Sunday as we draw nearer and nearer to Holy Week, both lessons from the Hebrew Scriptures speak to God's inscrutable goodness. Isaiah's text urges the faith community to forget what God has done on their behalf, including the magnificent liberation from Egypt. Why would the prophet write such a thing? Because God is about to do a new thing. In the modern vernacular Isaiah promises, "You ain't seen nothin' yet!" Israel's future hope is kindled by the promise that Isaiah makes as the Lord's spokesperson.

As brilliant as this Isaiahan promise is, for the purpose of stewardship we turn to another joyful text, Psalm 126, which radiates elation at every turn. When the Lord restores Zion's fortunes, the response of faith-filled stewards is that of a people whose mouth is "filled with laughter, and our tongue with shouts of joy." In other words, praise and gratitude develop into appropriate responses from people whom the Lord blesses.

The psalm begins by reminding readers that Israel's postexilic restoration is for the people "like those who dream." In a sense, the dreams of which the psalm speaks offer hope to a people who have given up on any stake in the future. Dreams help people get through the misery of the present. Dreams allowed believers to await better times when even surrounding nations, almost always perceived as enemies, would say of Israel, "The Lord has done great things for them." Dreams commonly make the unbearable tolerable.

Psalm 126 recounts the reversal of the Hebrew people's fortunes. While the pain of sowing in tears remains in their collective consciousness, the hope for reaping with shouts of joy lingers. This lingering hope constitutes the people's hope for fortune's reversal. We can say the same for "those who go out weeping," for they "shall come home with shouts of joy, carrying their sheaves." If there is a psalm of hope for a grief-stricken people, then this is the psalm. For stewards this psalm signals a fundamental reason for offering God our time and treasure.

Too often people simply surrender offerings to the church's ministries without much thought. These actions regularly are responses of those who feel as if they are doing their duty. Despite their understanding of returning a portion of firstfruits to God, this dutiful mindset lacks the joyful aspects of holy worship. Psalm 126 reminds faithful stewards that what we give is merely a response to God's rich generosity toward God's people in the first place. We give to others because God first gave to us.

Veteran pastors know the truth about people who give with open hands to the church's ministries. These pastors might tell us that the evidence is obvious. Generous people habitually reveal a character that is spiritually enthusiastic and happier than that of the ungenerous. The size of the gift has little to do with this stance. It has to do with the level of generosity with whatever we happen to have. Psalm 126 reminds stewards that all generosity is rooted in this: God's benevolence toward God creatures. When we respond to God as true stewards, then we reveal ourselves as "those who dream."

Passion/Palm Sunday
(Sixth Sunday in Lent)

Philippians 2:5–11 (Liturgy of the Passion)   Invest in Obedience
to Christ

"[Christ Jesus] humbled himself and became obedient."
(Phil. 2:8)

On the final Sunday in Lent in Years A and B, this commentary focused on the texts for the Liturgy of the Palms. However, in Year C we explore the Liturgy of the Passion as we turn to Paul's epistle to the church at Philippi. For stewards, Philippians 2:5–11 offers a clear expression of the mind of Christ, at least from Paul's point of view. In fact, there is a précis of this "Christ Hymn" in verses 3–4 of the epistle: "Do nothing from selfish ambition or conceit, but in humility regard others as better than yourselves. Let each of you look not to your own interests, but to the interests of others."

To be a Christian is to take the yoke of Christ. Farmers use yokes to harness or bind cattle or oxen together to plow. When believing stewards bear Christ's yoke, then Christ controls them; in the Philippians' case these stewards have the mind of Christ. In a biblical irony, the yoke is not a heavy burden. Rather, as Jesus tells the crowds who have ears to hear: "For my yoke is easy, and my burden is light" (Matt. 11:30).

On this Passion Sunday, we encounter a parallel irony regarding the Christian life. Our lives in Christ begin as the Christ Hymn suggests. We assume the yoke of Christ (the mind of Christ) and anticipate the heaviness of emptying ourselves and taking the form of a slave. However, by the Christ Hymn's conclusion, the formerly expected shame through obedience now evolves into joy. Because Jesus took the form of a slave, humbled himself, and "became obedient to the point of death," God designated Jesus as worthy of worship. The irony of the slave being worthy of worship comes full circle in the liturgical season of Lent/Easter. God exalts Jesus as risen Christ, but not until Jesus passes through the humiliation and death of Good Friday. By being brought low, Jesus is lifted up.

We live in a culture that denies death, as well as most other unpleasant things: servanthood, obedience, and surrender to God. People habitually deny reality without considering the consequences of that denial. This is too often true for churches and the stewardship gifts that make ministry and mission possible. Recently I met a woman whose church was in the same town where I was once the pastor of a smaller church. Because of our connection, she spoke freely with me. She said, "Our church is in real trouble. Many of our older members give and give—a tithe and more. But we can't seem to get our church finances under control, and it is hurting our church badly."

So I asked her a simple question: "Do your church leaders discourage your pastor from talking about giving and stewardship?"

She replied, "Yes! How did you know?"

If we do not allow our pastors and other leaders to teach us what God expects of Christian stewards, then how can we tackle our faith task? The point of Christian stewardship is not to repay God what we owe God. The point of Christian stewardship is to share what God has given us with those with whom God wants us to share. When we share God's bounty, then we live up to Scripture's promise. We stewards also possess the mind of Christ.

Holy Thursday (A, B, and C)

John 13:1–17, 31b–35   Jesus Sets Stewards Apart

"Unless I wash you, you have no share with me."
(John 13:8)

Maundy Thursday worshipers are unlike most in the church, who excuse themselves from this night's worship occasion. For many faithful Christian stewards, Maundy Thursday is worship at its most profound. Worship this night is serious business.

By way of contrast, in a cartoon that originally graced a cover of the *New Yorker* in 1995, Art Spiegelman depicts a rabbit in a suit and tie, crucified on a 1040A tax form. This form is part of the rite of spring and, along with Easter, represents what our cultural mind conjures up when it reflects on what mid-April brings. Plainly this satirical art shows a crucified taxpayer. Yet it would make no sense to someone unfamiliar with Jesus' story and what takes place during Holy Week. Thus, when preachers begin their homiletical work, rather than beginning from scratch they rather start in people's awareness—however vague—of Jesus' crucifixion. Preachers can build on this awareness and help deepen it.

The text from the Hebrew Bible tells the story of Passover. It also prescribes how the meal shall be prepared and eaten. It may have been the first and most famous case of "fast food." Israel is told to eat this meal with "your loins girded, your sandals on your feet, and your staff in your hand; and you shall eat it hurriedly. It is the passover of the Lord" (Exod. 12:11). In the Epistle lesson, Paul offers one of the earliest liturgies for Holy Communion, which focuses on the Seder meal Jesus celebrates with his disciples in the upper room.

In the Gospel lesson, John does not include the Eucharist per se, but instead relates the story of Jesus washing the disciples' feet. While some may argue about which moment in Jesus' life was the most important, it is worth noting that for John this moment comes when Jesus "got up from the table . . . tied a towel around himself [and] . . . poured water into a basin and began to wash the disciples' feet."

For stewards, the impact of this Gospel lesson comes in two ways. First, at his most difficult moment and while enduring Judas' betrayal, Jesus still displays the meaning of God's sacrificial love. When John records that "Jesus knew that his hour had come," this suggest the climax of John's story. Clearly Jesus might have taught many things to his inner circle. But at this weighty moment he puts aside all else to make sure that the disciples understand how everyone will know that they are his disciples.

The second impact upon disciples, then and now, is that Jesus enacts what he teaches. The shock of what Jesus did for the disciples in the washing of their feet cannot be understated. It must have cut them to the quick. Jesus not only speaks the message from God—he enacts the message. True leaders never ask from their followers those things that they are unwilling to do themselves. This is as sterling an example of servant leadership as we will find in Scripture.

Maundy Thursday reminds all stewards and believers that holy moments present themselves at odd times. Stewards are ever vigilant for these moments. John's Jesus demonstrates that if he stoops down to wash another's feet, then what excuse could we offer to evade any avenue of humble service? Authentic stewards will do whatever it takes to share God's love with others.

Good Friday
[See Year A]

Easter

Easter Day

Psalm 118:1–2, 14–24   The Easter Mystery We Steward

"I shall not die, but I shall live, and recount the deeds of the LORD."
(Ps. 118:17)

Crowds flock on Easter Sunday to any church with an open door. Only days ago, congregations were sparse on Maundy Thursday and Good Friday. Easter Sunday, however, is all about joy. People take the good news wherever they find it. Easter declares good news that "Christ is risen," and preachers pull few surprises. Even erratic attendees know why they are there. The lesson from the Psalter gives those almost-faithful a peek inside what gives life meaning and purpose. Perhaps such insight helps to grow faithful stewards—or at least puts them on the path to stewardship.

An unabashed confession of faith begins Psalm 118: "O give thanks to the LORD, for he is good; his steadfast love endures forever!" From this confession the church hopes to plant faith seeds. From the psalm's initial confession to its final counsel to "rejoice," we see a struggle to understand God's precious gift of life. Despite how well Israel or modern believers manage God's gift, they can rely on one thing—"the steadfast love" of God. It is present today and will last forever. It is ours to use or neglect.

Tucked away in a metaphorical corner of this psalm is the phrase "I shall not die, but I shall live, and recount the deeds of the LORD." Perhaps this is a call for stewards to manage the household that we can call "a household of witness." To what does God call us to witness? We witness to God's steadfast love, which lasts forever.

Modern people tend to reduce life to small, manageable pieces. A movie summarizes a world war by depicting a hero who willingly dies for a comrade in arms. A book recaps the Great Depression by showing a rural family that makes it though the harrowing experience intact. We get our nightly dose of the news of the world via thirty-second sound bites. In other words, we reduce life to parts that we can digest quickly and with little aftertaste. Psalm 118 reminds us that the life that God gives Israel and us is much bigger and much more unmanageable than we suspect.

People flock to church on Easter Sunday for reasons that they can scarcely articulate. In most cases they do not know why they are drawn to the Easter message. I suspect, however, that they sense that there is more to human existence than working and raising a family and paying bills and going on an occasional vacation to rest up and begin the whole frenetic process again.

When Psalm 118 relates, "I shall not die, but I shall live, and recount the deeds of the LORD," it offers us a purpose larger than the one we can see. One of the wonders of the Easter Sunday message is that we cannot put it into a thirty-second memo. Rather, the announcement that Christ has risen is so large and so deep that it will take us a lifetime to unpack. And that is where God calls forth those stewards who are willing to commit themselves to "live, and recount the deeds of the LORD."

As a small child I stood with my physician father at the bedside of our ten-year-old dying neighbor. As I watched the adults talk and cry, I knew I was in the presence of something much greater than I understood. We stewards may not be able to put in plain words the good news of Jesus' resurrection, but we can recount the deeds of the Lord and live into God's goodness. One need not understand a gift in order to appreciate it.

Second Sunday of Easter

Revelation 1:4–8   A Kingdom of Priests

"To him who loves us . . . and made us to be a kingdom, priests . . ."
(Rev. 1:5–6)

Many preachers pigeonhole Revelation from conflicting angles. It seems as if preachers in recent church tradition consider John's Apocalypse either as the

Bible's "end all" or as a document so prickly that wise preachers avoid it altogether. Still, many congregants hunger for what Revelation discloses to faithful people. Many believers yearn to hear about Revelation from known and trusted preachers. Today's lesson offers preachers a portal into Revelation that outlines what it means to be "a kingdom of priests." This priestly kingdom is God's gift to us to manage.

Revelation 1:4–8 is a solid Easter text for several reasons. First, it helps us see the world from a postresurrection perspective. John's message is to the churches, but it is a message mediated through each church's angel and Jesus Christ. When John describes Jesus as the "the faithful witness, the firstborn of the dead, and the ruler of the kings of the earth," John presents readers an eternal point of view. John portrays the eternal and cosmic Christ who in faith conquers death and reigns as the sovereign of nations.

Second, this text offers redeemed people a task. With Jesus' crucifixion, resurrection, and ascension, the New Testament has spotlighted what God does on humankind's behalf. Now, however, God fashions the redeemed into a kingdom of priests. As a result, a new focus is not so much on what God has done for us, but rather what we can do for God's creation. By definition, a priest is one who sacrifices on behalf of the household of faith or, in some cases, for an individual. Thus, a nation of priests is a collection of persons who sacrifice on behalf of others.

As early as Exodus 19:6, God called Israel to the task of being a "priestly kingdom and a holy nation" (see also 1 Pet. 2:9). Perhaps this legacy was in the divine mind as God fashioned God's people. Perhaps even from creation this is God's appeal to all God's people. We might even say that God created human beings to live in a distinctive community where all persons readily sacrifice for one another.

In today's lesson John suggests that the people offer glory to God. God has "freed us from our sins," or "washed us from our sins" as the KJV reads. Moreover, whether "cleansed" or "freed" from sin, pardoned people have a task—to become a kingdom of priests. In 2005 Hurricanes Katrina and Rita created dire circumstances for thousands of Mississippi and Louisiana residents. Churches throughout the United States opened their checkbooks and church buildings to assist displaced people from these natural disasters. In many cases, scores of churches and a multitude of individual believers made abundant sacrifices on behalf of persons whom they had never met. Additionally, individual churches provided health care and housing for those exiled from their homes. These benevolent actions offer a picture of what it means to become stewards on others' behalf and a kingdom of priests.

To become a kingdom of priests, Christian disciples who recognize their freedom in Jesus Christ appreciate David's insightful remark to Ornan in 1 Chronicles 21:24: "I will not take for the LORD what is yours, nor offer burnt offerings that cost me nothing." To be a part of a kingdom of priests, we stewards offer something that dearly costs us. We give not because we subscribe to our culture's consumer mentality, but we give because we believe that God has offered us much. Our response to God's grace in Christ is to sacrifice for others.

Third Sunday of Easter

Revelation 5:11–14   The Stewardship Household of Worship

"Worthy is the Lamb . . . to receive power and wealth."
(Rev. 5:12)

Easter is about pure joy. Easter expresses the joy of God's decisive and final victory over sin and death. Christians celebrate joy via worship. Believers steward the households God gives us to manage. Surely worship is one of these explicit households. Yet as we move further from the quaint 1950s, faithful Christians recognize that Christian worship is a decidedly neglected stewardship household. Within a culture that idolizes utility, worship appears as a nonutilitarian distraction. When people ask, "What good is attending worship?" and "What can I get out of worship?" we observe foundational fissures in Christian faith practice. For believers, the basis for worship is simple: the genuine Christian life begins and ends in the praise of God. Worship and the joy it offers is a worthy topic to address from the pulpit during the season of Easter.

The lesson today presents John's vision inside the heavenly throne room. A voice invites John into heaven, and "in the spirit" John observes one seated on the throne (4:2). The balance of chapter 4 communicates what John witnesses in a prophetic trance. As chapter 5 progresses, John sees "a scroll written on the inside and on the back, sealed with seven seals" (5:1). John also sees many other things, but plainly the scroll arrests his attention. This lesson represents a prelude to the opening of the scroll and its seals.

John watches the heavenly extravaganza, but he also hears. What he hears is "the voice of many angels surrounding the throne and the living creatures and the elders; they numbered myriads of myriads and thousands of thousands, singing." In a word, all the creatures described in this vision surround God's throne and worship. This worship honors the glory due God. John's depiction in heaven should give us pause.

Christians worship the image of God that we see most clearly in Jesus, portrayed in this Revelation text as "the Lamb that was slaughtered." If the "myriads of myriads and thousands of thousands" sing loving praises to God, then what does this say to mere mortals? If worship conveys the love and adoration of God by the heavenly beings, then worship is a worthy expression of our love and adoration of God.

Will Willimon writes: "Sunday morning is not 'working out' in the manner of the grim jogger who trudges past my home in the morning, sweating and groaning in order to live longer. Sunday is the person running to meet her lover, the child dancing wildly around the room when he hears there is a circus in town. Worship is an intrinsically valuable experience, gratuitous."* In other words, like many emotions and passions people experience, worship is among those that we carry out for its own elemental joy.

---

*William Willimon, *What's Right with the Church* (San Francisco: Harper & Row, 1985), 115–16.

When people sit down to a Thanksgiving meal, because it is such a singular occasion, typically they do not spoil the event by quibbling over calories or fat content. They eat heartily because Thanksgiving is a feast with family and friends. They can go back to the diet tomorrow. We worship God lavishly because it is fitting and right to do so. We worship because our ancestors from Abraham onward did so. We worship because as creatures we give God what God desires— praise and adoration.

We put forward our praise and thanksgiving as stewards of God's glorious bounty because we manage the stewardship household named worship. Although we may serve God and others, the confirmed Christian life begins and ends in divine worship of God.

Fourth Sunday of Easter

Revelation 7:9–17   Guided by the Shepherd

"The Lamb . . . will be their shepherd, and he will guide them."
(Rev. 7:17)

We may ask, implicitly or explicitly, why does God put us through the paces of worship and prayer and Bible study? Why doesn't God simply write the divine message so large in the sky that no one could miss it? Why doesn't God program us to be good and just and equitable to one another? Why doesn't God end terrorism, disease, war, and human malice? Perhaps the reason resides in creation. God created our ancestors and placed them in the garden of perfection "to till it and keep it" (Gen. 2:15). From creation, God sought partnership with God's creatures. God calls these partners "stewards." A root principle of stewardship is that God and human stewards collaborate to manage God's world. God furnishes every resource; we administer them.

Perhaps it is ironic, but the God we worship operates as if what people say, believe, and do is important on creation's grand stage. Regularly, even habitually, we humans forget our role and purpose as creatures. Perhaps we think our knowledge or sophistication will offer us meaning and purpose. Yet we too often overestimate our control.

Easter is about joy, but it is also about direction. God calls redeemed believers to share Christ with the world. Our Acts lesson recounts that Tabitha was devoted "to good works and acts of charity" (Acts 9:36). These deeds of service gave Tabitha direction. The other three lectionary texts use a shepherding image to suggest direction for Easter people.

Revelation 7:9–17 depicts those faithful "who have come out of the great ordeal." Their formerly soiled robes have been washed and are now "white in the blood of the Lamb." Then the elder tells John that the postordeal faithful now "worship God day and night." God offers them shelter. God now attends to every previous human need. As the text reminds us and as many preachers have intoned beside a six-foot cemetery hole, "They will hunger no more, and thirst no more; the sun will not strike them, nor any scorching heat." Why? Because "the Lamb at the center of the throne will be their shepherd." Jesus as the Lamb of God performs the functions of animal husbandry. Jesus guides us "to springs of the water of life" and will comfort us at our point of need.

In the ancient world, where most knew the agricultural rhythms of life, this image promised comfort, safety, and protection. The shepherd's chief task is to care for the sheep, who are unable to care for themselves. The Good Shepherd "lays down his life for the sheep" (John 10:11) and tells those who listen that "I know my own and my own know me" (John 10:14). Thus the Good Shepherd, ironically depicted as the Lamb of God in Revelation, is a model leader and guide for faithful stewards.

Often when I preach revivals at small, rural churches, Dorothy A. Thrupp's 1836 hymn, "Savior, Like a Shepherd Lead Us," is sung. It speaks of the believer's need of tender care and of God's promised mercy. When John alludes to Jesus' guiding us to living water, he speaks to the unqualified love and grace that only God provides. These meet our every need. As stewards who manage God's gifts, we would do well to keep our eye on the guiding shepherd. We faithful take our cues from the direction that Jesus provides. When Israel blessed Joseph, he said, "God . . . has been my shepherd all my life" (Gen. 48:15). This is a steward's blessing.

Fifth Sunday of Easter

Revelation 21:1–6   The Newness of Life

"I saw a new heaven and a new earth."
(Rev. 21:1)

A philosopher friend once shared with me a story about David Hume, the eminent eighteenth-century Scottish philosopher. Perhaps apocryphal, the story nonetheless makes a point. Hume's friends chided him because he attended church every Sunday to hear the minister John Brown preach. Defending himself, Hume said, "I don't believe what he's saying, but *he* does. And one day each week I like to hear someone who believes what he says." Stewards act upon their commitment to faith.

Easter offers Christians unbridled hope. It does so because one of the tenets of our faith is that God can make all things new. This belief means that people can begin life again in faith, even when life has taken some unhappy turns. Yet in our sophisticated, modern society, few believe that people get an authentic second chance. For example, if a person has paid a debt to society by serving a prison term, then few people can forget whatever crime or indiscretion put that person in jail in the first place. As we are prone to say, "I can forgive, but I can't forget." Whether issues are major or minor, we make starting over both painful and difficult.

However, the vision John offers in today's lesson from Revelation provides ample hope for beginning anew. This new beginning is not only for the natural order but for God's people as well. Only God can say, "See, I am making all things new." While Revelation never directly quotes any other part of the Bible, it does echo many other texts. Today's lesson brings to mind a couple of prophetic texts: Isaiah announces a God who is "about to do a new thing" (Isa. 43:19), and Jeremiah prophesies that "the LORD has created a new thing on the earth" (Jer. 31:22). John, the visionary seer of the New Testament, stands in good stead with his prophetic predecessors.

For Easter people, God's willingness to do a new thing in creating "a new heaven and a new earth" is the gospel's good news. Jesus' apparent cavalier attitude with respect to those perceived to be sinners prompts the Pharisees' question: "Why does he [Jesus] eat with tax collectors and sinners?" But taking a page from the prophets, Jesus speaks about new life. Jesus offers new life to those who have made a mess of theirs: "Those who are well have no need of a physician, but those who are sick; I have come to call not the righteous but sinners" (Mark 2:17). New life is the gospel's calling card.

John reminds his readers that the God he describes is one who "dwell[s] with them" and that "the first things have passed away." In other words, those who embrace John's vision for a new way of life can start over.

As a pastor I occasionally visit with someone who has experienced a fresh word from God and has received a new spirit. Sometimes people reflect deep remorse over the way they have lived. Even those who have never left the church say things like "I am ashamed of the way I have lived my life as a Christian" or "I have not taken care of my Christian life. Can God really forgive me?" If one subscribes to John's vision and the gospel of mercy and forgiveness that Jesus preached, then the answer is a resounding "Yes!"

To be stewards, faithful and true, then all we must do is begin living as if we believe that God owns all. Once we do this, then we are on our way to becoming the stewards God created us to be. We give because God first gave to us.

Sixth Sunday of Easter

Psalm 67:1–7   Managing God's Blessing

"The earth has yielded its increase; God, our God, has blessed us."
(Ps. 67:6)

The season of Easter is for many approximate to the agricultural season of planting. Not only is spring a time for hope to swell in our hearts, but it is also a time when faithful people celebrate Christ's resurrection as a sign of that hope. Today's lesson from the Psalter is the community of faith's prayer of praise for what God has done for Israel—and by extension for all the nations (Ps. 67:2). When the psalm addresses the theme of God's blessing, it implies that grateful people extend these blessings to others. Perhaps the way grateful people extend God's blessings is through the stewardship of praise and worship. After all, the psalm appeals, "Let the peoples praise you, O God; let all the peoples praise you."

Praise of God reflects a worshiping community's conviction that the creator of all life does not want us creatures to worry about material things. In the Sermon on the Mount, Jesus says as much: "Do not worry about your life, what you will eat or what you will drink, or about your body, what you will wear. . . . If God so clothes the grass of the field, . . . will he not much more clothe you? . . . Your heavenly Father knows that you need all these things" (Matt. 6:25, 30, 32). God wants us to have what we need to survive and thrive. A fitting response to such divine generosity is simply a steward's worship and praise.

A reader might assume from its context that Psalm 67 was most likely used in a harvest thanksgiving liturgy. It plainly fits that particular setting. Indeed, verse 6 says outright, "The earth has yielded its increase; God, our God, has blessed us." What does a nation like Israel do with its blessing? The answer may be even more remarkable than the fact of blessing. Israel is to declare this "truth reflected as thanksgiving" beyond the confines of its own national borders. Israel through praise and worship extends God's blessing "to the nations." This may be a theological variation on Isaiah's prophecy of Israel being "a light to the nations" (Isa. 42:6; 49:6). This notion is further signaled in verse 4: "Let the nations be glad and sing for joy." Thus, Israel shares the good news not only that God provides but that Israel's God as creator also judges and guides "the nations upon the earth."

Wendell Berry once wrote, "In losing stewardship we lose fellowship; we become outcasts from the great neighborhood of creation." Berry may have meant that one of the ways all earth's people are connected has to do with celebrating creation's magnificence and in preserving its grand gifts. Our gift back to God in thanksgiving is to manage these blessings as a stewardship household.

The task for faithful stewards is merely to care for God's creation. One of the purposes for the creation is to provide for God's creatures. But it may be just as true that the purpose for the creation is to occasion worship and praise from those who receive the gifts of creation, that is, the earth yielding its increase. For by earth's increase we know that "God, our God, has blessed us." Maybe a few readers will note ruefully that this psalm reflects a type of "natural theology." Yet for ancient Israel, as well as those who even today live close to the land, there are few more persuasive arguments for God's goodness. God does indeed provide. The faithful response of a steward is in praise and worship.

Ascension of the Lord
[See Year B]

Seventh Sunday of Easter

Acts 16:16–34   Saved From or Saved For?

"What must I do to be saved?"
(Acts 16:30)

For the final Sunday of Easter, the lectionary offers a first-class set of texts from which to preach, including several stewardship options. Psalm 97, for example, presents God as the ultimate sovereign of the whole earth. Thus, God is the one to whom all creatures owe fealty. A preacher could effectively explore stewardship from the Revelation text, which includes this verse: "I am coming soon; my reward is with me, to repay according to everyone's work" (Rev. 22:12). Finally, a preacher might probe the stewardship of prayer from John's Gospel text, which includes a section of Jesus' prayer for his disciples.

Instead we turn to the Acts passage, which is the story of a slave girl and her spirit of divination. Paul and Silas heal her of the evil spirit, causing her owners to lose their opportunity to make money from her. In response, they incite the magistrates and an attending crowd of onlookers against Paul and Silas, and the apostles are thrown in jail.

While securely locked up in stocks in an innermost cell, Paul and Silas pray and sing hymns to God. A timely earthquake looses the prisoners' chains and shakes open all the prison doors. The jailer, assuming blame for the circumstance, prepares to kill himself rather than face the wrath of his supervisors. But Paul and Silas stop him, saying, "We are all here."

Either in relieved gratitude or out of complete dread, the jailer falls down trembling. He then leads Paul and Silas out of the prison and asks them, "Sirs, what must I do to be saved?" For Luke, this is the classic gospel question. In fact, in Luke's Gospel a lawyer asks this same question, which initiates Jesus' parable of the Good Samaritan (Luke 10:25). The so-called rich young ruler, whom Luke calls "a certain ruler," asks similarly, "Good Teacher, what must I do to inherit eternal life?" (Luke 18:18). For Luke, this question gets to the heart of the gospel and our faith response.

Because we recognize the Bible's compact way of telling the faith story, we might suppose on good grounds that when Peter tells the jailer, "Believe on the Lord Jesus and you will be saved," this directive is essentially shorthand for the entire gospel message. Undoubtedly Peter taught the jailer more than this solitary thing. Believing in Jesus is a beginning, but Peter was far too skilled an evangelist to suggest that belief is merely all there is to salvation. We might speculate that Peter told the whole story of faith, for example, as Stephen did when called on to make his defense (Acts 7:2–53).

For many Christians, the "plan of salvation" is faith's terminal point. Some people reflect such thinking by offering the exact time and place when God saved them. For these persons, both Matthew and Luke put the idea in John the Baptizer's mouth: "Who warned you to flee from the wrath to come?" (Matt. 3:7;

Luke 3:7). However, rather than taking into account from what God saves a person, stewards are free to look on faith's opportunities. Good stewards ask, "For what did God save me?" In this understanding, God does not simply save us from wrath as much as God saves us to extend God's realm on earth—today. Perhaps in this way we may understand salvation as a call to discipleship and stewardship.

Pentecost

Day of Pentecost

Romans 8:14–17   Life in the Spirit

"All who are led by the Spirit of God are children of God."
(Rom. 8:14)

Acts records that "when the day of Pentecost had come, they were all together in one place" (Acts 2:1). On first blush it is hard to imagine all Christians being in one place. Yet if we remember the story, then we recall that the church on that fateful Pentecost day was small and no doubt fearful. Judas had met a bad end, and after casting lots the disciples replaced Judas with Matthias (1:26). Things did not look promising for believers after Jesus' ascension.

Still, the day of Pentecost revealed to believers what Isaiah prophesied about God long before: "I am about to do a new thing" (Isa. 43:19). From these dismal prospects at its beginning even now the church prospers. By the end of Acts Paul is "proclaiming the kingdom of God and teaching about the Lord Jesus Christ with all boldness and without hindrance" (Acts 28:31). What empowers believers and stewards to act boldly in the face of such adversity? The answer to such a question in part resides in God's Spirit. It is this Spirit that the church celebrates on the day of Pentecost.

The day's reading comes from the Epistle text (for a treatment of the classic story of Pentecost in Acts 2, see Year A). In the chapter preceding today's lesson, Paul addresses, even laments, the dangers of sin and people's misguided faith in the law. Beginning in chapter 8, Paul turns to what we might call the believer's life in the Spirit. Paul offers the life in the Spirit as an alternative way to look at the world and live in it.

Much of Paul's theology hinges on understanding God's way in the world by one of two alternative perceptions. One way to understand God is by the conventional Hebrew law. The law served traditional Judaism well, more or less, for centuries. Yet Jesus taught believers to go beyond the law as a border for human behavior. He said, "I have come not to abolish [the law or the prophets] but to fulfill" (Matt. 5:17). This is a second understanding of God's way. Perhaps Jesus offered grace, rather than the law, to fulfill God's will. Maybe this is what Jesus meant in quoting Isaiah that God will "let the oppressed go free" (Luke 4:18).

As to how people can trust in something that is not as concrete as the law, Paul assures the church at Rome that "all who are led by the Spirit of God are children of God." When we follow the strict letter of the law, then we have control over the interpretation and obedience to the law. However, when we let God guide us by the Spirit, then we must make our journey in faith. Thus, life in the Spirit is a life lived in trust.

Leaders as stewards are led by God's Spirit. Modern Christians are obliged to find new ways to midwife relationships between people and God. Our traditional evangelistic methods and our posture as having the church's authority behind us are now mostly fantasy. We live in a new world—a difficult world. We can no longer fall back on the old, customary ways of doing evangelism. But as God promised through Isaiah, "I am about to do a new thing." As frightening as the new may be, for those who steward a leadership household, we can trust in God. Rather than falling back into fear, we can be led by God's Spirit. It is this Spirit that gives believers and stewards the boldness to face the adversity of a new culture. If we can trust God's Spirit, then we know that we are heirs of the ancient promise of God.

Trinity Sunday
(First Sunday after Pentecost)

Proverbs 8:1–4, 22–31   Stewardship, Leadership, and Wisdom

"I was beside him, like a master worker."
(Prov. 8:30)

Naturally enough, on Trinity Sunday the lectionary texts focus explicitly or implicitly on Trinitarian matters. The Proverbs lesson is a wisdom speech.

Although "wisdom" is not part of the Father-Son-Holy Spirit triad, wisdom does disclose how God makes known the divine in the world. Wisdom, according to Proverbs and speaking in the first person, declares, "When he [the Lord] marked out the foundations of the earth, then I was beside him, like a master worker." Thus, wisdom was part of creation from its inception.

Beyond wisdom's task at creation, wisdom also led Israel. For example, Moses said to Israel, "I now teach you statutes and ordinances for you to observe in the land that you are about to enter and occupy. You must observe them diligently, for this will show your wisdom and discernment" (Deut. 4:5–6). Thus, those who follow God's law are those who employ wisdom. How may stewards access God's wisdom?

Good stewards pay attention to what wisdom offers. The foremost quality of wisdom, according to the speech by Lady Wisdom (as the church has tradition-ally designated wisdom) that covers most of Proverbs 8, is that wisdom offers human beings what they need to prosper. Most of the reasons given for follow-ing wisdom's guidance come from the portion of this speech omitted from the lectionary. For example, Lady Wisdom tells her audience, "From my lips will come what is right" (v. 6), "the words of my mouth are righteous" (v. 8), "wis-dom is better than jewels" (v. 11), and "those who seek me diligently find me" (v. 17). Within the heart and mind of a steward are aspects of what wisdom offers believers.

Yet perhaps the most compelling reason for human beings to heed wisdom's voice is simply because God established wisdom "ages ago." As Lady Wisdom reminds her readers, "I was set up, at the first, before the beginning of the earth." For the reason of longevity alone, wisdom has existed nearly as long as God has—which makes a convincing argument on its own merit.

Generally, wise leaders use wisdom as a stewardship household. We manage the wisdom and its accompanying discernment to build up God's kingdom. Wise leaders make good choices on behalf of the people they lead. Good stewards are those who are wise toward the things that God deems of value and meaning for God's people.

Solomon was reputed to be one of Israel's wisest kings: "All the kings of the earth sought the presence of Solomon to hear his wisdom, which God had put into his mind" (2 Chr. 9:23). Yet Solomon strayed from God's wisdom, for "he sacrificed and offered incense at the high places" (1 Kgs. 3:3). Stewards may vac-illate in their devotion to God and to wisdom. However, wise stewards will per-sistently return to the divine font of wisdom.

Today's stewards employ wisdom in various ways. I once heard the story of a farmer who slaughtered a hog and hung it in his barn. Soon after, it was stolen. The farmer did not mention the theft to anyone. When a neighbor asked him six months later if he had ever caught the thief, the farmer merely replied, "Just did."

To exercise wisdom as a steward, sometimes we speak, and sometimes we hold our tongue. To exercise wisdom as a steward, sometimes we step out as leaders, and sometimes we let others take the lead. Good stewards allow wisdom and discernment to guide their steps. To discern the way of God and God's wisdom is part of our life of prayer.

Sunday between May 29 and June 4
(if after Trinity Sunday)

Luke 7:1–10   The Stewardship of an Outsider

"He is worthy of having you do this for him, for he loves our people."
(Luke 7:4–5)

An issue that seems to trouble the church from time to time is whether or not it is truly open to outsiders. Does the church welcome outsiders, or does it merely tolerate them? In the spirit of evangelism, the church always claims that it has an open door. Yet human nature being what it is, often churches are suspicious of those who are different. Today's Gospel lesson is the story about a centurion's slave who appears close to death. As stewards, we might put the question of managing God's resources like this: Can stewards learn from those who are different from us? Is it possible to learn a lesson of stewardship from one whom we consider an outsider?

Jewish people in first-century Palestine could hardly have imagined anyone to be more of an outsider than a centurion. Not only was he a soldier of an occupying military force in their homeland, but also he was a pagan. This centurion was the walking definition of "outsider." Despite this, the Jewish elders appeal to Jesus on his behalf, saying, "He loves our people, and it is he who built our synagogue for us." Jesus goes with these elders to the centurion's house. Before they arrive, however, the centurion instructs some friends to tell Jesus, "Lord, do not trouble yourself." Citing his unworthiness, the centurion requests Jesus to heal his slave. After his humble request, the centurion via his friends tells Jesus that he too understands authority. He relates his experience of sending and summoning soldiers. Jesus marvels as he hears the centurion speak. Jesus announces to the crowd, "I tell you, not even in Israel have I found such faith," and he heals the slave.

In Luke's story we ponder a centurion, an outsider to the community of faith. Still, this outsider is one who loves the Jewish people. What a gift this outsider offers. Clearly the Spirit of God has touched him so much that he becomes one who contributes to the Lord's cause. This centurion becomes a steward in the midst of a community in which he represents the invader.

The theologically remarkable thing about this kind of story is that it occurs often in Scripture. A foreign woman, Ruth, was a steward of loyalty to her Jewish mother-in-law, Naomi. Ruth asks Boaz, soon to be her husband, "Why have I found favor in your sight, that you should take notice of me, when I am a foreigner?" (Ruth 2:10). The foreigner is always an outsider.

Luke regularly employs outsiders to make theological points with insiders. For example, when Jesus speaks of being a neighbor, he utters the parable of the Good

Samaritan (Luke 10:25–37). Or when Jesus speaks about to whom God reveals God's self, he speaks of the woman from Zarephath, reminding his listeners that "Elijah was sent to none of them except to a widow at Zarephath in Sidon" (Luke 4:26). In another circumstance when Jesus teaches about gratitude, he uses the occasion of healing ten lepers to make his point. After only one returns, Jesus asks, "Were not ten made clean? But the other nine, where are they? Was none of them found to return and give praise to God except this foreigner?" (Luke 17:17–18).

Stewards can learn from Ruth's management of loyalty to her mother-in-law. Stewards can learn that God sometimes comes to widows in Sidon. Stewards can learn that even Roman centurions may function as stewards. Sometimes good stewards can learn from outsiders that God pours grace on those whom we consider foreigners. Luke reminds stewards that God's grace can come from many amazing directions.

Sunday between June 5 and 11 inclusive
(if after Trinity Sunday)

Galatians 1:11–24   The Stewardship of Our Own Counsel

"I did not confer with any human being."
(Gal. 1:16)

I have a pastor friend who is fond of saying, "I would buy a book for one good sermon illustration." Perhaps you know what he is talking about. In communicating the gospel to a culture and church distracted by a thousand competing voices, preachers always look for an edge. After all, preachers are, to a degree, stewards of the gospel message. Sometimes in our eagerness to connect with our listeners we go overboard in the search of "performance enhancing" preaching materials. We attend conferences, listen to tapes or CDs, and read books, magazines, and journals for the latest technique or up-to-the-minute tactic to make our church "successful."

Our diligence and industry in finding fresh ways to do ministry makes Paul's Galatian assertions all the more startling. Paul writes that his gospel "is not of human origin." He continues: "I did not receive it from a human source, nor was I taught it." He even goes so far as to declare, "I did not confer with any human being." Paul wants the Galatians to know that his gospel comes directly from "a revelation of Jesus Christ." No human ideas—for example, "neo-orthodoxy" or "the church growth movement"—taint Paul.

For all human beings, and especially believers, there are some decisions we must make for ourselves. In these private decisions there are no authorities to consult. These decisions define our character. J. C. Watts, the Oklahoma-football-star-turned-politician, once purportedly said, "Character is doing the right thing when no one is watching." Our stewardship of God's gifts is one of these lonely places in which God forms character.

For the most part, Paul infrequently relates his personal circumstances. But here in the first part of the Epistle to the Galatians, Paul wants to establish his leadership authority. The gospel he will spend the rest of his life proclaiming is so sacrosanct to Paul that he wants the Galatian readers to know that he obtained his message directly from a divine revelation. Paul sees himself as a steward of holy things, and it is upon this basis—and this basis alone—that he claims his authority. When someone claims this kind of revelation today, we react with skepticism.

In the modern church we talk a lot about qualifications and certification. We require of our clergy diplomas, which we hope signify knowledge. Candidates for ministry seek approval from church bodies that in turn sanction those whom they find worthy. Paul's credentials, however, did not come from such sources. As Paul writes, "I received [the gospel] through a revelation of Jesus Christ."

Out in the wilderness, reminiscent of Jesus' desert testing, Paul meets God. In these revelatory years, Paul concludes that he is a steward of God's mysteries. In fact, when Paul later writes to another church, he puts it this way: "Think of us [probably Paul, Apollos, or Cephas] in this way, as servants of Christ and stewards of God's mysteries" (1 Cor. 4:1). As verification of his change of heart and mind, Paul appeals to his own life. The former church destroyer has now become the church's most ardent campaigner. Why? Because somewhere in the lonely wilderness of his soul, Paul reckons that God had plans for him much bigger than his own plans. When a believer has this realization, then a Christian has become a worthy steward.

Sunday between June 12 and 18 inclusive
(if after Trinity Sunday)

Luke 7:36–8:3   Stewardship's Remarkable Assembly

"The twelve were with him, as well as some women."
(Luke 8:1–2)

The Gospel lesson today illustrates two far-reaching stewardship principles. One principle is that God includes people as partners in creation. Surely God as creator can regulate the universe. Yet God has deemed people as creation partners (see Gen. 2:5, 15; 3:23). In the Christian life, God allocates stewardship responsibilities to humankind. Thus, we do our part, others do their part, and God does God's part. God created people as partners and stewards to make creation what God intended it.

We see another stewardship principle in God's providing believers with gifts necessary to accomplish the stewardship tasks that God gives them to do. This is a key principle, because believers often bear guilt for doing either too much or not enough as a response to managing God's generously given gifts and talents.

What is surprising, given the culture of the ancient world and the gender pigeonholing that existed, is that Scripture allots stewardship tasks to women. Today's lesson begins with the story of "a woman in the city, who was a sinner." She offers Jesus a precious gift in Simon's house. Ultimately, Jesus says to the woman, "Your faith has saved you; go in peace."

Jesus' praise of this woman doubtlessly surprised those gathered at table in this male-dominated culture. But Jesus' lesson, in part, was that everyone has a gift to offer God. Our gift is our faith response as stewards of God's gifts. In another surprising story, Jesus exemplifies faithful stewardship by way of a poor widow (Mark 12:41–44; Luke 21:1–4). This anonymous woman is an example of generosity as well as a person of deep faith. Yet she is also free from fear. She does not fear the future, for as Jesus tells the disciples, "This poor widow has put in more than all those who are contributing to the treasury . . . [,] all she had to live on" (Mark 12:43–44).

In Luke's lectionary text the story homes in on Jesus' highlighting individuals' gifts that are regularly and systematically overlooked. Apparently those eating with Jesus that day would have never expected Jesus to praise the woman who wiped his feet. After all, she was to their way of thinking "only a woman." But as Ephesians reminds people who think this way, God gave us all gifts "to equip the saints for the work of ministry, for building up the body of Christ" (Eph. 4:12). Each person receives a gift from God for ministry, and this woman's gift was gracious hospitality.

Finally, tucked away at the end of the reading is a small notation that readers might fail to notice. Luke reminds us that the band of Jesus' followers had a unique composition, especially for the ancient world. Luke notes that after Jesus and the others departed Simon the Pharisee's house, "the twelve were with him, as well as some women." Women, who by and large were overlooked in the culture, were among Jesus' followers. They contributed to the ministry and the building up of God's realm. They are part of a remarkable assembly because of their stewardship.

Luke tells us, almost in passing, the names of these women and that they provided for the disciples "out of their resources." In God's mysterious realm, the work God does among us is often carried out by those we didn't expect. In each of our lives there are persons waiting to exercise ample talents for God. Who can hinder them?

Sunday between June 19 and 25 inclusive
(if after Trinity Sunday)

1 Kings 19:1–15a   Our Stewardship Task Conquers Fear

"Then he was afraid."
(1 Kgs. 19:3a)

The Hebrew Scripture lesson addresses Elijah's intense fear after his face-off with the Baal prophets at Mount Carmel. After Elijah slaughters what appear to be

Jezebel's personal prophets, she in essence sends Elijah a death threat, prompting Elijah to flee for his life. Interestingly, while Elijah shows notable courage in the face of a multitude of prophets, he nevertheless runs for his life from Jezebel. Perhaps the yoking of fear and stewardship explains the lives of people who try to manage God's gifts. Often we want to be good stewards, but fear often thwarts our best intentions. In our worry and anxiety we do not always do the things that God calls us to do.

Many people are full of doubts. In our desire to control our future, we retire into postures of fear. We each fear a variety of different things, but when fear of the future grips us, it robs us of present joy. Some people fear failure, while others fear success. Some people spend restless nights anxious about what other people think of them. We fear for our children, our health, our nation, and our world. At times we fear things that ought to be feared, but far too often we fear things that need not be feared.

Perhaps the most fearless steward in the Gospels is a poor widow who performs like a stewardship superhero. Mark tells the story of Jesus' watching the crowd place large sums of money into the temple's treasury. Jesus draws the disciples' attention to a poor widow, who "put in two small copper coins." Jesus tells the disciples, "This poor widow has put in more than all those who are contributing to the treasury. For all of them have contributed out of their abundance; but she out of her poverty has put in everything she had, all she had to live on" (Mark 12:41–44).

No doubt the temple scene produced shame in those who watched. Maybe it brought to the disciples' minds a proverb: "Whoever follows perverse ways will be found out" (Prov. 10:9). Jesus' example of the poor widow reveals much, but mostly it reveals the widow's fearlessness. Certainly she possessed deep faith. But more than that—she was visibly free from fear. This widow evidently did not fear what her future held, but she did what was appropriate for her faith in the moment.

When the angel in Luke visits Zechariah, Mary, and the shepherds, he says, "Do not be afraid" (Luke 1:13, 30; 2:10). Perhaps this suggests that the good news casts out fear, as John's Epistle explicitly suggests (1 John 4:18). Again and again we find in Scripture allusions to fear and how faith and trust can conquer human dread.

Returning to Elijah, it appears that his fear has gotten the best of him. Yet God never forsakes God's prophet. Instead, God reveals God's self to Elijah "not in the wind," "not in the earthquake," and "not in the fire." Rather, God speaks to Elijah out of "a sound of sheer silence." God commands Elijah, "Go, return on your way to the wilderness of Damascus." Thus, God helps Elijah conquer his fear by giving him a task. In that task the prophet regains his courage. God's task for us enables us to control our fears as well.

Many modern believers are not the stewards God created them to be. Yet God has nevertheless charged us with the task of being faithful with the gifts and graces God has given us. We can overcome the fears that keep us from our stewardship by hearing God call us once again to be the stewards God created us to be. It is in response to such divinely appointed stewardship tasks that we receive our courage.

Sunday between June 26 and July 2 inclusive

Luke 9:51–62   Total Commitment

> *"No one who puts a hand to the plow and looks back is fit."*
> (Luke 9:62)

One of the chief principles of Christian stewardship is that God and God's realm will break into our world with or without our participation. A way to understand this stewardship principle is that God has fixed the outcome of creation and Jesus preached that the kingdom of God has already arrived. Mark opens his Gospel by writing, "The time is fulfilled, and the kingdom of God has come near" (Mark 1:15). This means that we can certainly duck our practice of stewardship and neglect our confession of faith, but if we choose to bypass the obligation of Christian stewardship, then we are the ones diminished. With us or without us, God's reign will come on earth.

A pastor friend told me the heartbreaking story of a young woman in his church. Several years earlier she had wanted the lead in a school play, but the directors chose another girl instead. The directors did offer her a subordinate, although substantial, role in the play. However, their decision wounded her pride. She refused to take part in any way whatsoever. Her mother pleaded with her, but she stood by her decision tenaciously. Later the young woman told her pastor that it was the biggest mistake she had ever made. She said, "Because of my stubbornness and failure to admit I had made a mistake, I spent the whole spring semester of my senior year isolated from my best friends. While they had fun rehearsing, I sat in my room and pouted. The funny thing was that the play was great. Worse than that, I am not sure anyone missed me, but I know that I sure missed them. I learned a painful lesson the hard way." This young woman demonstrates that when we fail to participate, we devalue our gifts. We can squander God's gifts by misusing them or even not using them at all.

In the Gospel text for today, Luke begins a new section. We see this change in a literary signal. Luke alerts readers that as "the days drew near for him to be taken up," Jesus "set his face to go to Jerusalem." After reining in the disciples' zeal toward some who did not receive him, Jesus is approached by several people on the road to Jerusalem. The first offers a profession of loyalty. Jesus offers the enigmatic response about the Son of Man having nowhere to lay his head, suggesting tough going ahead for Jesus' followers. To the second prospective disciple, who offers a plausible reason for a delay in his response, Jesus curtly says, "Let the dead bury their own dead." The last also wants to follow Jesus but appeals to him to "let me first say farewell to those at my home." Jesus offers a glimpse into the gospel's absolute earnestness by saying, "No one who puts a hand to the plow and looks back is fit for the kingdom of God." So much for human excuses.

In each of Jesus' responses we see the common theme that what Jesus is doing is so important that all else pales in comparison. Whether the excuse for delay is duty at home for an aged parent or simply a word of explanation for an extended absence, it matters little to Jesus' task at hand. All is to be sacrificed for God's kingdom.

In our modern world we often look for shortcuts and bargains. We hedge our bets and play both ends against the middle. In the gospel world, Jesus commits himself absolutely. He calls us to do likewise. As stewards, we pledge our time, talents, and treasure wholly to God and God's work in us and through us. If we can commit ourselves fully, then perhaps we too can turn our faces to Jerusalem.

Sunday between July 3 and 9 inclusive

2 Kings 5:1–14   The Source

"Am I God, to give death or life?"
(2 Kgs. 5:7)

A true steward assumes an essential convention of stewardship, which is that God owns everything. This convention, of course, we predicate on the premise that God as creator holds title to all that was, and is, and will be. In a sense, modernity bears a guilt that Isaiah prophesied against Israel: "Shall the potter be regarded as the clay? Shall the thing made say of its maker, 'He did not make me'?" (Isa. 29:16). As creator, God's dominion is over all. Paul echoes this prophetic theme: "Has the potter no right over the clay, to make out of the same lump one object for special use and another for ordinary use?" (Rom. 9:21). We modern folk want control. We exert our influence over our days. We function as if, under our fantasy, we have effective influence over our life.

The Hebrew Scripture lesson introduces readers to Naaman. He was the king of Aram's army chief, "a great man and in high favor with his master." But for all Naaman's greatness he suffers from leprosy. "Leprosy" in the Bible refers to several skin diseases, one of which may be what modern medicine calls Hansen's disease. Whatever the nature of Naaman's disease, it has made him a social outcast. People in the ancient world recognized the disease as a punishment from God. This social stigma went along with the Deuteronomic theology that accepted that reward and punishment were meted out directly from God. Therefore, leprous people were persistently shunned (see also Luke 7:22 and 17:12, among many references to leprosy and lepers). Naaman was a successful military leader, but a pariah nonetheless.

Military leaders, in ancient times as today, command respect. At Capernaum a centurion encountered Jesus, and Jesus healed his slave. What is of interest is not only the humility of the centurion, but what he said to Jesus: "I also am a man set under authority, with soldiers under me; and I say to one, 'Go,' and he goes, and to another, 'Come,' and he comes, and to my slave, 'Do this,' and the slave does it" (Luke 7:8). Clearly Naaman's military authority is similar to the centurion's in Luke's account. Although a pariah, Naaman still perceives himself as in control of his destiny. The text tells us what he brought for healing—the equivalent of our best health-care insurance: "ten talents of silver, six thousand shekels of gold, and ten sets of garments," as well as a letter of introduction from the king of Aram. Armed with these treasures, perhaps Naaman believed he could buy his healing.

Yet there is a twist in this story of a person who thinks he controls his destiny. The hand of God enters the mix, almost preposterously, in a chain of encounters that introduces Naaman to Elijah. If we read this story with care, we will observe a chain reaction of those who conspire with God to grant healing to Naaman. First, there is a slave girl who tells Naaman's wife about the prophet in Samaria. After hearing from his wife, Naaman approaches the king of Aram, who writes a letter to the king of Israel. Other intermediaries enter the picture as well. In time, God heals Naaman.

Few were more powerful in his domain than was Naaman. Yet his healing begins in a tentative word spoken by a slave girl. God owns all and is our source. When God's people do their small parts in the divine realm, then through us God's gifts multiply. Our small ingredient causes a stewardship chain reaction of faith that serves Christ's realm.

Sunday between July 10 and 16 inclusive

Luke 10:25–37   The Neighbor

"Go and do likewise."
(Luke 10:37)

With the technology that continues to expand and the uses to which modern people put it, our world appears to steadily contract. People today can sit in their homes and watch on television events that are occurring continents away—and watch them as they unfold. Yet despite the world's perceptible shrinkage, we still must cope with the people who live next door. For this reason, Jesus' parable from Luke helps inform daily life in ways that we can barely imagine. The self-justifying lawyer's question, "Who is my neighbor?" is a persistent question for us as we aspire to become Christian stewards.

The parable of the Good Samaritan begins with a simple enough question. A lawyer stands, perhaps to exert his authority, and asks Jesus, "What must I do to inherit eternal life?" Luke offers a clue to the lawyer's motive when he notes that the man "stood up to test Jesus." Jesus conforms to good rhetoric in argumentation by throwing a couple of questions back to the lawyer: "What is written in the law? What do you read there?" The lawyer quotes from Leviticus 19:18 and Deuteronomy 6:5. Jesus commends the lawyer on his answer.

But not satisfied to leave well enough alone and wanting to justify himself, the lawyer presses Jesus with yet another question: "Who is my neighbor?" Jesus' reply has become in our faith tradition the model for caring people. Jesus now begins the parable proper. This adored parable needs little amplification.

Rather than trying to define who the neighbor is for the lawyer, Jesus instead offers a representative story of what a neighbor did on behalf of a man "who fell into the hands of the robbers." Good neighbors, as perhaps good stewards, are those who go beyond requirements and do what is essential in particular circumstances. As Matthew writes, "If anyone wants to sue you and take your coat, give your cloak as well; and if anyone forces you to go one mile, go also the second mile" (Matt. 5:40–41). Significantly, after writing these words as part of Jesus' Sermon on the Mount, Matthew continues, "You have heard that it was said, 'You shall love your neighbor and hate your enemy.' But I say to you, Love your enemies and pray for those who persecute you" (5:43–44). Matthew and Luke link earthly neighbors to divine love.

Stewards are people who are generous with the things that God has loaned them to build up God's realm. This Samaritan is the least likely person to go the second mile to help a Jewish person—let alone be extravagant in his generosity. Earlier, perhaps out of obligation to the Mosaic law, a priest and a Levite "passed by on the other side." Yet it is the one that Jesus' audience would have least suspected as showing mercy who is the one to show compassion. The generosity of the Samaritan (who can measure the value of such without looking at his tax return) is demonstrated in his care for the one in the ditch who had been left to die.

It is probably to the lawyer's credit that he asks a religious question on many people's minds: "What must I do to inherit eternal life?" When Jesus answers this query, he counters not so much quantitatively as we might today—who is the richest or has the greatest possessions? Rather, Jesus' answer is qualitative. The one who lives abundantly is the one who shows mercy to the neighbor—who is anyone in need.

Sunday between July 17 and 23 inclusive

Luke 10:38–42   The Mary and Martha Controversy

"Mary has chosen the better part, which will not be taken away from her."
(Luke 10:42)

Luke knows how to tell an engaging story. Readers may even recognize various parallel conflicts that occur under our own roofs, for this is a conflict-laden story. The conflict perhaps arises from sibling rivalry, about which most of us know far too much. But the story may also apply to conflict that arises from our expected roles within a household. We all know about teaching young children about responsibility. Years ago my wife asked our youngest son to take his shoes from the stairway and put them in his closet. As he stomped loudly up the stairs, he dramatically put his forearm over his forehead and sighed in a loud stage voice, "I have to do everything around here!" His mother said he had heard me say this, while I was certain he had heard the phrase from her. In any case, most of us assume, at work or at home, that we do far more than our share most of the time. This realization influences our understanding of stewardship.

In today's Gospel lesson, Martha welcomes Jesus and his companions into her home. It is a gracious act of hospitality, which from the context seems a characteristic of Martha's. Luke tells us that Martha's sister, Mary, "sat at the Lord's feet and listened to what he was saying." No cooking or cleaning or the like for Mary. All seems to go well until Martha asks Jesus to arbitrate the evident conflict between the sisters. This brings to mind another Lucan story, in which someone asks Jesus to help brothers divide an inheritance. In this instance Jesus says, "Friend, who set me to be a judge or arbitrator over you?" (Luke 12:14). Surely Jesus' reputation for honesty occasioned these requests. Martha asks in effect the same question here. She wants Jesus to put Mary in her place.

In terms of stewardship this story reminds us—and we derive this from Jesus' answer to Martha—that each of us has stewardship tasks to perform. In Mary's defense Jesus tells Martha, "Martha, you are worried and distracted by many things; there is need of only one thing. Mary has chosen the better part, which will not be taken away from her." In essence Jesus tells Martha that Mary's enthralled attention to his words is okay. This is part of Mary's stewardship—to listen and learn from the master.

Yet for far too long Martha has gotten a "bad rap" in that church tradition often perceives her as nothing less than a grumbler or moaner. However, to offer gracious hospitality to guests involves a certain amount of manual labor. Martha is clearly aware that all her work is intrinsic to offering hospitality, and Jesus does not criticize her work per se. Rather, he points out that her domestic work has produced worry and that worry has led Martha to a distracted anxiety.

The church is little different. All churches have members who want all their offerings to go to foreign or local missions—and this is laudable. Still, the church has a responsibility for sustaining its own local mission site. A church provides heating and cooling for worship gatherings as well as for Sunday school. Churches also have the responsibility to compensate fairly those who are in full-time Christian service, whether lay or clergy. When a church shirks its nominal obligations to its own ministry, it reminds me of the father who lavished expensive gifts on his child but failed to provide court-mandated child support for her welfare. "Feel good" giving is quite fitting giving, but not at the expense of doing the things that allow for the local preaching of the gospel. Mary was undoubtedly doing the *right* thing. But we do Martha wrong when we fail to recognize that she did the *necessary* things.

Sunday between July 24 and 30 inclusive

Luke 11:1–13   Primacy of Prayer

> *"Ask, and it will be given you; search, and you will find."*
> (Luke 11:9)

Of all the requests that Jesus' disciples made, it may seem puzzling that among them is "Lord, teach us to pray." After all, we believe prayer arrives part and parcel with faith. Yet judging from the numerous biblical citations regarding prayer, there must have been much unease and confusion about prayer and its essential nature. Thus, when Jesus teaches the disciples what to say as they pray, among his directives is "Forgive us our sins, for we ourselves forgive everyone indebted to us." Readers may well conclude that what God does for us we then in turn do for others. This supposition is a first-order stewardship attitude. We share our time and treasures with others because God has loaned these talents to us in order to build up God's realm.

Luke's Gospel text has three parts. First is the response to the disciples' question, which is Luke's account of the Lord's Prayer. Next Jesus tells the "friend at midnight" parable. Finally, Jesus tells the disciples, "So I say to you . . . " In these verses of paraenesis (exhortation or counsel) Jesus uses several analogies that follow the parable's logic. He employs the rhetorical argument from the lesser to the greater. The logic states that if a friend is willing to arise at midnight to accommodate a neighbor, then how much more will God do to grant our petitions. Preaching this entire text might be problematic, although the prevailing concern focuses on prayer and how to pray. Thus for stewardship, we could argue that all gifts offered to God are gifts offered in prayer.

Of course, a careful reading reveals that in the final section of the text Jesus changes the metaphor slightly from the parable's "friend" to images regarding what parents want to offer their children. Perhaps Jesus' point is twofold. First, because God has forgiven us, we now are free to forgive others. Second, as God gives to us we now are free to give on behalf of others. Too often, however, both forgiveness and stewardship take on a "you scratch my back and I'll scratch your back" flavor. We think, "I'll forgive others, God, if you first forgive me." At best this is a kind of bartering prayer for forgiveness (or stewardship) with God and, at worst, it looks like an out and out bribe.

An amusing example of this self-serving tit-for-tat mentality comes from James W. Moore's book *Healing Where It Hurts*. In a love letter to her former fiancé, a woman expresses her recent change of heart:

> Dear Tommy:
>
> Can you ever forgive me? No words could ever express the great unhappiness I've felt since breaking our engagement. Please say you'll take me back.

No one could ever take your place in my heart, so please forgive me. I love you! I love you! I love you!

Yours forever,
Marie

P.S. And congratulations on winning the state lottery!*

Authentic prayer is the source for forgiveness and giving. We do not forgive to gain God's mercy. We do not give to obtain God's blessings. We receive God's mercy, and God's forgiveness frees us to forgive. Likewise we give because God has given to us beyond our grasp. God's act of forgiving us and giving to us is always a prior act. An authentic link to God begins and ends in prayer. Prayer spiritually prepares stewards to do for others what God has done for us. Giving and forgiving are among the most difficult things our faith asks of us. In prayer perhaps we prevail over these obstacles.

Sunday between July 31 and August 6 inclusive

Luke 12:13–21   On Building Bigger Barns

"One's life does not consist in the abundance of possessions."
(Luke 12:15)

People often asked Jesus direct questions and received for their trouble nothing but a story. In today's reading Luke introduces the readers to a person in the crowd who asks, "Teacher, tell my brother to divide the family inheritance with me." It was not an unusual question, for even people today in settling family estates commonly rely on judges and courts to settle such matters. But rather than play the role of judge, Jesus warns listeners to beware of greed, because "one's life does not consist in the abundance of possessions." Luke here offers his readers a stewardship lesson.

Jesus' parable of the Rich Fool implies that anything that replaces God as a person's ultimate concern thrusts that individual into idolatry. Although Jesus does not use the explicit term "idol" or "idolatry" in the parable's NRSV translation, savvy readers recognize that idolatry is the issue at stake. In this parable barns become symbolic of mammon, or money, in Luke's telling about a rich, foolish man.

In modern culture, money has certainly become a god we worship, but perhaps this is no different than in antiquity. Faithful stewardship nonetheless overcomes this temptation to become possessed by possessions. Even the biblical writers knew that money is a god that never satisfies. Ecclesiastes noted this long

---

*James W. Moore, *Healing Where It Hurts* (Nashville: Abingdon Press, 1993), 81.

ago: "The lover of money will not be satisfied with money; nor the lover of wealth, with gain. This also is vanity" (Eccl. 5:10). The stewardship question may well be "When is enough, enough?"

Jesus' antihero in the parable seemed to have no larger life purpose than to build bigger barns. If the barn builder was intent on storing grain to feed the hungry, then he would have had a realistic stewardship cause. Yet the parable's context suggests he wanted "bigger barns" for the simple purpose of having "ample goods laid up for many years." He could then say to himself, "Relax, eat, drink, be merry." His barns were bluntly for his security. Cautioning believers about the last days, 2 Timothy 3:2 prophesies as a warning, "People will be lovers of themselves, lovers of money, boasters, arrogant, abusive, disobedient to their parents, ungrateful, unholy." When people seek security in anything but God, idolatry flourishes. For this man, barns are money.

Money is a tool like anything else. It can be used for good or it can be misused and thereby create evil in a social sense. The epistle we know as 1 Timothy never suggests that "money is the root of evil," as people regularly misquote it. Rather, the text reads, "The *love* of money is a root of all kinds of evil" (1 Tim. 6:10). In this regard money is value-neutral; it can be used for good or ill. Good stewardship knows this difference.

The barn builder has two primary troubles with his barn construction project. One concerns his community, and the other concerns his life perspective. The first concern is that the man who wants bigger barns wants them for his own ease and not for the community's security. The story never mentions what happens when drought or famine comes to his region. Will he help others ward off starvation? Such thoughtlessness may remind us of another Lucan story of a rich man (see Luke 16:19–31). The rich fool's blunder was regarding only himself. If the Bible is clear about anything, it is clear about a positive answer to Cain's question (Gen. 4:9).

The rich fool's second problem is that his hoarding smacks of a person only trusting his own skill to supply his need. This is not only self-aggrandizement but clearly idolatry. True stewards trust God so that they will not need to stockpile—or build bigger barns.

Sunday between August 7 and 13 inclusive

Luke 12:32–40   Faithful Preparedness

"Be like those who are waiting for their master to return."
(Luke 12:36)

People loathe waiting. Maybe it is a symptom of modernity that everything speeds up as culture evolves/devolves. Maybe no one ever liked waiting. Yet even today we recognize that much about life is simply waiting. Fast food, microwaves, and high-speed computer networks all symbolize our aversion to waiting. Even credit cards (perhaps the single modern convenience that most puts us into grave fiscal troubles) have to do with our bias against waiting. To be a faithful disciple or a faithful steward, believers are obliged to cultivate a nonanxious ability to pass God's time.

Luke's chapter 12 attends to stewardship. The first 12 verses address the disciple's gospel stewardship, while verses 13–34 address stewardship of property. In the Gospel lesson's first few verses, Jesus tells the disciples not to be afraid, because God has given them God's kingdom. In contrasting earthly with divine treasures, Jesus teaches that "where your treasure is, there your heart will be also." The text's conclusion reveals Jesus' teachings about being good stewards of time. Jesus instructs believers about how they can view and redeem the time until his return.

If the Christian life requires waiting, then good stewards need to learn how to do it. Jesus teaches us "the way to wait" for his return. In verses 35–36 Jesus spells out three elements involved in waiting, three descriptions of the readiness for and expectation of his return. Verses 37–38 promise the blessings on those who wait as Jesus has taught. Verses 39–40 offer a warning; some do not wait in readiness for Jesus' return. In Jesus' words we may see that stewardship of time requires us to wait in readiness.

If we summarized three characteristics of good waiting, they might be the following: (1) preparation—"be dressed, ready," (2) maintenance—"keep your lamps burning," and (3) expectation—"[and be] like people waiting for their master." "Be prepared" is the Boy Scout motto, but it also serves as a good slogan for Christian stewardship.

To be prepared is to be a believer who has vision and a contingency plan ready. A youth group once joined with another group at a lake house, where they were to prepare for a musical performance. Rolling out an extension cord, someone realized that the socket would not accept it. The group panicked because no one could figure out how to plug a three-pronged cord into an outlet with only two inserts. One of the youth leaders said, "Don't sweat it. I always carry an adapter with me." This is what being prepared means. This youth leader had been in this situation before. He was set to address it and with ease. He was prepared. Not only that, but in his practice of waiting between events like this, he had used his time to plan accordingly.

Jesus teaches believers to prepare for his return. In his absence, we attend to the things Jesus desires. Jesus' parable of the sheep and goats (Matt. 25) outlines Jesus' and the prophets' wish: feeding, watering, clothing, visiting, praying. When Jesus comes, like our lesson's parable master, will he find us about God's work? This is what being prepared means. It means redeeming God's time as faithful stewards.

We all wait in life. As a child I remember waiting for my father to return from work. I would sit at the window and wait and watch. But I always did so because I expected him to return. Similarly, we expect Jesus to return. Sometimes the waiting is long, hard, and discouraging. Our zeal flags. The way we wait for the return of the master is a genuine measure of the kind of disciples we are—and what kind of stewards too.

Sunday between August 14 and 20 inclusive

Hebrews 11:29–12:2   Stewards Walk by Faith

"By faith the people passed through the Red Sea."
(Heb. 11:29)

As a prime precept of stewardship and as a foundation for this commentary, we assume that God owns everything. This principle derives from the theological tenet that "the LORD is the everlasting God, the Creator of the ends of the earth" (Isa. 40:28). But we also believe that God has sent the Spirit, a continuing guide for believers. Paul suggests as much when he writes, "For all who are led by the Spirit of God are children of God" (Rom. 8:14). Stewardship thus takes its prompting from God's Spirit, which has created and continues to create. Today's Epistle lesson hammers home the point about the saints of old that their walk as God's covenant people was done "by faith." Today's text uses the phrases "by faith" or "through faith" four times. Even more remarkable is that in Hebrews 11 the phrase "by faith" occurs eighteen times—a repetition that has a jackhammer effect on the reader. Hebrews is serious when it relates that our heroes of faith lived "by faith."

Perhaps this passage that underscores the reality of our forbears' faith is a good antidote to the way modern people grasp life. We moderns tend to be self-absorbed and far too often trust our own abilities and instincts. For stewardship this is clearly antithetical to biblical teaching. Left to their own devices when they discovered they were naked, the aboriginal man and woman sewed fig leaves together for clothing—comparable to making underwear out of an abrasive, graded sandpaper. When left alone we make poor choices.

Recently I attended what was euphemistically called a "worship of life celebration"—in other words, a funeral. At the service I witnessed an attitude of self-confidence in its most naked manifestation. Among several inappropriate songs used in the service was "My Way," one of Frank Sinatra's signature songs. Of course, doing it our way is the problem with human beings in a nutshell. We do it our way and not God's way. Each time Israel did it Israel's way, destruction loomed around the corner. The same is true for us as well. The writer of Hebrews will have none of this. Rather, this text reminds us repeatedly that those who surround us with "so great a cloud of witnesses" are those who walked "by faith." Paul puts it this way: "So we are always confident; . . . for we walk by faith, not by sight" (2 Cor. 5:6–7). Our confidence is in God and not in ourselves. Stewards are called upon by God to manage what God has offered us. We offer back to our world the time and treasures God has loaned us. This is the source of our confidence. We add our small part, and God performs the rest.

Whether passing through the Red Sea, receiving spies in peace, or breaching the walls of Jericho, we do our part "by faith." Good stewardship begins with the recognition that the God of the covenant is our God of the promise. The concluding part of our Epistle lesson invites us to "run with perseverance the race that is set before us, looking to Jesus the pioneer and perfecter of our faith." Faithful stewards keep their eyes on Jesus as the final and decisive sign of God's covenant promise. We understand that none of the gifts we employ as modern people would be worth a fig if it were not for God's prior gift to us. Therefore, when we function as stewards, we manage as those who before us did great things "by faith." For it is in the crucible of faith that God fashions authentic stewards.

Sunday between August 21 and 27 inclusive

Luke 13:10–17   Being Sabbath Stewards

"Ought not this woman . . . be set free . . . on the sabbath day?"
(Luke 13:16)

Of all the robust rites that Christian and Jews observe, modernity has thrust aside Sabbath keeping. Believers throughout the centuries regularly followed the commandment to "hallow the sabbath, and keep it holy" (Exod. 20:8). Yet Sabbath keeping today fights for its pride of place, even in faith communities. For stewards, Sabbath keeping is a foundation that keeps our stewardship management grounded in God's word and God's design for creation. Today's Gospel lesson reminds us that people struggled with Sabbath's meaning even in Jesus' day.

The Sabbath has been a day set apart in the Judeo-Christian sphere since at least the middle part of Exodus (see 16:23ff.). When the Babylonians carried the people of Jerusalem away to exile, Judah was shaken to its roots. During captivity Isaiah prophesied about the nation's theological underpinnings: "If you refrain from trampling the sabbath, from pursuing your own interests on my holy day . . . I will feed you with the heritage of your ancestor Jacob" (Isa. 58:13–14). Our Lucan text might appear as merely another of Jesus' miracles, but its focus is Sabbath keeping.

Aligned on opposite sides of the Sabbath-keeping question Jesus and a synagogue leader debated the matter. Jesus suggested that the healed woman's health took precedence over keeping Sabbath law—at least in this actual case. Lest we devalue the synagogue leader's position, we need to remember that for Jews the Sabbath was sacrosanct. Jesus would have affirmed this attitude as well. Jesus' point, nevertheless, was that some things override the sanctity of Sabbath keeping—and healing this woman was such a case.

If he were here today, the leader of the synagogue might point out that we have been carried away. We have not been carried away bodily like Judah, but our culture has lapsed into Sabbath forgetfulness. Regardless, the Sabbath is important to Israel, as it still is to modern believers.

For stewards, our management of our God-given abilities flows from our rest, worship, and remembrance, which are, after all, the basis of Sabbath keeping. Why is keeping the Sabbath so important? On the grounds of utility alone, what is the point of resting? What is a useful reason or a pragmatic motive for resting and worshiping weekly?

In a chapter entitled "Sharpening the Saw" in his book *The 7 Habits of Highly*

Effective People, Stephen Covey writes about a Sabbath-like habit that is akin to Sabbath keeping.* Covey's point is that stepping back, resting, and getting perspective on our work makes our labor time more effective. Covey likens resting to the process a wood chopper uses when he sharpens his saw as he rests. With a sharpened saw the work goes more efficiently. We do better work when we stop and rest periodically—and we do the work more quickly.

For stewards, the Sabbath is not idle time. Rather, it gives believers the chance to recoup our energy and focus our attention. It also allows us to celebrate God's gifts to us. God builds into our week an idea of rest and re-creation. Stewards use the Sabbath to remember who we are and to connect with life's spiritual facet, which God gives as a gift.

The dispute between the synagogue leader and Jesus was not over the importance of the Sabbath. Rather, Jesus' point was that at times human need overrides Sabbath keeping. In this case it was a crippled woman, but in every circumstance the Sabbath is a great gift from God.

Sunday between August 28 and September 3 inclusive

Luke 14:1, 7–14   Christian Hospitality and Preserving Pride

"When you give a banquet, invite the poor, the crippled . . ."
(Luke 14:13)

For Luke, meals enact a powerful metaphor for God's dominion. In Luke-Acts there are no fewer than forty references to "eating" or "at the table." Perhaps Luke uses this device in order to give Jesus a more personal setting for teaching. Today's Gospel lesson shares one such intimate moment as guests jockey for positions of honor around a banquet table. After Jesus notes "how the guests chose the places of honor," he tells a parable. For stewards this parable is a superb guide on how to share with others.

Luke earlier suggested that food is to be shared with the community (see the commentary on Luke 12:13–21 on page 222). Regarding stewardship, one insight this parable offers is that the method by which a person offers assistance to another may be as important as the assistance itself. That is to say that when someone is on the giving end of a gift, it is often easy to make the receiver feel not so much gratitude as embarrassment—even shame.

Examples abound for ministers about this principle of reciprocity. One of my pastor friends has a daughter who got married. The family received many, many gifts from his rather large congregation. But rather than feeling gratitude, my friend instead felt shame. Why? Because he had never bought a single wedding present for any family in his congregation and felt he should reciprocate the people's kindness.

*Stephen R. Covey, *The 7 Habits of Highly Effective People* (New York: Simon & Schuster, 1989), 287–307.

In part, this is what Jesus' parable addresses. Jesus first speaks about the choosing of seats of honor. We strive to sit in important places—to see and be seen. Yet Jesus says that it is better to be asked to "move up higher" than to be asked to surrender a seat to someone worthy of more honor. Of course, in the ancient world honor was among a person's most prized assets. Jesus then offers up gospel wisdom: "For all who exalt themselves will be humbled, and those who humble themselves will be exalted." When people attempt to create honor themselves, the endeavor is doomed.

Jesus recognizes the human desire for competition, whether for honor or wealth, at the parable's closing. Then Jesus shows stewards how to be truly generous in God's realm. Jesus directs his words to the host, but all pay rapt attention to his words. In our give and take world, we offer hospitality to those who are capable of returning the favor. Christmas gifts often are not deliberated based on relationship but rather on what is likely to be a suitably reciprocal gift. When someone offers too lavish a gift, it may plant tension in a relationship. Lavish gifts may also create the shameful feelings that my pastor friend felt regarding his daughter's wedding gifts from parishioners.

Instead of showing honor by bestowing invitations (or gifts) on those who can without question repay such a debt, Jesus tells the host to "invite the poor, the crippled, the lame, and the blind. And you will be blessed, because they cannot repay you." In other words, the gift's motive should not be based on some sort of reciprocity, but rather on what the gift contributes to the recipient's well-being.

At Thanksgiving or Christmas, sometimes people of genuine goodwill give gifts in ways that shame the poor. In God's realm there is a better way. Once I had a large bag of aluminum cans. I stopped and offered them to an evidently poor fellow gathering cans in a highway ditch. He refused the cans, saying, "I don't need no charity." So over the next hill I pitched the cans into the ditch. Later as I drove back, I noticed that he had picked up every can—and preserved his dignity and pride to boot. Stewardship perhaps?

Sunday between September 4 and 10 inclusive

Philemon 1–21   The Stewardship of Altered Relations

"Welcome him as you would welcome me."
(Phlm. 17)

Philemon appears only on this Sunday in the three-year lectionary cycle. Perhaps for this reason alone we might take a closer look at a household that stewards manage that we might call "a stewardship of altered relationships." How stewards handle the constant flux in human relationships certainly merits a faith perspective.

Handling the transition that children make toward adulthood can be stressful. One day a child is simply a child whom parents direct by filling her plate, telling her when to go to bed and what to wear. Suddenly, so it seems to parents, this heretofore malleable child begins to exert her will. She refuses to eat certain foods, demands to stay up an extra hour, and begins to dress in ways that befuddle the most patient of parents. The child begins to exercise her will.

In our lesson today Paul writes to his "dear friend and co-worker," Philemon. The recipient of the letter is worthy of honor, as revealed in Paul's noble tone throughout the epistle. Not only this, but as a respected member of the local church community, Philemon hosts the congregation in his house. Paul reveals the depth of his relationship with Philemon when he says, "I say nothing about your owing me even your own self." Paul may mean that he has birthed both Philemon's and Onesimus's salvation. In this epistle, Paul helps define new relations in Christ Jesus.

When people experience a change in status, they often incur changes in their relationships with others. We may all know a person who at one time was simply our friend. Then that individual became a bishop or a doctor or a mother-in-law. Abruptly the ease we had with this person needed new clarity. In John 9 after a man who was born blind receives sight from Jesus, suddenly he is no longer simply a "blind man." His neighbors even argue whether or not he is the same man: "Some were saying, 'It is he.' Others were saying, 'No, but it is someone like him.' He kept saying, 'I am the man' " (John 9:8–9). When someone changes status, then relationships also change.

Paul bases his appeal to Philemon on the fact that the slave owner is a Christian brother and that Paul had "received much joy and encouragement from your love." Now Paul asks Philemon to accept back "Onesimus, whose father I have become during my imprisonment." Paul never negates Philemon's legal claim over his slave. Rather, Paul appeals to Philemon's scruples and "in order that your good deed might be voluntary and not something forced." Paul asks such a thing by virtue of their shared ministry in Christ.

In Galatians, Paul makes a claim about the absolute uniqueness of the Christian community in the ancient world: "There is no longer Jew or Greek, there is no longer slave or free, there is no longer male and female; for all of you are one in Christ Jesus" (Gal. 3:28). Christian community is distinctive.

In our parish there is a fellow who was recently released from prison. People's reactions are genuinely mixed, but as a rule, the former inmate has found a place in our congregation. The way we offer ourselves to people whose circumstances change—through divorce, a handicapping condition, HIV-positive status, loss of job, criminal conviction—exposes how we steward relationships in flux and transition. It is a gift to help people in life transitions.

Sunday between September 11 and 17 inclusive

Luke 15:1–10   The Odd Economy of God's Realm

"Rejoice with me, for I have found the coin that I had lost."
(Luke 15:9)

Commonly when pastors teach the Bible, questions arise about how we *really* know this or that happened. These questions arise out of our post-Enlightenment mindsets and penchants for scientific data. Someone surprised me recently when he asked with respect to the prodigal son, "Why didn't Jesus give names to the father and sons?" It was a question that had never occurred to me.

In today's Gospel lesson, the characters, the finder of a lost sheep and a woman who found a lost coin, are collective characters. Their reactions to finding something represent typical responses. They are unnamed because they signify all people.

Luke sets the context for these parables by writing, "The Pharisees and the scribes were grumbling." As Jesus teaches "tax collectors and sinners," the religious establishment ridicules Jesus for involvement with such riff-raff. Thus, these parables address a bottom line theological truth. When God finds sinners (or perhaps when sinners find God), "there is joy in the presence of the angels of God." Typical of Luke, the protagonists are those who would have been near the bottom of first-century society—a shepherd and a woman. Luke also makes use of both male and female characters to make the point (see also Luke 1:13; 2:34, 36; Acts 17:34; 18:2, etc.).

Although modern people tend to overvalue the individual, we nonetheless understand utility. From our perspective it seems imprudent to abandon ninety-nine sheep in the wilderness and search for one. Losing 1 percent of a person's holdings seems like a necessary cost of doing business. We could suggest the same with regard to the nine coins that were in the woman's hand. Why risk losing what we already possess in order to regain a small amount?

Of course these parables are truly concerned with God's finding the last, the lost, and the least as represented by the parable's initial audience—tax collectors and sinners. Yet the real listeners—the Pharisees and the scribes—may have been Jesus' intended audience. Jesus may be saying that in God's realm it is often the unseen or at least the overlooked that concern God. Therefore, the finding of a single sheep and the finding of one coin well embody what God sees as vital in God's realm.

We live today in a "throwaway society." After we use a product, we simply toss it in the trash. Perhaps this is simply the nature of twenty-first-century culture. Yet at the same time a comparable attitude pertaining to human beings often rears its head as well. We hear about our nation's "throwaway children." These are youngsters who are products of broken homes and often come from poverty. They often fail in school and are in trouble with the legal system. Some social architects simply suggest that society cut its losses with these children and ware-house them in institutions.

Today's lesson reminds us of the worth of each individual—whether a coin, sheep, or a child. Jesus taught that each human life was worthy of God's love and concern. If God values every person, can we do less as faithful stewards?

Sunday between September 18 and 24 inclusive

Luke 16:1–13   Surprising Praise for a Dishonest Steward

"And his master commended the dishonest manager because he had acted shrewdly."
(Luke 16:8)

Luke continues throughout this portion of the Gospel his narrative theme of peo-ple's relationship to possessions via a troublesome parable, that of the Dishonest Steward. It is a parable that often creates palpable discomfort among believers. Even the parable's text is knotty concerning where it actually ends. David But-trick writes, "Clearly the parable embarrassed Luke, for he keeps adding verses— 8b, 9, 10–12—trying to find an acceptable moral for the story."* We will focus on the parable's first eight verses.

Luke uses the image of a "rich man," as he sometimes does, to begin this para-ble (see Luke 12:16; 16:19). Evidently the steward's master lives some distance away from his business but, nonetheless, catches wind of his steward who is "squandering his property." After calling him to account (the steward never denies his neglect of his stewardship) the master mercifully does not fire him but rather asks for an "accounting of your management." This act of clemency buys some time for the steward, who ponders what he shall do, saying, "I am not strong enough to dig, and I am ashamed to beg." Without a job recommenda-tion or the prospect of another job, he hits on an idea.

The steward's idea is to place others in his debt by discounting their bills to his soon-to-be former master. Of course, the master's debts will not come due until the harvest, and the intervening time will allow him to scramble for the next idea to save his skin. The dishonest steward acts hastily before word of his dis-missal spreads to those who are indebted to the master. Luke describes two cases of debt reduction: a hundred jugs of olive oil become fifty, and a hundred con-tainers of wheat become eighty. We can assume that the dishonest steward uses this practice again and again. In defense of the steward we might infer that he reduces his commission on the collection of debts, but the parable never explic-itly tells us this. The parable ends with a surprise: "The master commended the dishonest manager because he had acted shrewdly." What kind of parable is this, and why did Jesus tell it as a positive model?

No doubt one reason Jesus told this parable is that those who seek God's realm

*David Buttrick, *Speaking Parables* (Louisville, KY: Westminster John Knox Press, 2000), 210.

must be willing to employ drastic measures. Thus, the master praises the steward not so much for his dishonesty as for quick thinking in a pinch. When it comes to matters of salvation and eternal life, we might apply Jesus' words: "See, I am sending you out like sheep into the midst of wolves; so be wise as serpents and innocent as doves" (Matt. 10:16). At times to be wise, faithful stewards must do some fast thinking. When faithful stewards face desperate times and circumstances, then these occasions call for rash actions.

The dishonest steward perhaps puts the creditors in his debt. Later he can appeal to them on behalf of his prior favor. Perhaps the master praises him for his chicanery that has gotten the master into the good graces of those who first owed him. Either way, in a tight spot the dishonest steward does what is required to save his neck. In the realm of God, those who "make friends for [themselves] by means of dishonest wealth" also know how to make friends with a God who ushers them into their eternal homes. This parable speaks to the issue of the wise use of resources at hand. Faithful stewards on occasion do what needs to be done in order best to manage God's resources.

Sunday between September 25 and October 1 inclusive

1 Timothy 6:6–19   The Dangers of Lusting after Wealth

"Those who want to be rich fall into temptation and are trapped."
(1 Tim. 6:9)

In the last portion of 1 Timothy, Paul offers counsel to his young protégé. He writes Timothy to "teach and urge these duties" (1 Tim. 6:2), which subsequently he cheerfully outlines. In some ways these words appear as Paul's closing words of guidance to Timothy. Paul wants to offer Timothy, presumably now on his own, some final observations. Key to the text is when Paul writes, "But as for you, man of God . . . ," for this sets the context. Timothy is not just another person. God has called him to lead congregations and thereby manage the stewardship household we might call leadership. Paul wants Timothy to be faithful to this stewardship calling.

In a sense, Paul wishes Timothy to live a life that befits the gospel. Today we hear a lot of chatter about lifestyles. Television boasts of one 1990s program for voyeurs who want to spy out the *Lifestyles of the Rich and Famous*. Yet from Paul's perspective, a lifestyle is more style than life. What is important is to live "in godliness combined with contentment." If Timothy achieves this aim, then he will indeed be a "man of God."

Perhaps the supreme temptation that any modern believer faces is trying to fit in. We crave acceptance and approval. Certainly, as Paul shares with Timothy, food and clothing are necessary. But now and again the world yanks us into competition so that we are like others. In striving for more and better, we become more and more like those around us who have "gain[ed] the whole world and forfeit[ed] their life" (Mark 8:36). Paul plainly recognizes what is at stake for Timothy. Because he is a leader, people will watch Timothy and imitate him; as a result, his ministry will influence many.

The words of warning for Timothy are as pertinent today as they were in the first century. When Paul writes, "But those who want to be rich fall into temptation and are trapped by many senseless and harmful desires that plunge people into ruin and destruction," he does not suggest that it may happen—he knows it is inevitable. As the character Lou Mannheim says in the film *Wall Street*, "The main thing about money, Bud, is that it makes you do things you don't want to do." Why? Because money and possessions become idols to "lust after" (Ps. 68:30). Too many of us, even when we know better, believe that more money and possessions can somehow secure life. But then we hear Jesus' words ringing in our ears: "Guard against all kinds of greed; for one's life does not consist in the abundance of possessions" (Luke 12:15).

Paul's admonition is easier to hear than it is to live. Immersed as we are in consumerism, we are like a fish who might ask, "Where is the water?" Paul's phrase is exact: we are "trapped by many senseless and harmful desires that plunge people into ruin and destruction." For Christian stewards, a new perspective becomes vital. For Paul, this viewpoint is Jesus' gospel, which teaches, "I came that they may have life, and have it abundantly" (John 10:10). Herein dwells freedom for us.

If nothing else, common sense helps us here. Most people know that the best things in life are free. Loving family and friends, the satisfaction we derive from helping others, and the blessings of health and old age rarely derive from our work. They are complimentary products of unmerited good fortune that Christians name "grace." Still, too many of us live as if the gospel may or may not be true—even as we are confronted with the brokenness among the rich and famous. As stewards we trust that God provides, and because of that providence we, like Timothy, are free to live righteously.

Sunday between October 2 and 8 inclusive

Luke 17:5–10   Doing Our Duty

"We have done only what we ought to have done."
(Luke 17:10)

Faith's function in a believer's life is the focus of today's Gospel lesson. Faith is a stewardship issue too. Jesus responds to a request to "increase our faith," no doubt needed in light of Jesus' demanding discipleship. He then offers a test case of a faithful person ordering a mulberry tree, "Be uprooted and planted in the sea." It obeys. Although surely an outlandish circumstance, Jesus' point is that faith does impossible things.

One sin of modernity is a propensity to confuse humanity with divinity. Perhaps this is in part the issue for Jesus' hypothetical slave in the short parable that follows the story of the mulberry tree. We might ask, "What kind of slave would expect red-carpet treatment?" Real slaves recognize their roles and grasp the strict separation between masters and slaves. Likewise, when we mar the distinction between God and people, we skew our way of knowing and being. We confuse ourselves with God, which is exactly what occurred in the garden when the serpent said: "You will be like God, knowing good and evil" (Gen. 3:5). Stewards should always recognize that God is our ultimate master.

About Jesus' story of the slave, no one would thank a slave for doing what slaves do. The slave's nature is to do slave work. Today we rarely speak of slaves. But our lack of experience with slavery should not hinder our understanding of Jesus' image. In our lives where does this attitude manifest itself?

Recently I saw a notice in the newspaper that a Senate committee was investigating abuses of power by the IRS. How many of us ever expect the IRS to send us a thank-you letter in response to our sending our taxes to the government in prompt fashion? Even after a public rebuke, the IRS will likely not be so contrite as to send us thank-you notes in the mail. An idea like this one makes us laugh. Paying taxes is what taxpayers do!

In our culture, most of what passes for gratitude is nothing more than social convention. We tell restaurant servers, "Thank you," when they bring our food, or we thank someone who opens a door for us. However many times we say thanks, we can still find ourselves at a loss for words when someone has shown us extraordinary kindness. Thus, when Jesus asks the rhetorical question, "Do you thank the slave for doing what was commanded?" the answer to his question is an obvious no.

The issue before us is how Jesus talks about faith and the tasks of a servant, one who would claim to be a Christian steward. How do they relate to us? We all need a deeper sense of faith and its power. Too often we use faith as a common noun, as a possessed object. We better value faith, however, as a verb: "we faith through life" or "we faith our suffering." Faith is active relationship between the creature and the Creator. Jesus offers an image of authentic faith that is potent enough to plant trees in the sea.

When Jesus teaches his apostles in a subtle way about an appropriate relationship between master and slave, he alludes to the profound relationship between God and human beings. To forget who is God and who is not is a grievous theological error and, in a word, sinful. Our faithfulness to God is required by the nature of the relationship we have with the Creator. To be a fully engaged steward of the households that God has given us to manage, it is helpful to think of ourselves as slaves. We act as stewards not because of who we are or what we want, but rather because we serve a sovereign God.

Sunday between October 9 and 15 inclusive

Jeremiah 29:4–7   Stewardship in Jerusalem or Babylon

"Seek the welfare of the city where I have sent you into exile."
(Jer. 29:7)

God's gift of imagination is one of life's most useful assets. The gift of imagination can help us to negotiate reality and to envision what can be. Imagination can also lead us into mere daydreaming. In this case, people at times can lose their grasp of reality. When our imaginations deter us from attending to real life, then they simply become yet another way to sidestep the truth.

The Hebrew Scripture lesson today cites part of a letter that Jeremiah wrote to those whom "Nebuchadnezzar had taken into exile from Jerusalem to Babylon." No doubt these exiles were despondent over losing their way of life, the temple, and every vestige of home. Yet Jeremiah offers words of hope and guidance. These are words that 2,600 years later Christian stewards can appeal to for guidance as well.

God had blessed the chosen people for centuries as occupants of the land that God had given them, "a land flowing with milk and honey" (Jer. 11:5). Around 597 BCE the nation found itself without land, without the temple, and without a home. Nationalism in this circumstance would naturally include talk of subversion and defiance. But as always, here Jeremiah is akin to a fish swimming against the current. Instead of lamenting the exiles' situation, Jeremiah offers encouragement: "Build houses . . . plant gardens . . . take wives . . . multiply there. . . . Seek the welfare of the city where I have sent you into exile . . . for in its welfare you will find your welfare." How odd.

Jeremiah's counsel to these exiles should not surprise those familiar with the prophet's tendency to offer peculiar words from the Lord. Jeremiah has made a prophetic career of doing the offbeat and the uncanny. When the nation faces doom, Jeremiah buys a field from his cousin Hanamel (Jer. 32:9). The Lord's word via Jeremiah encourages the exiles to embrace "the welfare of the city where I have sent you." This is a good word for stewards too.

We all know people who are never quite satisfied with their life circumstance. At our annual denominational meetings, one can hear laypeople hint that if they just had a different preacher, then their church would thrive. Ironically, in the preachers' cluster some preachers imply that if they only had a better church, then their gifts and graces would shine. In each case overactive imaginations avoid a truthful assessment of reality. All of us play the "if only" game: "If only I had gone to a different school . . . ," "If only I had married someone else . . . ," "If only I had chosen a different career path . . ." This game allows us to avoid dealing with our reality.

Jeremiah's word benefits faithful stewards because he suggests to the exiles that God will not return to recreate their past. The past is past. Instead, Jeremiah helps the people recognize that the only true reality is the one they live in now—in Babylon.

A tempting excuse to avoid managing those gifts that God has given us is to discount them. But as the poor widow in Mark's Gospel (12:41–44) reminds us, it is not the size or quality of the gift that matters. Instead, it is the heart and faith from which stewards offer their gifts to God. Whether a steward lives in Jerusalem or Babylon, God calls stewards to be faithful where God plants us.

Sunday between October 16 and 22 inclusive

Luke 18:1–8   A Persistent Way of Life

"Grant me justice against my opponent."
(Luke 18:3)

When Jesus tells his disciples a parable about a widow's persistence, he notes that the story is "about their need to pray always and not to lose heart." We may presume that prayer's many obstacles parallel stewardship hurdles. In any case, we know that as we should pray, we should also manage God's gifts given to believers. Yet for things as simple on their face—for example, prayer or stewardship—we might ask why each of these faith measures appears so daunting.

Jesus knows the difficulty of sustained prayer. Luke describes him in the Garden of Gethsemane: "In his anguish he prayed more earnestly, and his sweat became like great drops of blood falling down on the ground" (Luke 22:44). Jesus knows about prayer. Jesus also knows about giving everything, as he confirmed not only in his life but perhaps even more especially in his death. For stewards, it is important to recognize that Jesus' intent in the parable of the persistent widow concerns diligence. Diligence or persistence is a requisite faith trait for stewards. It is easy to give emotionally, even impulsively, to causes that tug at our heartstrings. But like prayer, sustained, systematic giving is a difficult path to follow.

Prayer is hard work, although many people see it as a quick fix to solve daily problems. "O Lord, let me find a parking space near the door of my office building," we might pray. Or "O God, protect my investment from the ravages of the stock market." When Jesus offers this parable about prayer, he implies that prayer is a way of life. So too is faithful stewardship.

Jesus knows about our predilection to give up, whether the subject is managing our God-given resources or our prayer life. Jesus' Gethsemane prayer reveals his temptation: "If it is possible, let this cup pass from me" (Matt. 26:39). Jesus also knows that we are apt to capitulate to evil forces about us when things get tough, whether we are praying or giving. When we are ready to quit, earnest prayer to God takes our focus off of ourselves and our circumstance and places it squarely on God—where it belongs. We are only stewards to the extent that we recognize that all we have to give is merely an extension of God's prior gift to us. In the real world we recognize that persistence is the key to an effective life. Whether we are learning to play the piano, entering school as an adult, overcoming an addiction, or digging out of a financial quagmire, persistence is key.

I know an African student who has a literal grasp of life. Recently a professor told him he would meet him in his office after lunch, although the professor wanted to put the student off and so went home for lunch and for the day. But the student did as he was asked and sat outside the professor's office after lunch. That night, about 9:00 p.m., as a caretaker locked the office building, she told the student that the professor would not return. He protested, "But the professor said he would be here after lunch." The next morning at 7:00 a.m. he returned to the same place right outside the professor's door and waited. This African student reflected the essence of persistence.

The point of Jesus' parable is not that persistent prayer promises a petitioner her or his desire. Rather, Jesus' parable teaches that prayer offsets cowardly resignation. Whether our life circumstance is rising or falling, we recognize that stewardship, like prayer, is a way of life.

Sunday between October 23 and 29 inclusive

2 Timothy 4:6–8, 16–18   Looking Back

"The time of my departure has come."
(2 Tim. 4:6)

Today's text includes some of Paul's final words to Timothy. Paul has guided and nurtured Timothy, as recorded in the middle part of Acts. Paul has been a friend of Timothy's family (2 Tim. 1:5). They have evangelized together, taught together, and broken bread together for much of Paul's ministry. Now Paul has some final words of counsel for his young apprentice. Paul's angle for the writing of his epistle to Timothy is one of retrospective. As he looks back, Paul offers encouragement to one who must look ahead.

One of the ways that all of us take stock of our lives is to look to our past. Where are the places that we have succeeded, and where have we failed to do our best? This is the kind of perspective that can help believers measure their stewardship. Paul helps all of us make this measurement.

Paul uses sacrificial language about his ministry. He writes that he has been "poured out as a libation." This sounds much like those who sacrificed to God during the time of Israel's wilderness wanderings (Num. 15:5, 7). Then with regard to Paul's own faith, often tested, he uses a few sporting metaphors that would have been familiar in Greek culture in the first century. Paul has "fought the good fight . . . [and has] finished the race." Such language gives Paul's words a ring of authenticity. Paul knows what he is writing about. Paul's own experience in proclaiming the gospel gives his words credence for the young Timothy.

I once visited an older man in one of my parishes who was exceedingly wealthy but lived as an ordinary person without pretension. We became fast friends over the years. This man did nothing outside of caring for his wife who was a stroke victim. On my first visit to his house he told me that a man from the church had asked him to make a large contribution to the church's endowment fund. Evidently as a way to evaluate his new pastor and to shed some light on the person who asked him about the endowment, he asked me, "Preacher, what would you have done if you had been in my shoes?" Plainly, the endowment promoter seemed slightly disingenuous to my friend.

I thought for a moment and said, "I think I would have asked him what he had done for the church's endowment." This struck a chord with my new friend because he said to me, "That is exactly what I asked him." Over time, this man offered much to our church by way of financial support. Yet he never gave anything to the church's endowment. My guess is that he avoided the endowment because he did not feel the person who solicited him on the endowment's behalf was genuine.

As stewards, to use an old cliché, we must practice what we preach. When Paul counsels Timothy, he does so as one who walks the faith path. As stewards, the chief element in sharing a stewardship message with others is to make certain our own house is in order. The most influential stewardship witness we can make is to be good stewards. Our lives offer the most persuasive argument possible about what we believe. Looking back over our stewardship offers proof about our faith's sincerity.

Sunday between October 30 and November 5 inclusive

Habakkuk 1:1–4; 2:1–4   A Steward's Ultimate Decision

"Then the LORD answered me."
(Hab. 2:2)

At November's start many churches enter what we might euphemistically call "stewardship season." Although not a liturgical season resembling Advent or Lent, stewardship season is still vital for churches trying to balance a budget. On this Sunday the lectionary offers from Habakkuk words of hope. In the three-year lectionary cycle this minor prophet appears only this Sunday. Yet Habakkuk's is a word that modern people need—as believers and as stewards.

One of the first issues addressed in Habakkuk, merely three chapters long, is the matter of God's justice, or the doctrine of theodicy. Sounding like a lament psalm, Habakkuk launches his prophetic word: "O LORD, how long shall I cry for help, and you will not listen?" Such a question reveals an all-too-human doubt about God's willingness to defend God's people. Another way to understand Habakkuk's word is simply as an honest plea for God to come to the people's aid.

A great barrier to believers exercising stewardship is the engrained idea that what people do matters little in the big picture. Many people function as if giving gifts and offering service is no more than a drop in the bucket. Accordingly, believers often set aside their stewardship responsibilities by thinking that they are futile. As a result, believers sometimes hoard their God-given talents and treasures in order to protect themselves from whatever may come. Faithful people in Israel would have called this stance idolatry.

Our perspective, of course, determines our response. Habakkuk prophesies that although God often seems far away, in reality God still rules and overrules. If we are to be truly free with respect to our God-given free will, then we may question God's providential care for us. After all, it seems a natural human response to calamity. But even in the most dire of human conditions, Habakkuk's affirmation is unambiguous: "I will stand at my watchpost. . . . I will keep watch to see what he will say to me." Habakkuk refuses to yield to an abyss of fear. Rather, he decides for faith, a decision that he puts like this: "Then the LORD answered me and said . . . there is still a vision for the appointed time. . . . It will surely come, it will not delay." His trust in God facilitates his decision.

The initial decision that believers make as disciples and as stewards is that the God we profess is the God we trust. This is a chief article of faith: God is the owner of everything simply because God is creator. But there is an important corollary for stewardship. This corollary is that the creator God includes people as partners in creation. In the divine wisdom God offers us another stewardship standard. This principle reminds us that although God can do everything, God nonetheless invites human beings to help keep the garden that we call our earth.

A steward's decision is important, mainly regarding how we manage the gifts God places in our hands. But human decisions also must be genuine decisions. Indeed, our decisions are authentically free; they do not simply appear to be free. Thus, although God can know all the possible outcomes of a certain decision or action, God does not determine what we will do or decide. Stewards must do this. This is what makes the ethical life possible and empowers our stewardship decisions with genuine meaning.

All Saints' Day
(November 1, or may be used on the first Sunday in November)

Ephesians 1:11–23   Embracing Our Inheritance

"This is the pledge of our inheritance toward redemption."
(Eph. 1:14)

The church has two primary understandings about what a saint is. Customarily when the church celebrates All Saints' Day, we remember departed believers who handed to us the faith experience in Jesus Christ. This notion of saint suggests that these departed persons "now rest from their labors" (Rev. 14:13). These saints have, as Paul writes of himself, "fought the good fight" (2 Tim. 4:7).

In addition, the term "saint" can refer to any person, living or dead, who belongs to the body of Christ. Saints are, biblically speaking, not merely persons placed in stained glass windows upon death, but rather believers who roll up their sleeves here and now. They work for justice and equity today. When the church observes All Saints' Day, it remembers those who have passed from the human scene. Yet as we remember these persons formerly among us, they inspire us as God's saints even today.

The Epistle lesson today addresses the concept of the inheritance that believers have received from God. Many scholars detect in the first chapter of Ephesians a collage of early Christian hymns and creeds. The logic is thick and in some ways nearly impenetrable. In fact, many modern translations divide verses 3–14, which is one sentence, into multiple sentences to amplify understanding. Regarding stewardship, we focus on the notion of inheritance found in verses 11, 14, and 18. The inheritance is primarily for saints to "live for the praise of his glory." We saints, or believers, receive this divine inheritance "with the seal of the promised Holy Spirit."

In the briefest possible way, the inheritance is a summing up of all of God's benefits to believers. To be precise, "in Christ we have also obtained an inheritance . . . so that we . . . might live for the praise of his glory." The inheritance sets our hope on Christ and on hearing gospel truth about salvation. These divine benefits mark the saints with the seal of the Holy Spirit. What does it mean to "live for the praise of his glory" (verses 6, 12, 14)? Perhaps it means that stewards live lives that please God. Thus, stewards express both gratitude and praise. Nothing pleases God like people living in faith.

The word the church employs for stewardship derives from the Greek word that in English we render as "economy." Stewardship basically means "to manage a household." Sadly, when many hear the word stewardship, the only household that comes to mind is the household of money. Yet everything Christians manage is a household. For example, we are stewards over our power, devotion, spiritual life, listening, prayer, worship, support of others, and benevolence. Whatever we manage or control is a stewardship "household." Our households include money, but stewardship is a richer concept than merely money.

In modern parlance we usually think of an inheritance as consisting of land, stocks and bonds, or other financial assets. In the first century, people doubtlessly conceived of inheritance in a comparable manner. However, the author of Ephesians writes about believers' divine inheritance that can never be taken away. People can lose almost anything that they enjoy as a benefit—health, wealth, prestige, and the like. However, no one can remove our inheritance of salvation from God in Christ. Genuine stewards practice managing the household of faith and salvation that God gives us as our inheritance. The inheritance God gives stewards is a divine trust that God expects us to value.

Sunday between November 6 and 12 inclusive

2 Thessalonians 2:1–5, 13–17   Stewards of the Traditions

"So then . . . stand firm and hold fast to the traditions."
(2 Thess. 2:15)

While the word "tradition" is not a four-letter word, many church quarters treat it as such. For far too many people today, both young and old, history and its corresponding tradition smells of dingy, dusty archives from which we moderns garner little useful data.

Jesus was cautious about the uncritical use of tradition when he said to the Pharisees and scribes, "You have a fine way of rejecting the commandment of God in order to keep your tradition!" (Mark 7:8–9). Given Jesus' words, legitimate stewards will handle church tradition with care. It is true that we need to discard many elements of tradition—traditions of male domination, traditions of slavery, traditions of spiritual hierarchy of clergy over laypeople, and so on. But a culture that discounts its tradition is a culture that will soon lose its anchor when the winds of change blow, as they always do.

Paul urges the Thessalonians to "stand firm and hold fast to the traditions that you were taught by us, either by word of mouth or by our letter." Paul writes this because he knows that the embryonic church must establish itself in the faith realities of daily life. Paul also is aware of "false witnesses" (Acts 6:13), "false apostles," "false brothers and sisters" (2 Cor. 11:13, 26), and "false believers" (Gal. 2:4). As a safeguard against false doctrine, Paul urges his beloved Thessalonians to rely on the fixed value of the tradition. It is tradition's unchanging consequence that provides believers an anchor in the storms of change.

Good stewards heed the words of both Jesus and Paul with respect to the church's tradition. On the one hand, the church can and has used tradition as a weapon against just causes and helpful advances for Christ's realm in the world. On many occasions the church has exploited tradition to hide from the Hebrew Scripture's mandate to "do justice, and to love kindness, and to walk humbly with your God" (Mic. 6:8). Church tradition has sometimes "neglected the weightier matters of the law: justice and mercy and faith" (Matt. 23:23). Like patriotism, tradition can become a refuge for cowards or scoundrels.

On the other hand, good stewards also recognize the value of tradition rightly interpreted and used. Tradition protects the church from theological fraud, as Paul well knew. Tradition shields the faith from acutely renegade theologies and their proponents, for example, "the prosperity gospel." For stewards, the role of Christian tradition steers us by our remembrance of prior issues of faith and belief. Used in this fashion, tradition supplies a defense against flawed doctrine and theology. Finally, the Bible stands as the decisive test for stewards to judge tradition's merits—and then to live by them.

Sunday between November 13 and 19 inclusive

Isaiah 65:17–25   The Joy of God's Realm

"I am about to create Jerusalem as a joy, and its people as a delight."
(Isa. 65:18)

Today's lesson is God's word of promise to a specific group of people. In Isaiah 65:1–16 the prophet distinguishes between "a rebellious people" (v. 2) and "my servants" (v. 9). God's subsequent promise in today's lesson extends to obedient believers. Perhaps this signifies authentic stewardship—obedience with respect to God's gifts loaned to us to build up God's realm.

The steward's reward, as is the reward for Isaiah's obedient and returned exiles, is to live in God's new creation. As God is about to "create Jerusalem as a joy, and its people as a delight," the people's response is pure joy. In the end God's servants or stewards will experience joy and thus become stewards of joy. This joy is a blessing of eschatological consequence. Indeed, from the beginning of the gospel story, Matthew writes of the magi, "When they saw that the star had stopped [over Jesus' birthplace], they were overwhelmed with joy" (Matt. 2:10). From the beginning to the end of the gospel narratives, a blessing of faith is unrestrained joy. Joy is a gift from on high. Jesus tells his disciples, "I have said these things to you so that my joy may be in you, and that your joy may be complete" (John 15:11). The writer of 1 John confesses, "We are writing these things so that our joy may be complete" (1 John 1:4). Even Paul expresses his gift of joy by writing: "Yes, you are our glory and joy!" (1 Thess. 2:20)!

Nonetheless, as often as Christians appeal to joy, we also know the reality that little in church life reflects the joy we trumpet. Those things Isaiah invokes as passing away—death, plunder, vain labor—remain today. We seem to have misplaced our joy.

Today's lesson from Isaiah helps remind us of God's promise to obedient stewards and believers. Recognition is always the first step in learning to be a steward. Consequently, Christians recognize that God owns everything because God is the creator. To live in that knowledge is to live a life of joy.

John 9 includes a story about Jesus healing a man born blind. The long (41 verses) and exquisite narrative has numerous twists and turns. After his healing, which is told in spare detail (vv. 6–7), everyone the man encounters cross-examines him. He has been healed of a lifelong infirmity, yet what the story's characters want from him is the gory details: When? How? Why? John's story elicits not one ounce of joy from those who should be jumping with delight at this man's good fortune. No one—neighbors, parents, and religious authorities—offers congratulations. Is this a story of the current church? Do we rejoice when we can?

Years ago I read a small book entitled *Clowning in Rome* by Henri Nouwen. The book's controlling image for the Christian life was the clowns that Nouwen encountered in Rome. Nouwen compares the clowns to the way that Christians are to be in the world. The clowns did not take themselves too seriously, yet they offered themselves to all who watched as reminders of life's joy and mirth. Perhaps all of us can be stewards of the joy God offers us as reminders of life's gift and blessedness.

A beautiful quilt hangs over the end of the bed my wife and I share, a gift from a dear church. Stitched into it is each church member's name. These names continually remind me of my joy in serving that congregation. Could we imagine that God looks at our names stitched into the heavens? We are stewards and manage God's resources because we express the joy of our salvation. Stewards derive joy from being part of God's realm.

Christ the King/Reign of Christ
(Sunday between November 20 and 26 inclusive)

Luke 23:33–43   Is There a Stewardship of Irony?

"There was also an inscription over him, 'This is the King of the Jews.' "
(Luke 23:38)

Today's Gospel lesson offers one of the Bible's many ways of "telling the truth slant." Luke uses the ironic title "This is the King of the Jews." Irony (from the Greek *eiron*) is fundamentally what a speaker does who hedges in speech or says less than the speaker thinks. Often irony states one thing but really means something else, even the opposite of the words' literal meaning. An ironic statement is often self-evident to those who understand the statement's context. When a Hollywood casting director rejected Ronald Reagan for the part of president of the United States, he supplied a prophetically ironic statement: "He doesn't have the presidential look." Irony is subtle, and listeners frequently hear it as sarcasm, as when the Romans use the inscription "King of the Jews" to ridicule Jesus. Still, the inscription declares truth absolutely—Jesus is King!

As "servants of Christ and stewards of God's mysteries" (1 Cor. 4:1), we handle sacred truth, and on occasion we disclose truth in unequivocal ways. Yet life's situations crop up in which truth's fierce honesty is too severe for humans to abide. Often a person who needs such truth is not mentally or emotionally prepared to receive it. When such circumstances arise, then we do well to pursue Emily Dickinson's suggestion: "Tell all the Truth but tell it slant." She implies that at times we couch truth indirectly in order for others to appropriate it. Søren Kierkegaard regularly used this rhetorical strategy.

The Bible is bursting with irony—Moses, the "slow of tongue," becomes God's mouthpiece (Exod. 4:10); Rahab, a foreign prostitute, saves Israel's spies (Josh. 6:25); and Judas betrays the Messiah with love's most familiar emblem (Luke 22:47–48). At times irony reveals God's power working through imperfect, fallible human creatures. But sometimes irony simply states truth too painful not to tell "slant."

Christian stewards manage Holy Scripture. On balance the Bible tells its story in a straightforward manner. But in an astonishing number of ways, the Bible reveals its truth "slant." For example, when the Bible addresses love, Paul will write devoid of rhetorical convention, "Love is patient; love is kind; love is not envious or boastful or arrogant or rude" (1 Cor. 13:4–5). John's epistle reminds believers to love in fairly clear ways: "Let us love, not in word or speech, but in truth and action" (1 John 3:18). But on occasion, Scripture needs additional and penetrating scrutiny. Perhaps as stewards of Holy Scripture, we believers need to be as "wise as serpents and innocent as doves" (Matt. 10:16). As stewards of God's word we need to know when each kind of reading is required to arrive at truth.

This is a critical distinction, because we live in a "me first" culture and take inordinate pride in the possessions that we control. As stewards, the most faithful way for us to respond to the gospel is to live as if we really believed that God owns everything. To live as obedient stewards is a profession of faith. To live as if God's ownership matters entails a life of discipleship—and perhaps irony. If we can live this way, then we will raise eyebrows—perhaps even God's eyebrows.

Thanksgiving Day

Philippians 4:4–9   Stewards of Thanks

"Think about these things."
(Phil. 4:8)

By biblical standards Paul's epistle to the Philippians is not particularly long, but perhaps more than any of his other letters it reveals Paul's emotional connection to a church. To be sure, Paul knows how to cajole and how to censure. Yet this letter shows Paul's earnest affection for this Philippian congregation.

Philippians 4 closes the epistle, and verses 4–9 express Paul's final litany of untreated themes. Thus, we read here of topics Paul might have explored further with the church: "Whatever is true, whatever is honorable, whatever is just, whatever is pure, whatever is pleasing, whatever is commendable, if there is any excellence and if there is anything worthy of praise, think about these things." At the beginning of the chapter Paul writes explicitly about "Euodia," "Syntyche," and a believer named "Syzygus"—maybe an anonymous believer—whose name is often translated as "loyal companion" or "true yoke-mate." But our text for today is in summary generic.

Pastors frequently receive little notes from people in the congregation—sometimes signed, often not. As a rule, these notes have a dismal tone. They cover a variety of subjects: sanctuary temperature, hymn selection, why the preacher persists in speaking against war, and so on. Yet it is a delight to receive a note of thanks. Each time someone writes a word of appreciation about a sermon, I feel joy—and relief!

Too often we dwell on the negative messages we receive. Recipients of some of Paul's epistles would certainly recognize this reality—Paul was on occasion quite severe. Yet here Paul goes to great lengths to offer words of thanks and appreciation for the Philippians' gift. In the first chapter Paul tells them of his prayer for them: "that your love may overflow . . . having produced the harvest of righteousness that comes through Jesus Christ for the glory and praise of God" (1:9–11).

If Paul can wax so effusively about the gifts a church offers him, then what can we say about Christian stewards and the manifold gifts God presents to us in so many ways? One way, biblical from start to finish, is to offer God praise and thanksgiving. It is the ability to give God thanks that distinguishes us in perceptible ways from pagans. It is about pagans that Paul writes elsewhere, "They did not honor him as God or give thanks" (Rom. 1:21). Thanksgiving Day provides a liturgical opportunity to offer thanksgiving to God. Our thanks help us remember the One "from whom all blessings flow." Perhaps we also recall a text from James: "Every generous act of giving, [as] with every perfect gift, is from above" (Jas. 1:17). To worship God fully, stewards as disciples begin with thanksgiving.

For many people, Thanksgiving Day means a time with family and friends. Our culture designates the day as a celebration of football, overeating, and relaxation. Most churches do not even hold worship on Thanksgiving Day. Yet Thanksgiving Day represents liturgically for Christians what we should be about every day. We offer thanks to God. Paul knew the importance of thanking the church at Philippi. Good stewards understand thanksgiving as an act of worship.

Scripture Index